CW00920933

VOICES FROM ASIA

TOKYO STORIES

The publisher gratefully acknowledges the contribution to this book provided by the Literature in Translation Endowment of the University of California Press Associates, which is supported by a generous gift from Joan Palevsky.

TOKYO
STORIES

A LITERARY STROLL

TRANSLATED FROM THE JAPANESE
AND EDITED BY
LAWRENCE ROGERS

UNIVERSITY OF CALIFORNIA PRESS
BERKELEY LOS ANGELES LONDON

University of California Press
Berkeley and Los Angeles, California

University of California Press, Ltd.
London, England

© 2002 by Lawrence Rogers. All rights reserved.

Photograph on pages 1, 58, 200, and 240 by Lawrence Rogers.

For acknowledgments of permissions, please see page 267.

Library of Congress Cataloging-in-Publication Data
    Tokyo stories : a literary stroll / translated from the Japanese and
edited by Lawrence Rogers.
        p. cm. — (Voices from Asia ; 12)
    Includes bibliographical references.
    ISBN 0–520-21786-1 (cloth : alk paper) — ISBN 0–520-21788-8 (pbk. :
alk paper)
    1. Short stories, Japanese—Translations into English—History and
criticism. 2. Japan—Social life and customs—Fiction. I. Rogers,
Lawrence William. II. Series.
    PL782.E8 T65 2002
    895.6'301083252135—dc21   2001007075

Manufactured in the United States of America

12   11   10   09   08   07   06
10   9   8   7   6   5   4   3

The paper used in this publication is both acid-free and totally chlorine-
free (TCF). It meets the minimum requirements of ANSI/NISO Z39.48–
1992 (R 1997) (Permanence of Paper). ∞

Dedicated to the memory of Igarashi Hitoshi,
translator into Japanese of Salman Rushdie's
The Satanic Verses, murdered July 12, 1991

Contents

Preface

This anthology was compiled to serve two ends, one literary, the other utilitarian. I hope that readers who are interested in Japanese literature will find this book useful and that the work will appeal to those whose focus is more on the city of Tokyo, either because they are wayfarers come to it or because they simply want to add another dimension to their knowledge of one of the world's most fascinating cities.

I would like to thank the people who have helped me in various ways during the preparation of this collection. I am grateful to Susan Maesato of the University of Hawai'i at Hilo library and to my colleagues Kamila Dudley and Rick Castberg for the information they provided, as well as to Jacqueline and the late Richard Howell for their comments over many a shared meal. I am also grateful to Theresa Conefrey and Donald Richie for reading the introduction, to Michael Godley for scrutinizing the page proofs, and to Edward Fowler for directing my attention to the San'ya stories of Ikeda Michiko. I want to thank Alisa Freedman and Richmod Bollinger, who are translating *The Crimson Gang of Asakusa* in its entirety, for allowing me to make a partial translation, and Mr. Richie, who holds the translation rights. I am also grateful to Cecilia Segawa Seigle and two anonymous reviewers for their helpful comments on the manuscript, and to Laura Driussi, Rachel Berchten, Kristen Cashman, Edith Gladstone, and Linda Norton of the University of California Press for their sure editorial touch. I owe a debt of gratitude to the Nishikawa family in the Yotsugi 3-chōme district of Tokyo's *shitamachi* for their generous hospitality over the years.

I also wish to thank Ikeda Michiko, Inaba Mayumi, Hino Keizō, and Saegusa Kazuko for allowing inclusion of their works in this anthology.

Research and copyright costs for this book were paid by the University of Hawai'i Japan Studies Endowment, which is funded by a grant from the Japan Foundation.

Finally, I am indebted to the steadfast encouragement and support of my wife, Kazuko Fujihira, vigilant smiter of all ambiguity.

Needless to say, I am responsible for the selections and for any errors therein.

L.R.
Hilo, Hawaii
rogers@hawaii.edu

Tokyo

Mitaka

Kichijōji

Inokashira
Park

Chūō Line

Inokashira Line

Jindaiji Temple

Ikebukuro

Takatanobaba

Tokyo City Hall

Shinjuku

Meiji Shrine

Yoyogi Park

CHŌFU

Shinsen-chō Shibuya

Ebisu

0   1   2   3 km.

0   1   2 mi.

Only selected place names are included.

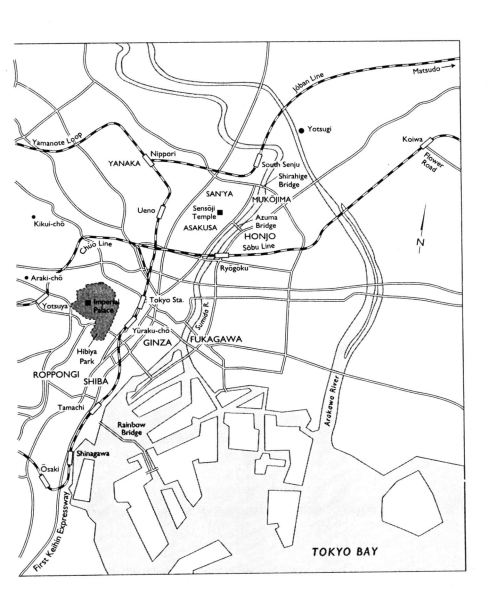

Jōban Line

Matsudo →

Yamanote Loop

Nippori

YANAKA

Yotsugi

Koiwa

Flower Road

South Senju

Shirahige Bridge

SAN'YA

MUKŌJIMA

Ueno

Sensōji Temple

Kikui-chō

ASAKUSA

Azuma Bridge

HONJO

Chūo Line

Sōbu Line

Ryōgoku

N

• Araki-chō

Imperial Palace

Tokyo Sta.

Yotsuya

Sumida R.

Yūraku-chō

GINZA

FUKAGAWA

Hibiya Park

ROPPONGI

SHIBA

Arakawa River

Tamachi

Rainbow Bridge

Ōsaki

Shinagawa

First Keihin Expressway

TOKYO BAY

Introduction

LAWRENCE ROGERS

THE BIG PERSIMMON

Tokyo is one of the most fascinating cities in the world, and one of the most rewarding for the visitor, though doubtless most newcomers are not immediately aware of its bounty. It has, for example, more restaurants than Manhattan, safer streets than London, nightlife incredibly rich in its variety. It boasts a transportation system second to none amongst the great cities of the world, and it is, most significantly, the lodestar of Japanese culture in modern times. Its citizens once breathed what must have been the world's most polluted air, but the people of other capitals now contend for that notorious distinction. According to recent statistics published by the metropolitan government, Tokyo spews less nitrogen dioxide into the atmosphere than either New York City or London, and it generates less garbage per capita than the Big Apple.[1]

This is not to say that Tokyo is without its shortcomings. It is not, for example, a particularly impressive city visually. Certainly among the world's metropolises its cityscape does not yet awe the newcomer with a vast and prickly stand of skyscrapers as does Manhattan, nor can it charm with antiquity as do so many European capitals. Naturally the casual and unimpressed tourist is unlikely to consider the disastrous history of the city during the twentieth century when, in a span of less than twenty-five years, Tokyo was destroyed by earthquake and fire, rebuilt within the constraints of a then-frail economy, then leveled yet again, this time by the incendiary bombs of General Curtis LeMay and his 20th Air Force. We can safely assume that Paris would have rather less charm today if it too were subject to seismic whimsy and had suffered the carpet bombing of World War II.

Beyond the effect of wholesale destruction is the absence of significant and comprehensive planning. Japanese bureaucrats are seen abroad as omnipotent and implacable, certainly capable of sweeping aside landowners, petty or powerful, to plan and execute a grand scheme for the city. Yet in limited projects carried out since the Edo era—the widening of certain streets in the commoner districts, for example—no grand plan has been imposed to reorder the layout of the city as in the Haussmannization of Paris. In fact, the artificial divisions of the city underlying the ever-changing structures have remained remarkably constant over the generations. The architectural historian Jinnai Hidenobu, comparing old Edo-era maps with those of modern Tokyo, found in his research that the old Edo streets, the pattern of district divisions, and even lot boundaries "corresponded, in almost every instance, to the contemporary map."[2]

Structures or clusters of structures on the land have disappeared, of course, and even entire districts and architectural styles have vanished, as has the improbable and charming brick Londontown of the Marunouchi business district. Yet changes can be even more profound and disorienting, altering the very geography of the city. In Tokyo Bay the shore creeps seaward and artificial islands rise above the bay. Rivers and

canals yield to expressways that ooze implacably over the city. The Sanjukken canal, so significant to the narrator of one of the Takeda Rintarō
short stories in this collection, was filled in decades ago and the Izumo
Bridge that spanned it pulled down as superfluous.³ Nihombashi, the
elegant late Meiji bridge that has, in its present and earlier forms, functioned as the accepted geographical center of all Japan since the Edo era,
stands blighted by the elevated highway that since the early sixties gro-
tesquely straddles and obscures it.

The relentless rebuilding continues, even in the current recession, de-
stroying what has come before, good or bad, to raise glass palaces of
commerce and often questionable public works projects. But some consider this a sentimental and subjective view and look on change more
positively, or at least without sentiment. The city's adaptability has led
the architect Ashihara Yoshinobu to an optimistic biological simile: Tokyo is like an amoeba, "with its amorphous sprawl and the constant
change it undergoes, like the pulsating body of the organism."⁴ In this
view the city has a physical integrity and the capacity for regeneration
when damaged.

The residential texture of the city has certainly altered over the years.
To some this means Tokyo is less drab than it was thirty years ago; to
others the city now offers fewer examples of what is *shibui*. For better or
worse, the culture of weathered wood has ineluctably given way to the
culture of painted stucco, bare concrete, and other exotic innovations.
Unpainted wood-frame houses have been replaced by a variety of buildings, usually larger and more assertive, with lighter, brighter facades.
Size and color saturation aside, however, the city remains for the most
part a visually ungainly place, an incongruous mixture of this style and
that, ersatz Swiss alpine next to Spanish colonial next to early American
whatnot, creating an architectural dissonance much like that of Los Angeles, but on a more compact, and therefore harsher scale.

I frequently stay with friends who live in the *shitamachi* area of Tokyo,
the older, more plebeian, part of town. They have a very pleasant house,
well built and handsome, that you might call twentieth-century traditional. The entryway floor is Japanese cypress, a beautiful golden wood
that the passage of stocking feet helps keep in high burnish. The carefully

tended garden is magnificent in the Japanese style of such oases, and hidden from the street behind a relatively high wall. The street outside, however, is an entirely different matter. Immediately in front of the building a grand total of sixteen wires, telephone and electrical, are suspended from massive rat-gray concrete utility poles that stand, stolid and thuggish, on the near side of the street, and to which are grafted a bulky gray transformer and a clutch of unidentifiable electrical geegaws.

Utility lines have been put underground on the larger thoroughfares of the city, in the Ginza district, Kasumigaseki, Shinjuku, and so on, but elsewhere the poles and wires are strung about in unsightly profusion. The writer Morimoto Tetsurō is harshly critical of his compatriots and mocks the widely held belief that the Japanese are a people who love beauty or are the possessors of a fine-tuned aesthetic. He holds that the citizens of Paris, London, or the other capitals of western Europe—he has wisely excluded North America—would rise up in arms if the utility poles and wires that overspread Tokyo were to be strung up around those cities. He adds,

> As for the Japanese, they are unfazed. They have absolutely no interest in how a city looks. They put down such a scene of disorder as quite natural, or rather, they are convinced that this indicates a civilized city.[5]

Young minds are often cautioned not to celebrate mere beauty over character, and this is wisdom the Tokyophile can champion in illuminating the cosmetic virtues of the city. Surely, he or she might say to a doubtful visitor, the attraction of a city lies not in the clever arrangement of its bricks and boards, but in the sense of its vitality, or in the ambience of its individual neighborhoods. Who can walk through Araki-chō in the Yotsuya district and talk of ugliness? Another response is to take the detractor—particularly the seeker after "the real Japan" of *Madama Butterfly*—to Yanaka, one of the few areas in Tokyo that escaped the fire-raids of 1945, and thus still has the traditional wood-frame buildings, some from the Meiji era, fine old houses with their gracefully weathered, broad semi-clapboard siding, each of which elegantly complements the vast Yanaka Cemetery and the brood of Buddhist temples that make Yanaka such an enchanting borough of the past.

Should the disenchanted visitor discover that even a Japanese critic has observed that the city's townscape "is like a set of badly aligned teeth" because of the city's irregular building sites,[6] a Tokyophile can profitably retrieve the useful principle of asymmetry, an important cog in the gear of Japanese aesthetics for centuries, or shamelessly offer the observation that architectural conflict is the ideal catalyst for urban progress and vitality.

Whatever the city's sins to the eye, it has not been reduced to a homogenous plain of social and architectural undifferentiation. Like any large city, it has its distinct districts. The sophisticated Ginza can never be mistaken for the apartment sprawl of, say, Kōenji, along the Chūō train line, or for down-to-earth Asakusa, and certainly never for down-and-out San'ya. As for individuals, recent economic prosperity has tended to lift most, if not all, boats and works to some extent against obvious social differentiation. In prewar Japan the keener observers of Tokyo's sidewalks claimed the ability not only to identify a stroller's calling by apparel, but also the part of town he or she hailed from. Such Holmesian deduction would be considerably more difficult today.

THE BRIGHT LIGHTS

Of course, it is still possible to have an experience that will confirm one's preconceptions or prejudices. I recently lunched at the Kamiya Bar—really a multistoried beer hall—in Asakusa, an establishment best known as one of the haunts of the writer Nagai Kafū, author of "Azuma Bridge" and the premier chronicler of the plebeian *shitamachi*, the "low city," until his death in 1959. In the course of the meal there were three instances where a man in his cups had to be semi-carried from the premises, so great was his intoxication or relaxed his inhibitions. Two of the men assisted out were tie-and-suit salarymen; the third, a blue-collar worker of middle years, was more thrown than helped out, cursing his escorts as he was whisked through the front door. Needless to say, such rowdiness—and the rough dispatch of patrons—is less common in the upscale Ginza district, which certainly has its share of beer halls but also has in its backstreets what is said to be the greatest concentration of art galleries in the world.

But Asakusa is coming up in the world, too. One of the side streets has been repaved and gentrified with large flower planters set on the sidewalk next to the curb—the curbs themselves are fairly recent—two or three meters apart. Each of the planters has a speaker in it that gently and relentlessly sends forth music, film scores, pop tunes, and even baroque. The crusty traditionalist Kafū would not have approved.

Across the Sumida River from Kafū's Kamiya is Super Dry Hall, Asahi Beer's shiny new black slab of a building, topped off by what is said to represent a golden flame rising above the roof, though unkind critics see it as a gigantic dollop of rancid mayonnaise. Next to it stands the Asahi Beer Tower, the company's luxurious head office, which has a large picture window in the twenty-first-floor men's room, surely the only restroom in Tokyo that offers such a spectacular aerial view of the Sumida River and its bridges to anyone standing at the urinal.

A *Bierhaus* is not the symbolic heart of Asakusa, however. That honor rightly belongs to the ancient Sensōji temple complex, Kaminari Gate, and the touristy shopping arcade between the two; these draw swarms of visitors daily from all over Japan. The towering main hall—yet to be rebuilt when the couple in Hayashi Fumiko's "Old Part of Town" visit it—is an imposing structure, but first-time visitors may also be impressed by the collection box, which equals the hall in the generosity of its dimensions, about the size of a small swimming pool. The clink of coins thrown by petitioners of all ages is never-ending, at least in the daytime. A monk reads from a sacred text to drum accompaniment several times a day, providing a more solemn ambience in the main hall.

The Shinjuku district in the western quarter of the city, by contrast, is a country of the young, especially at night. Teenage couples, college students, amorphous masses of young people flow along the streets on their way to countless restaurants, bars, karaoke clubs, "love hotels" on the far side of randy Kabuki-chō, movie houses, coffee shops, department stores, game arcades, bookstores, porn parlors, and several dozen other potential divertissements that the bustling area provides.

There are relatively few post-twenties people about. The relinquishing by older Japanese of places like Shinjuku, nearby Shibuya, and Harajuku to the young is an interesting phenomenon, doubtless related to perceptions of social roles, but for Japanese over sixty it may stem from something rather more complex than the unpleasant feeling of being outnumbered and out of place. Morimoto Tetsurō was born in Tokyo in 1925 and spent his young adult years on and about the gentle slopes of the Shibuya district. There was nothing gentle about his life then, however. Those were the immediate postwar years; he, and most Japanese, led a difficult, hand-to-mouth existence in a devastated country, and this has left its mark. Morimoto writes in a recent collection of essays that he rarely goes to Shibuya now unless he has to, although he has no aversion to strolling the streets of Shinjuku, notwithstanding the radical changes there and the flood of young.

> To be jostled by the waves of humanity in Shinjuku does not bother me that much, but to find myself in the sea of youths that Shibuya is awash in really depresses me. I suspect it comes from the incredible gulf between my impoverished youth there and the spectacle of the overly affluent young people of today enjoying the good life.[7]

The immediate west side of Shinjuku station, once known as Tsunohazu, is now the site of imposing skyscrapers and world-class hotels, but it was very different a generation ago, a proletarian warren of seedily pleasant two-by-four bars and eateries where, as a young and eager student of the Japanese language, I happily put my classroom knowledge to the empirical test of beer and real-life conversation with salarymen red-faced from drink. Tsunohazu stays in my memory because it was here I first heard the word *amekō*, "damned Yank" in conversation—not in disparaging connection with me, I hasten to add, but in the context of a discussion on the virtues of American cigarettes. The speaker, the plump, middle-aged woman who managed the bar, quickly caught herself and assured me she meant no offense. I was startled at the word but quite pleased with myself, a budding lepidopterist who had snared a particularly furtive butterfly he had heard about from more experienced colleagues yet never seen himself.

Later, when the area was redeveloped, the name Tsunohazu was apparently judged to be in bad odor and unsuitable for posh luxury hotels and government offices and was changed to the bland, if descriptive, West Shinjuku.

Until recently the moving sidewalk there took pedestrians from the grand opulence of the city hall complex—described here in the Hino story "Jacob's Tokyo Ladder"—and the luxury hotels around it and ironically delivered them into the midst of a phalanx of Tokyo's homeless clinging to the western edge of Shinjuku station. Arrival there was foretold by the smell of stale urine and attenuated disinfectant. The small, cramped encampment—homeless living in large cardboard containers— was the remnant of an even larger settlement that at one time extended along the passageway leading from the station to the city hall area before the police rousted its luckless inhabitants. A fire in 1998 took the lives of four of the squatters and led to the forced dispersal of the homeless and the apparent end of the cardboard shantytown, only "apparent" because of the demonstrated tenacity of these unfortunate people to regroup and reclaim.

The homeless of Tokyo can be found elsewhere in the city, of course.[8] Many live in parks or along the banks of rivers such as the Sumida, sadly conspicuous under their bright blue tarp shelters. The best thing that can be said about this persistent social problem is that it has not reached the grand Reaganesque scale seen in U.S. cities.

Across the tracks from the municipal bureaucrats and liveried doormen of West Shinjuku is its antithesis, the misnamed Kabuki-chō, which has nothing to do with Kabuki and a good deal to do with commercialized sex: massage parlors, porn shops, peep shows and the like, and extortionate bars with muscular bouncers. Kabuki-chō also has first-run movie houses, good restaurants, and pleasant coffee shops, but visitors should be aware that it is the premier crime quarter of the nation. According to a recent report, during 2000 approximately 5,400 crimes were committed per square kilometer of Kabuki-chō. This is 40 times the national average.[9] It is a more than worthy successor to the bulldozed Tsunohazu.

Gaijin, or foreign, street entertainers were to be seen all over Tokyo in the early 1990s—certainly a testament to the draw of Japan's then vigorous economy—but were most heavily concentrated in Shinjuku. One-man bands, guitar players, Irish fiddlers, dancers, or singers, rap and otherwise, seemed to be plucking, dancing, or singing for their dinners on every corner, and at an entrance to the train station commuters might see a five-man band, the centerpiece a superb Beiderbeckian trumpeter. Each performer or group had a generous receptacle to solicit money, and if he or she was a regular at a particular location, one can assume the local *yakuza* got a cut of the action, or at least considered it his due. Most of the street entertainers are gone now, swept into the ash heap of history by a gloomier economy and impatient municipal authority. On the weekends when the main street through Shinjuku and the Ginza district is a "pedestrian paradise," open to strollers and closed to vehicles for several blocks, the local police sometimes post a sign in the middle of the street for all to see. "WARNING!" it says in English in large red letters, "Act of vending performance on the street is prohibited."

Aside from the Immigration Department, where a disregard of the niceties is not surprising, I've come across very few such displays of cautionary signs specifically directed at the non-Japanese of Tokyo. I was, however, brought up short recently by the following three separate notices posted—in English—in an Asakusa bank.

POLICE PATROL STOP
THIS BANK IS PROTECTED BY AN EMERGENCY ALARM SYSTEM.
ANTI-CRIME CAMERAS IN ACTION

Such signs suggest that certain of the English-reading *gaijin* of *shitamachi* have not been on their best behavior, and, unfortunately, recent statistics support this. Police say that compared with 1980, serious crimes committed by foreigners have seen a twenty-five-fold increase.[10]

The name Shinjuku is synonymous with urban adventure, but it also has its ungaudy areas. I recently wandered one overcast Sunday afternoon down a street to see where it could take me and came upon a funeral service in progress at the Taisōji, a temple on a subdued side street in 2-chōme.[11] In an annex next to one of the temple buildings a class in *nagauta* was in progress, a woman singing in accompaniment to the samisen. A sign on the fence announced classes in flower arranging (the Sōgetsu school), English, calculation, and arithmetic. I sat on a low wall and listened to this serendipitous performance; it reminded me that I was, modish Shinjuku notwithstanding, in Japan. I could see through the window that most of the students were middle-aged women.

Paradoxically, the Shinjuku district appears only infrequently in this anthology, in the Hino story and in "From Behind the Study Door," Natsume Sōseki's recollections of his childhood. This is less a result of happenstance or the compiler's literary biases than the fact that when it came to setting, the colorful *shitamachi* and the sophisticated Ginza and environs tended to be favored, at least until well into the last half of the twentieth century.

Though it will not be obvious to the modern eye, old Edo and early Tokyo relied a great deal on the waterways of the city. In the Edo period goods now transported by bellicose, fuming trucks went by boat through the many rivers and canals. And a dandy bound for sex in Yoshiwara could go ostentatiously by boat, if he wished; even a visitor to the theater district in Saruwaka-chō in Asakusa might be ferried there, as we read in Sōseki's memoir "From Behind the Study Door." The *shitamachi* of an earlier day was, in fact, compared favorably, we are told, with Venice. Now much of the traffic on the remaining waterways falls under the category of urban amusement: the still-popular river bus rumbling its way up the Sumida, mentioned in Nagai Kafū's midcentury "Azuma Bridge," or *yataibune*, roofed restaurant boats that take diners out on the river for an agreeable meal and a refreshing breeze in the heat and humidity of a Tokyo summer.

A picture postcard from the 1920s shows Sukiyabashi Bridge in the heart of the city as almost bucolic,[12] a waterway through which flowed apparently clear, clean water under a graceful double-arch bridge. A tree is visible on one bank. By the fifties the tree was gone and the water was a foul-smelling, inky-black pool, seemingly too burdened with the offal of the city to move. I would like to report that the canal was subsequently restored to robust health, but in fact it was euthanized prior to the 1964 Olympics and filled in to serve in death as a foundation for two formidable symbols of rampant consumerism in contemporary times, an elevated expressway and a shopping center.

Two remarkable buildings that stood by that same canal are also gone, but certainly not forgotten by those who saw them. It would be hard to find two more architecturally incompatible structures than the rotund building that housed the Nichigeki theater, perched under its white-tile facade like a massive coconut cake at the edge of the Yūraku-chō district, and its immediate neighbor, the very unrectangular *Asahi* newspaper building. It is said the latter was designed to resemble an ocean liner, and, in fact, had porthole-style windows on the upper floors. The Asahi building must have been a spectacular sight when it was first built, berthed on the riverbank, the crimson and white company pennant, the rising sun, flapping in the wind. By the time it and the Nichigeki were demolished in the early 1980s, however, the exterior of the building had taken on a dingy olive-drab patina more suggestive of tombstones and mold than an ocean-going vessel. These two architectural landmarks have been replaced by a massive work-and-play complex known as Mullion, a much more fitting venue for a risen Japan and its more materialistic citizens. The two buildings house cinemas, two large department stores, restaurants, coffee shops, an art gallery, and even office space. The gilded practicality of the complex is symbolized by a huge mechanical clock of polished brass that emerges from the front of the building in a spectacular flourish of rambunctious tintinnabulation, climaxed by the chiming of the hour. Impossible to ignore, it has made itself one of the landmarks of Yūraku-chō. Years ago there was a popular song that beckoned lovers: "Let's meet at Yūraku-chō." Now the invitation, though not yet immortalized in song, has become more precise: let's meet at the clock.

For those who hope that the city will see its way occasionally to preserve at least a fragment of its past, it is a pleasant surprise to discover that across Harumi Boulevard from the clock—and here the Ginza district begins—the Taimei Elementary School is still educating children from the area. The present building dates from 1929, which, of course, is ancient by Tokyo standards. Like many such schools in the city it shares its precious urban space with a small public park.

Back in the early eighties someone writing for the *Asahi* counted the number of Ginza back alleys—that is, people-friendly walkways too narrow for cars and lined with sundry commercial enterprises—and came up with the figure 55.[13] These cozy alleys are in addition to the regular side streets that crisscross the roughly eight square blocks of the district. Unfortunately, there are fewer of these passageways now, many having been obliterated by the recent construction of large buildings, which put the incredibly expensive open space to use as part of the new building or reduce what were inviting urban walkways to functional, but barely passable, service alleys. The future only promises more encroachment and destruction of such charming passageways. Of course, these delightful Ginza walkways are a Faustian bargain in a city that is not a stranger to fire and earthquake, inaccessible as they are to emergency vehicles. The cynically hopeful response is to point to the common spectacle of a procession of fire engines, sirens wailing, crawling up a rush-hour Harumi Boulevard at the same leisurely pace as amblers on the sidewalk: the trucks are not likely to arrive in time to do any good in any case, so let us enjoy our back alleys.

For some the ultimate Sunday stroll is along Chūō-dōri, the main street through the Ginza district, arm in arm with the companion of your choice, leisurely making your way toward one of the Lion beer halls— the middle of the street on no-car days will permit an unhurried pace— for Pilsner and sturdy German sausages, and perhaps an amiable chat with someone like the elderly *shitamachi* man I shared a table with not long ago who had been a *tobi,* a fireman, who had taken part in acrobatic competitions atop the high ladder as a young man and had proudly brought his award certificates to prove it. Modern history buffs would be advised to continue on down to Shimbashi, where it is still possible to walk through the inviting backstreets beyond the JR station and see undemolished sections that date back more than forty years. The narrow alleyways of 2-chōme are lined on both sides with an uncountable variety of restaurants and libatoriums for every taste, and even the occasional coffee shop. By late afternoon the alleys are filled with smoke from what seem to be a hundred charcoal fires broiling and frying away, with the attendant smells of beef and chicken and pork dishes of every sort, and chestnuts roasting as well. You can turn a corner and still find—shades of an earlier, impoverished day—a traditional Japanese pawnshop, rather less common in these still relatively flush times.

Akasaka, a good stone's throw from the palace moat, has been a playground for adults for over a century, its geisha and exclusive *ryōtei*, or traditional Japanese restaurants, at one time the height of fashion and the talk of the town. Geisha can still be seen if one pays attention, and the sound of the samisen is never too far away, but most places where the good times roll are the bars and nightspots, where the burden of entertainment has shifted more to the customer. Akasaka, given its proximity to Nagata-chō, the bailiwick of the prime minister and the other political heavy lifters, has always attracted government bureaucrats and pols and been the natural site for *ryōtei* politics, so-called; it was here in the seventies that then–prime minister Tanaka Kakuei notoriously took his hefty hard cash payoffs.

I consciously avoided the lure of Akasaka when I was a student studying the Japanese language and culture and was never a habitué of the district, day or night. The district had a reputation as Tokyo's "foreign concession," an iniquitous playground for the sybaritic *gaijin*. I was not opposed to sybaritism, but I was then in the process of immersing myself—as thoroughly as the national ethos would permit—in the Japanese environment and considered contact with other non-Japanese a distracting, if not contaminating, influence. And experience had suggested that many such foreigners—people who were in Japan only because they or their kin were posted there by their company or the military—sat around and told each other that the country was a tiresome place and the maid utterly incompetent. And all this would be in English, a language I already spoke.

Akasaka was also known then for its scowling *yakuza*, and for huge and gaudy nightclubs, the latter now mercifully gone. These fleshpots were straight out of a thirties Hollywood film, and said to be capable of emptying a rich foreigner's wallet in the batting of a pretty eye. And of course all foreigners were rich.

Foreigners, less rich now, still live, work and play in Akasaka and

environs, as they have for over a century. There would seem to be relatively fewer Euro-American *gaijin* in the cosmopolitan mix now. There
is, for example, an unmistakable Korean flavor in the Tamachi district
of Akasaka, seen not simply in the number of Korean restaurants, but in
more subtle forms, as when a Chinese restaurant prominently advertises
that its luncheon special for the day is a kimchee dish.

At some point it came to me that it was perfectly safe, even reasonable,
to visit Akasaka in the daytime. I have since discovered that a stroll
through the area has rewards that extend beyond the transient pleasures
of overpriced restaurants and grog houses. A few minutes from the Akasaka Mitsuke subway station there is a Buddhist cemetery all but hidden
on a steep slope that rises up from a busy street, and next to it a holy
place dedicated to the steadfast Acalanatha. From higher up the hill the
sound of someone practicing the samisen. A few minutes away a narrow
walkway climbs, Telegraph Hill–like, to the top of a hill on which sits
one of the serendipitous pocket parks that are sprinkled about the city.
A sign informs the visitor that the park used to be the Tokyo residence
of the lord of the Hiroshima domain during the Edo era (and, more
relevantly, that the reader ought not go off with strangers). One does not
expect to find a small tree-shaded park sitting atop a hill in fast-track
Akasaka, yet here it is, right next to the studios of the Tokyo Broadcasting
System and placidly overlooking the busy streets below.

The fashionable Roppongi district, abutting the south flank of Akasaka, is also largely courting turf for the young adult. The population
that comes to play and the area itself, site of a large number of embassies,
share something of an international flavor. Before the Second World War
it had been an curious combination of well-to-do neighborhoods and
units of the Imperial Japanese Army, but this radically changed with the
arrival of the American military when the Occupation began in 1945.
The restaurants, bars, and nightclubs that sprang up to divert GIs have
been replaced over time by similar establishments catering to a broader,
international clientele, including people from the Japanese theater and
television.[14] The character of the area has continued to be dominated by
adult amusements and obsessions of one sort or another, not excluding
fashionable clothing shops and chichi beauty salons, but it is still possible

to turn off such a thoroughfare and soon find oneself on an intermittently serene lane given over to older, more substantial residences.

Aoyama, immediately west of Akasaka and Roppongi, is also known for its high fashion and its boutiques, but those are only the pricier tip of the iceberg. Almost any district of Tokyo has room for what is antithetical to its principal theme. Having had more than my share of excellent Fukienese dumplings at a ramshackle restaurant at the southern tip of Aoyama Cemetery, I decide I should take a brisk walk through its shaded, quiet grounds. On the street outside, an endless line of taxis parked along the boulevard in the hot early afternoon sun winds around a distant curve, the drivers catching a bit of noon shuteye. The cemetery, municipally owned, is known as much for its fine old cherry trees, lushly spectacular when in bloom, as for the once-notable dead who are interred there.

The raucous cawing of fat and saucy crows, of which there are many in the well-tended necropolis, is incessant, but—their funereal black notwithstanding—they are not exclusively companions of the dead. The birds are to be found all over the city and throughout Japan, though Tokyophiles naturally associate these in-your-face creatures with the energy of the capital. According to people who pay attention to such things, most of the crows to be seen flying from rooftop to rooftop in the Ginza, for example, are not residents there but fly in every morning from Meiji Shrine.[15] Which is to say, their daily routine is much like that of the people of the Ginza: they live somewhere else and come to the Ginza for their livelihood and—one suspects from the mocking tone—their amusement.

A stonecutter is chiseling in a new name on a family tombstone. I take his picture as he works, then, to my surprise, he calls after me and begins a conversation so wide-ranging and persistent as to suggest that his is indeed a lonely trade: the current state of the world economy, Japanese-American relations, black holes in space. He tells me the cemetery is permitting no new plots because the city wants to turn it into a park. He says the city is attempting to empty the cemetery by removing graves where it can be demonstrated there are no survivors, but that it would

be prohibitively expensive to move the plots of those with survivors—
many of the dead were prominent citizens in their day—since each family would have to be given considerable compensation.

Our expansive chatting is terminated by the roar of a large U.S. military helicopter that quite suddenly comes skimming over the treetops
and, passing directly overhead, disappears on the other side of a slate-
gray building of breathtaking ugliness. This relic of the Occupation, behind a high, equally charmless chain-link fence, is Hardy Barracks,
which the United States continues to use as a military base here in the
very heart of the city.[16] One can understand the attachment of the families
to their ancestral plots in Aoyama cemetery, but the Pentagon's continuing need for its barrack building more than half a century after the end
of the Second World War and a dozen years after the Cold War is considerably more obscure.

THE NEIGHBORHOODS

A suggestion of the somewhat less harried past can still be seen in the
neighborhoods of Tokyo. Araki-chō is an excellent example, a comfortable mix of elegant and semi-elegant *ryōtei*, sushi shops, residences, bars,
and sundry commercial enterprises set down in a warren of narrow,
winding streets in the Yotsuya district of western Tokyo. It is a hilly and
hidden enclave out of the indeterminate past that cannot be imagined as
one stands amidst the exhaust fumes and hurly-burly of the noisy thoroughfare that skirts it only a block away.

This is not to say that the essentials of city life have bypassed Araki-
chō. The metropolitan government recently laid various underground
cables along the main street of the quarter. Instead of tearing up the
surface of the street and disrupting the daily routine, the city, incredibly,
chose to go to the extra expense of boring underground and then de-
positing the dirt on a lot it had hidden behind a high wall.

Araki-chō has a small Inari shrine, built in 1683, and now stoically
suffering encroachment and encirclement by modern condominium
buildings. The low wall surrounding the shrine is incised with the names

of long-ago contributors to the cost of its construction, restaurants, traditional dance instructors, geisha houses, and even an ice dealer, all callings related in varying degrees to the so-called *mizu-shōbai*, or water trade, businesses engaged in satisfying the appetites of an essentially male clientele. I am startled by two loud handclaps behind me. A woman in her late thirties is getting the attention of *Inari-sama*. She bows and says a three-second prayer. I ask her if she comes often and she tells me she comes to the shrine every night, that she works "upstairs." There is a bar on the second floor of the building next to the shrine.

Women in kimono come down the street on their way to work in the various restaurants. It is not yet dark, but the lighted signs are already coming on. The district has enough houses—early postwar—to give Araki-chō a down-home neighborhood atmosphere, notwithstanding the commercial enterprises all about. Women stop in the narrow streets and chat. A fiftyish woman in kimono opens a can of cat food and gives it to her pet in the street in front of her home. I talk with a tiny woman in her eighties who has lost most of her teeth. She tells me she has lived in Araki-chō since the end of the war, having lost her home to a fire-raid elsewhere in Tokyo. She tells me there are still *okiya*—where geisha live, as oppose to entertain—in Araki-chō and says that the area was a red-light district in the old days, though she uses the term *karyūkai*, the "blossoms and willows quarter."

Araki-chō appears not to have lost its sense of community. A flyer pasted to a building wall proudly informs passersby that not only had the district's recently formed merchant association become the one hundredth such organization to be officially recognized by the ward, but, more important, the main street and a side street now have names. Suggestions for names had been solicited and voted on by the people of Araki-chō for the two streets—theretofore nameless—from some 100 entries.

Whereas Araki-chō is largely dedicated to the water trade, Shinsen-chō, an attractive residential area off Dōgenzaka, that is, Dōgen Hill Road, in Shibuya, is mostly residential, with only a spare sprinkling of bistros and boutiques about. It is a pleasant place to live, a quiet yet convenient retreat not too far from the good things of urban life, but not a congenial setting for Kafū's tarts and pimps. I'm struck by the stillness on the street within the mix of single-family houses, many neatly hidden behind stone or wooden fencing, and low-crouching apartment buildings. I can hear the footsteps of the occasional pedestrian approaching and the sound of Saturday afternoon piano practice coming from a nearby apartment house. This near-silence is not insignificant in a country where the greatest number of pollution complaints are concerned with noise.[17] Shinsen-chō is not quite as posh as the wealthy Shōtō area on its northern flank with its fine homes, art museums, and other high-culture venues, but it is only fifteen or so minutes on foot from Shibuya station and the statue of the eternally faithful canine Hachikō.

It should be noted that areas like Shinsen-chō, one station out from a large terminal, are said to be zones enjoying a relative absence of noise and commercialization, islands of calm in a sea of commotion. South Shinjuku on the Odakyū line is another such example of this terminus-plus-one law.

A two-story apartment building, a pale, yet jarring, powder blue stucco-walled intrusion, built on a rather steep slope, signals that I am leaving placid Shinsen-chō for a lesser elevation, and one with a more colorful past. Neighboring Maruyama had at one time been home to a flourishing geisha quarter and red-light district and a dozen fashionable restaurants toward the end of the Meiji era.[18] Some *ryōtei* still remain, but to those who wander a block or two in one direction, Maruyama will appear to be merely a slightly downscale version of the sedate Shinsen-chō. If approaching from another direction, however, the stroller will see that a phalanx of "love hotels" has invaded Maruyama and transformed it—in this more individualistic age—from a place of sexual provision to one of the do-it-yourself ethos.[19]

Having translated the Nagai Kafū story "Azuma Bridge," which mentions the former red-light district of Koiwa, a quarter I had never heard of, I decide that a visit is in order. My wife and I do not know precisely where to go, so we head for South Koiwa's Flower Road, since the term flower can be the metaphorical equivalent of the demimonde's red light.

Flower Road—the English words are used—is lined on both sides of the street with large flower planters in which grow all manner of flora. Quite charming and, intentional or not, an apt visual pun on Koiwa's gaudy past. Asked about said days, a middle-aged shopkeeper allows that there might have been bordellos "somewhere around here" before the war. Of course, we know from Kafū's short story that such was the case in the immediate postwar period. And the poet and novelist Sekine Hiroshi (1920–94) writes how when the Koiwa cell of the Communist Party, of which he was a member, formed something called the Koiwa Youth Cultural League at the end of World War II and set up a dance workshop at the local bathhouse to attract the young men of the area, attendance increased dramatically, at least at first. The youths, however, were apparently not that interested in Leninism and started drifting off to the nearby Tokyo Palace—mentioned in Kafū's story—a dance hall complex that also served as a massive bordello. The young men earnestly assured party members that the women there had asked them for dance lessons.[20]

On our brief stroll through South Koiwa we see no obvious traces of the area's bawdy past, only an Inari shrine, a still-thriving pawnshop, a public bath, "snacks" (these are bars), a "Philippine pub," and a sauna, all not too far from the station. The area appears to be a rung below the western suburbs of Tokyo—Kōenji, Asagaya, Kichijōji, and so on—on the socioeconomic ladder. The style and quality of women's clothes, my wife suggests, are a bit inferior to those found, for example, along the modest shopping arcade in Asagaya, just as Asagaya's are more than a jot below the quality in the Ginza. I see only one bookstore in an hour's leisurely stroll, not counting a small vacant lot beneath a forlorn wooden sign proclaiming it to be—or rather, to have been—the Yamashita Bookshop. The sole surviving bookstore—doubtless having seen the writing on the wall—is doing a brisk business selling fluff magazines and *manga*, that is, comic books for all ages. Having sniffed at South Koiwa, however, I must add that it is a pleasant place in its own way and certainly boasts a crime rate that many urban neighborhoods overseas would envy.

·   ·   ·

A VIEW FROM THE WINDOW

I look out the window of my room in Yotsugi, a cheek-by-jowl mix of small commercial and industrial operations and residences in the *shitamachi* tradition, hard by the Arakawa river. The woman next door, a widow in her late sixties with suspiciously black hair, is taking advantage of the sun after yesterday's thunder, lightning, and hail; she has put out her bedding on the railing on the laundry deck that extends from a second-floor window out over her garage and is vigorously beating the quilts of the house. Across the narrow street the barber's poles—he has two, one on either side of the entrance—spin in unison, displaying his readiness for custom. I can't see into his window from mine and can't tell if he is clipping and trimming, but there is a motor scooter in front of the shop, perhaps a customer's. Next door to the barbershop, on the low stone wall that indicates a boundary more than it provides privacy, a candidate from a recent election grins in duplicate at passersby from two identical political posters. Official posting boards for all candidates are scattered throughout the city at places that see heavy foot traffic, around train stations, and so on, but candidates also want to catch your attention on a quiet side street and cadge your vote. The city has gone to extra lengths and considerable expense recently to stop the proliferation of posters by wrapping telephone poles in aluminum plates that confront poster-pasters with a bumpy, no-stick surface, and this appears to be a successful ploy, but the city cannot bumpify all the walls and fences of the city. Besides, who would want it to deprive strollers of food for thought and, perhaps, ironic reflection?

A bald man in a pale green shirt that goes quite nicely with his walnut-colored head, so shiny it reflects the sun, hurries past the barbershop on an obviously important errand, or does he always rush past barbershops?

Sounds of the neighborhood. A motor scooter, then a car passing slowly, a sliding door opens and shuts—you know you are in Japan when you hear that—a baby crying, a machine thumping inscrutably behind the closed doors of a nearby shop (not a sound you would hear in the hills, in the better-off Yamanote district), the rolling, squeaking wheels of a baby buggy—simple back-carriage is long out of fashion—the distinct and muffled sounds of human voices, the sudden, deafening roar of a truck engine as the driver downshifts to the corner.

The sounds draw me outside and down the street. There is no sidewalk, but then no board-covered drainage ditch to sprain an ankle in, either. Another purely Japanese sound, the hollow bop of wooden pails hitting the floor of the public bathhouse and reverberating authoritatively in that tile echo chamber (doubtless with the inevitable pastoral scene painted on the wall . . . and who does those paintings?), brings me to a small shop—was the thumping machine here?—where a middle-aged man sits at a whirling buffer and polishes small metal objects, his door open to the street a meter away. I ask him what he's doing. He smiles and tells me he's buffing women's belt buckles. Three doors further down is another small shop, but they are taking the day off; the door is closed. Outside two large metal drums are overflowing with brass turnings, sinuous and shiny. On the floor above a faded coverlet hangs from a windowsill. Near the corner a forklift truck scurries across the street with its load of coiled cable and sets it down at the back of a tiny vacant lot. Workmen at a shop that makes gears take a break in front of the shop and are talking baseball. All are smoking, of course. And all the men are Japanese; I've noticed no workers from western Asia elsewhere either. The economic bubble has indeed burst, to use the tired media cliché, and blown away many of the young Pakistanis and Iranians, so numerous several years ago, who had come to Japan to work. The neighborhood is not without signs of affluence—two cars for that household, two satellite dishes for another—but there are also indications of poverty, or inattention. A two-story wood-frame house, boards out of true and its dull brown paint peeling, has stood empty for months, a FOR RENT sign nailed to a wall.

SAN'YA

Since its rise economically, Japan has been characterized by certain critics as a monolithic "Japan, Inc.," a society that moves in confident lockstep toward the goal of worldwide economic hegemony that is said to be just around the corner. Anyone who has had the opportunity to live in Japan knows that this is a caricature, and that the society, whatever its special qualities, is peopled with individuals of divergent abilities, temperaments, and life experiences. Those who doubt these differences exist should visit San'ya, by far the largest of Tokyo's several skid rows, which also functions as a *yoseba*, an assembly area for casual labor.

I went to San'ya recently because I was planning to translate Ikeda Michiko's short story "An Unclaimed Body," which is set there.[21] I wanted to get a feel for the place, and I was curious. I'd heard about San'ya for years and wanted to see it for myself. I had also recently read a firsthand account by Edward Fowler, an American academic who had briefly lived and, in fact, worked there.[22]

It is a lazy, sunny Sunday afternoon, but my introduction to San'ya is abrupt and pungent. I turn a corner at the edge of the district and am confronted by a very old and frail man urinating into the street. One sometimes sees—though much less often in Tokyo now than a generation ago—a man watering a wall or a fence, his back to passersby, but I have never encountered someone standing on a city sidewalk and urinating *into* the street. Beyond him, the roadway is littered with discarded newspapers and miscellaneous refuse, and the smell of stale urine hangs in the air. Further down the block several men lie on the sidewalk, passed out or merely asleep; one man is shirtless. Other men sit on the sidewalk, their backs against drab, weathered storefronts, and stare off into space. Several are elderly, but others are relatively young or middle-aged. I am struck by the banks of coin lockers in sheds off the street. One normally thinks of a coin locker as a temporary place for one's bag when traveling. Here it obviously has a long-term purpose, a place to keep those things for which there is no room in the cramped dormitory-like rooms that most men, and a handful of women, live in.

As I walk down the main street that bisects San'ya I feel I am stepping back in time. The storefronts—though certainly not the people—remind me of a rundown commercial neighborhood in nearby Asakusa of at least thirty years ago, before the Japanese economy had gotten back on its feet. I sense no hostility, no overt attention even directed at me, but I feel uncomfortable, nonetheless. I am, after all, an outsider come to slum the sights and go back to what can only be a better place. After a ten-minute walkabout I hail a passing taxi and leave, and not without a sense of relief.

IN THE OPEN AIR

Tokyo may seem as flat as a tabletop at first glance, but it is, in fact, a city of hills and dales, its slopes not as steep as those of San Francisco but inclined more than one might like on a hot and humid July afternoon walk. Most of this rolling topography is obscured by the buildings that blanket the city, but an extended stroll through most anywhere save for the landfill areas along the bay will confirm that topographical fact and take one up and down some of the 433 sloping roadways that are said to crisscross the city.[23]

As noted earlier, the quality of Tokyo's air has improved considerably since the very bad old days when, in 1970, for example, forty students at a single high school were bowled over by photochemical smog, and this was only one of the more newsworthy episodes of such egregious pollution.[24] The somewhat less noxious brew that often hovers over the city is referred to innocuously—even by NHK newscasters, otherwise figures of probity—as "haze," a term that brings to mind bucolic vistas of shimmering meadows early of a summer morn and a Bashō haiku on the hinterlands. This sort of obfuscation is a common pettifogging stratagem, quite like the enduring preference of TV weathercasters in Hawaii for the benign and tourist-friendly "showers," not "rain." Whether pure self-deception or for the benefit of the municipal ego, on a bad day in Tokyo both resident and visitor may still find themselves blowing lampblack into their tissues.

But haze or no haze, Tokyo is a city of green whenever the seasons will allow. It is a staple of Tokyoite pride that visitors coming up from Osaka are inevitably surprised to see how green the city is, whether in the form of parks or the unexpected tree. Greenness costs money, which for the Osakans—or so Tokyoites insist—is to be valued above all else.

Tokyo has over the years managed to set aside parks, large and small, which now remarkably number several hundred. Some of these, of course, are tiny, little more than green playgrounds; many were created in the wake of the 1923 earthquake and the destruction of World War II. This does not mean that no thought was given to park building before the twentieth century. Much of Sumida Park, a welcoming strip of shrubs, benches, and willow trees stretching along the river of the same name, dates from the eighteenth century.[25] Naturally, one can become inured to the sight of vegetation simply from repeated exposure. Returning to Japan last summer after an absence of almost a year, I noticed with pleasure the lush swath of green visible from the Chūō line where it bisects the midsection of the Yamanote loop, but a week later my eyes were either off in the default distance or reading that day's newspaper piece about the Liberal Democratic Party scandal du jour.

On an individual level, one can only be impressed by the seemingly universal ability of urbanites to create a patch of green, no matter how unpromising the surroundings. This cherishing of nature is a commonplace observation by outsiders, but it is especially striking in the *shitamachi* area of Tokyo, where there is precious little space for anything but two-man ironworks and the like, and the houses that are sprinkled amongst them on the omnipresent asphalt and concrete. The meanest dwelling inevitably boasts a line of potted greenery. A cryptomeria shoot, an aloe plant, some bamboo, and, in the lusher collections, a young pine of some sort, stand hard against the wall in the usual six-inch strip of land between house and street that such residents can presume to call their own. For the more ambitious or better off there are the traditional home gardens, and even rooftop or balcony gardens, some with unexpectedly impressive shrubs and trees. Rushing about the Matsuzakaya department store in Okachimachi in a desperate search for a foreign Visa-friendly ATM one day, I took a wrong turn, came out onto the roof of the building and quite suddenly confronted an entire Inari shrine. The shrine area, perhaps 20 by 30 feet, was completely natural: stone walkway, trees, *torii*, bushes, a pond with running water, even moss. It was tucked away in a quiet corner, but not languishing in isolation. A fortyish woman in business clothes was praying, doubtless for success in some endeavor, public or private.

Placid Yoyogi Park at the lazy end of a pleasantly warm, not too hot July day. A cooling breeze blows gently. Couples strolling, crows cawing, children playing, but in a very un-Tokyo environment: wide open spaces (and no cars!). Under a pedestrian overpass a man plays funky riffs on a saxophone but only moderately well, going flat and sharp here and there in the style of Bill Clinton. Another, however, practices scales on his trumpet flawlessly. I stand on a grate in the middle of a broad expanse of grass and am surprised to find I'm over the Chiyoda subway line. There is little wasted space in Tokyo. Every five or so minutes a train roars by under my feet, intruding into the bucolic illusion. Two young mothers pushing strollers—apparent strangers—admire each other's babes and chat briefly on the almost deserted walkway. I hear the metallic burr of the cicada.

Young people still gather in Yoyogi Park on weekends, but the *takenoko-zoku*, the Shedder Tribe young who used to change into outlandish costumes and befuddle bystanders with their coordinated group dancing have faded away, leaving behind a handful of now middle-aged men in leather who gyrate without the women, who have probably settled into respectable home and marriage two train-hours from the park. A student of Yoyogi Park fads, a fiftyish dispenser of fried noodles and shaved ice at his stall in the park, tells me that the Shedders more or less disappeared at the end of the eighties.

Tokyo has not been spared the curse of graffiti, though it is not as sorely afflicted as America's big cities. A nice wide, concrete wall, usually isolated, seems to be a tempting target. Yoyogi Park has a good bit, as has the wall in the aforementioned park along the Sumida River. Most of the scrawling is in Japanese, of course, though some is in English as well, usually of the simple four-letter sort.

Finally, although Tokyo is not known for its al fresco dining, there are many rooftop restaurants and beer gardens to enjoy in the summer, and even in winter one has choices. A Yūraku-chō or Ginza office worker looking for a quick and tasty bite and a beer after work can always repair to the simple restaurants that cling, year after year, to the massive concrete base of the elevated railway in Yūraku-chō like barnacles to a piling. Munching on a skewer of barbecued chicken liver underneath the tracks—*gaado no shita*, literally "under the girder"—I ponder the mel-

ancholy fact that several similar proletarian eat-and-drinkeries nearby
have been replaced by proper middle-class restaurants that choose to
seal their frail customers off from the elements with four walls. The three-
walled Tōunton, however, established in 1953, continues to enjoy considerable renown and patronage in spite of—or perhaps because of—its
lack of pretension as it carries on in its cave of concrete. Whatever the
fugitive fashions that flit through the trendy scenes of Aoyama or Harajuku or Shibuya, there will always be, I hope, healthy patronage for
the uncomplicated pleasures, for sitting in simpleminded contentment
in barbecue smoke and steam, laughter and chatter.

LOCOMOTION

How one moves about a city naturally affects one's experience of it. Pe-
dantically put, the mode of locomotion delivers sensory information in
inverse proportion to the efficiency of the transport. Pedestrians can hear,
see, smell, touch, and taste, if need be, everything in their immediate
space. Motorists' perspective is limited to where they can drive, and is
certainly without the luxury of leisurely regard. Subway riders, of
course, are the most deprived, whipped from point A to point B with
supreme dispatch, but ignorant of all but the immediate subterranean
environment. This is not to say that riding the subway in Japan is an
uninteresting experience. It can, in fact, be a sensual event, particularly
in summer if the air conditioning fails: tunnel air redolent of the oleo-
electric bouquet of train tracks and midrange technology blasting
through the open windows—if the windows open—the sense of speed,
the roar and grind of the undercarriage, the endless variety of intently
unconcerned faces.

Yet pedestrianship, for all its health-giving and educational virtues,
has always been a perilous choice in Japan. Losing a space dispute with
a car can be fatal, of course, but bicycles present the more immediate
hazard in the Tokyo neighborhoods, since the cyclist pedals along on the
sidewalk, where there is one, and usually at an practiced urban clip. It
doesn't take too long for malleable *gaijin* to adjust their conduct accord-

ingly: walk in a perfectly straight line and never veer left or right without a quick glance to the rear. Cyclists may warn of their approach with their bells and until recently bicycle brakes when applied gave off a hair-curling, high-pitched screech, but technological progress has largely eliminated this clear warning of possible collision. Thus whizzing handlebars may claim you, or at least whack your arm and put the fear of the sidewalk into you. Nature maintains its balance, however, since the pedalist, in turn, is prey for the motor vehicle.

Since the vast majority of workers must commute to work by rail, train stations on the Musashi plain continue to occupy a special place in the minds, if not the hearts, of the populace.[26] This in spite of an absurd and needless increase in car ownership. An outlying station naturally serves as a commercial hub for its immediate area, drawing a collection of shops about it, usually in the form of a user-friendly, roofed arcade. As for the business end of the commute, the writer V. S. Pritchett once observed somewhat grandly that the urban station a worker commutes to is "a quotidian frontier, splitting a life, a temple of the inexorable."[27] Bifurcation aside, it is unlikely your day-to-day Japanese strap-hanger, or any of the characters who people this anthology, would see the urban terminus as a temple of any sort. And for good reason. With notable exceptions—Tokyo Station foremost among them—train stations are utterly functional structures, steel beams, concrete, and heavy corrugated steel roofing to keep the nastier weather at bay. The labyrinthine Shinjuku Station is perhaps another exception, not because of any architectural merit, or even because it is the busiest station in all Japan, but because of its baffling maze-like structure and its role as the bête noire of tourists and Tokyoites alike. No one has described it more colorfully in English than the architectural critic Peter Popham: it is a "megastructure extraordinary . . . multistory shopping centers topped by floors of restaurants, endless promenades, seedy underground plazas, a station used by two and a half million people every day, home to hundreds of bums, place of assignation for scores of assorted fiends and deviants, yet neither sinister nor dangerous; only impossible."[28]

THE JAPANESE SHORT STORY TODAY

Having dilated on the neighborhoods and playgrounds of Tokyo, the lay of the land, the buildings and those bits of artifice and infrastructure that seem to be worthy of comment, I must quickly add, of course, that it is the citizens of the capital, the people who live here, who have made the city one of the more fascinating places on our planet, and—with the notable exception of Hino Keizō—they themselves are the focus of the writers translated here.

And here we must take note of an agreeable, if complicating, dynamic that is said to be at work on a broader stage than the 837 square miles of greater Tokyo. The people of the whole of Japan, with varying degrees of awareness and commitment, are in the process of embracing the somewhat amorphous concept of internationalization, reconciling their society, both economically and psychologically, to the outside world or, to use the current hopeful metaphor, to the global village, an equally ill-defined construct that has nonetheless captured the attention, perhaps even the enthusiasm, of citizens and subjects around the world.

Whether or not internationalization is eventually realized, much of the fiction being written in Japan today also partakes of these diverse moves toward globalization. Thus in looking for short stories and literary sketches that reflect the ambient vitality of Tokyo, one soon discovers that many of Japan's writers have likewise left capital and country behind for newer literary scenes, setting their tales in San Francisco, New York, Paris, and points beyond and between. The emergence of this adventuring literature in our age of relative affluence and ease of travel is certainly a welcome, even liberating, development, but it means that at the onset of the new century there is relatively less to choose from if we fancy a good Tokyo story in the fashion of Nagai Kafū or Hayashi Fumiko, notwithstanding the fact that Tokyo is the literary capital of Japan, the site of most of its publishing industry and the base for the majority of its established writers.[29]

This expanding literary locus, of course, is really an ongoing dynamic that dates back at least to the Edo era, when the center of popular culture was the vibrant Yoshiwara demimonde, itself only a part of the plebeian *shitamachi* district. By the end of the nineteenth century the setting for much of popular fiction was the *shitamachi* itself, where relative lack of socioeconomic mobility intensified the district's appeal to writers and artists, at least until the midtwentieth century. The *shitamachi*'s thematic charm faded over time as fire, war, and modernization destroyed its fabric, leaving us today, exceptional isolates aside, with little more than the Edokko spirit. Thus while roughly one-third of the stories in this collection are set here, it is significant that, save for Ikeda Michiko's "An Unclaimed Body," all the *shitamachi* pieces were published before 1955.

It should also be noted that all but one of those authors in this collection who write about *shitamachi*, Akutagawa Ryūnosuke, came from somewhere else, suggesting the not-unexpected attraction of "otherness" at work in a writer's choice of setting.

If a global perspective, abetted by affluence and ease of travel, has brought the outside world under the closer scrutiny of the contemporary Japanese novelist, or at least provided an exotic backdrop, there is a second impulse that these writers also share with literary colleagues around the world, the exploration of a domain that transcends world capitals and their ancillary provinces: the realm of fantasy. This natural impulse toward exploration—and the impatient belief that fiction today has reached a creative dead end—has propelled some writers beyond realism into fantasy, or into the more restrained subgenre of magic realism, where the story can evolve in a plastic environment just this side of surrealism. Murakami Haruki's diverting novel *A Wild Sheep Chase* is perhaps the best-known example of the latter to reach a non-Japanese readership, but what the literary and urban critic Maeda Ai observes about Murakami's works generally, that he has thoroughly expunged place-names, turning the city into an abstraction rather than an actual place, can also be said of many other writers today.[30] Each month in Japan literary journals that fly the belletristic flag provide examples of such fiction for the stalwart minority of the reading public that still buys them.

While, as we shall see in Saegusa Kazuko's "Firefly Tavern," the fantastic imagination has not forsaken Tokyo entirely, we must step back a generation or so to round out our survey of the urban literary environment. We will then find we are able to exploit the familiar tradition of the I-novel, feet-on-the-ground autobiographical fiction that, since it centers on the writer, also describes, with varying degrees of verisimilitude, her or his immediate environs, which for a healthy majority naturally meant Tokyo, the Big Persimmon, the political, economic, and cultural center of modern Japanese civilization. Much maligned by Western critics, the I-novel has the additional virtue of more readily exposing the reader to the ruminations of another mind, which, of course, is one reason readers read. Such ruminations can be banal and self-absorbed (though they may satisfy our own banal curiosity), but we may also encounter thought or scene or simulated act that resonates, or an insight that we can grasp with gratitude.

As for the short story, it is a congenial genre in Japan and still enjoys an impressive popularity, notwithstanding the recent encroachment of *manga*, the ubiquitous adult- and youth-oriented cartoon books and magazines, said to account for 30 percent of new titles annually. It is obvious from a perusal of the bargain tables that front the used bookstores of Tokyo's Jimbō-chō district, for example, that short-story collections are at least as abundant (and cheap) as full-length novels. The form seems to have a more loyal readership in Japan than in the English-speaking world, and particularly in the United States, where readers' tastes run to longer fiction. While the case can be made that a narrative like *The Bridges of Madison County*, outrageously popular several years ago, was a short story dressed in hardcover for the children of the telly age, it is certainly true that collections of short fiction in North America are less available than in Japan, whether in hardcover or paper.

It is too broad a generalization to say that the short story in Japan differs from its Western analogue in all specifics. Nonetheless, certain pieces here may at first baffle the foreign reader accustomed to fine-lined plotting and characterization. Such concerns often take a back seat to an imagistic focus on surface detail and to intense narrative subjectivity, as we see in Kajii Motojirō's "Mire," for example, or Hino Keizō's "Jacob's Tokyo Ladder." The Western reader may expect more process than texture, more story development than apparently idle rumination. But it is just this sort of writing that we turn to in our search for the flavor of an individual place, for the expression of its particular character or ambience.

This collection spans over eighty years, but it does not pretend to be comprehensive. Nothing less than a small library could adequately honor Tokyo as literary landscape for the men and women who have lived in and written about their city. The reader will find none of Tanaka Yasuo's neighborhood vignettes or Takami Jun's *shitamachi* fiction, and nothing by the all-but-forgotten Hamamoto Hiroshi, whose gritty descriptions of the seamier urban venues still fascinate the cognoscenti, and only a snippet from Kawabata Yasunari's sprawling *shitamachi* novel *The Crimson Gang of Asakusa*.

Yet even the most generous collection of urban stories can only present a transient take on its setting. A city is a place of growth and decay, and in the century plus of Tokyo's existence as the capital of Japan it has always been at the frantic forward edge of change, of destruction and renewal. Each story here can only be, at best, an artificial instant in time, an idiosyncratic cityscape that is subject to chance. Yet the ambitious aim of this collection is to provide the reader both glimpses of Tokyo in our time and a suggestion of other times that were once so much a part of the lives of millions of people who no longer walk the streets of the capital, a place that Edward Seidensticker, an explicator of Japanese culture not given to blandishment, calls "the world's most consistently interesting city."[31]

An important criterion for selection, aside from a coherent and appealing focus on Tokyo, has been previous inaccessibility. Any work not readily available in English that illuminated in an interesting fashion life in Tokyo was a candidate for inclusion. As far as I can determine, all but two of the pieces presented here, Hayashi Fumiko's "Old Part of Town" and Mishima Yukio's "Fountains in the Rain," are appearing in English for the first time. I have also included examples of what some Japanese critics call mass literature, middle-brow fiction that is usually omitted from short-story anthologies of Japanese fiction in translation, but read by a larger audience in Japan than the so-called pure literature included in such collections.

The anthology has been divided into Central Tokyo, *Shitamachi*,

West of the Palace, and the South End. This pigeonholing, of course, is for convenience's sake and overlooks the geographical untidiness of some pieces. The stories are arranged chronologically in each category.

All Japanese names are given surname first.

NOTES

1. Kankyō kanribu (department of environmental management), *Heisei nananendo Tōkyō-to kankyō hakusho (gaiyō)* (Environmental white paper for metropolitan Tokyo, 1995, summary) (Tokyo: Tōkyō-to kankyō hozenkyoku [metropolitan Tokyo environmental protection agency], 1995), 14.
2. Hidenobu Jinnai, *Tokyo: A Spatial Anthropology*, trans. Kimiko Nishimura (Berkeley: University of California Press, 1995), 9.
3. The Izumo Bridge was only one of many to be destroyed. At the time of the 1923 earthquake there were some 400 bridges in Tokyo. Most of the canals were filled in after 1945. See Edward Seidensticker's *Tokyo Rising: The City Since the Great Earthquake* (Cambridge, Mass.: Harvard University Press, 1991), 28–29.
4. Yoshinobu Ashihara, *The Hidden Order: Tokyo through the Twentieth Century*, trans. Lynne E. Riggs (Tokyo: Kodansha International, 1989), 58.
5. Morimoto Tetsurō, *Boku no tōkyō mukaroku* (An account of my paradisiacal Tokyo dream) (Tokyo: Shinchōsha, 1995), 171.
6. Ashihara, *Hidden Order*, 62.
7. Morimoto, *Boku*, 272.
8. A 1999 government survey estimates the number of homeless in Tokyo to be 5,800, but the actual number is presumably higher.
9. *Daily Yomiuri On-Line*, May 17, 2001.
10. This estimate excludes foreigners who have permanent residence status. Article in *Asahi Shimbun*, evening edition, September 24, 1999, reprinted in *Gekkan Shimbun Daijesuto* (monthly newspaper digest), no. 400, November 1999, 186.
11. The 2-chōme district is perhaps better known for its gay bars. See John Wittier Treat's *Great Mirrors Shattered: Homosexuality, Orientalism and Japan* (Oxford: Oxford University Press, 1999).
12. Jinnai, *Tokyo*, 188.
13. Ibid., 131.

14. For a study of a Roppongi hostess club by an anthropologist who actually worked in such a club, see Anne Allison's *Nightwork: Sexuality, Pleasure, and Corporate Masculinity in a Tokyo Hostess Club* (Chicago: University of Chicago Press, 1994).

15. Izumi Asato, *Tōkyō nijūsan-ku monogatari* (Tales of Tokyo's 23 wards) (Tokyo: Shinchōsha, 1988), 31.

16. In fact, the U.S. military was accused several years ago of illegally expanding the base. See the *Shūkan asahi*, April 26, 1996, 154–55.

17. Mitsuyasu Yamashita, "The Soundscape of Japan," *The Japan Foundation Newsletter* 24, no. 6 (March 1997): 1.

18. *Kadokawa nihon chimei daijiten* (The Kadokawa dictionary of Japanese place-names), Takeuchi Rizō, et al. (Tokyo: Kadokawa Shoten, 1991), 13:664.

19. Where prices are prominently displayed, English is now used in the signage, e. g., "Stay ¥9000, Rest ¥5000."

20. Sekine Hiroshi, *Pabirion* Tokyo *[sic] no machi* (Pavilion Tokyo, the city) (Tokyo: Sōjusha, 1986), 81.

21. Actually, the name San'ya was eliminated in 1966 by a wave of the bureaucratic wand. The district is made up now of Kiyokawa, Nihonzutsumi, and bits of surrounding Tokyo jurisdictions.

22. Edward Fowler's groundbreaking *San'ya Blues: Laboring Life in Contemporary Tokyo* (Ithaca: Cornell University Press, 1996).

23. An estimate in Yokozeki Hideichi, *Edo no saka, Tōkyō no saka* (The hill roads of Edo, the hill roads of Tokyo) (Tokyo: Yūhō shoten, 1970), 228.

24. Ōhama Tetsuya et al., *Edo Tōkyō nempyō* (A chronology of Edo and Tokyo) (Tokyo: Shōgakukan, 1993), 229.

25. With its high population density, however, Tokyo enjoys roughly only a quarter of the park space of New York and a tenth that of London, figured on a per capita basis.

26. According to government statistics, roughly one in four of those who commute to school or work in central Tokyo spends three hours commuting. See *Heisei 11-nen nihon no hakusho* (Japan white paper, 1999) (Tokyo: Seibunsha, 1999), 288.

27. Quoted in Paul Bailey, ed., *The Oxford Book of London* (Oxford: Oxford University Press, 1995), 281.

28. Peter Popham, *Tokyo: The City at the End of the World* (Tokyo: Kodansha International, 1985), 104.

29. This creative departure from Tokyo is especially noticeable in the fiction of younger writers, and particularly the women, whose considerable experience of living or traveling abroad, largely in North America and western Europe, has led to the creation of an orthographic

subgenre, the pages of which are leavened with distant place-names and people, a *katakana*-ized literature, to identify it with the Japanese syllabary used for transliterating foreign words.

30. Maeda Ai, *Maeda Ai chosakushū, daigokan: toshi kūkan no naka no bungaku* (The writings of Maeda Ai, book 5: Literature in urban space) (Tokyo: Chikuma Shobō, 1989), 397.

31. Edward Seidensticker, *High City, Low City: Tokyo from Edo to the Earthquake* (New York: Alfred A. Knopf, 1983), vii.

CENTRAL TOKYO

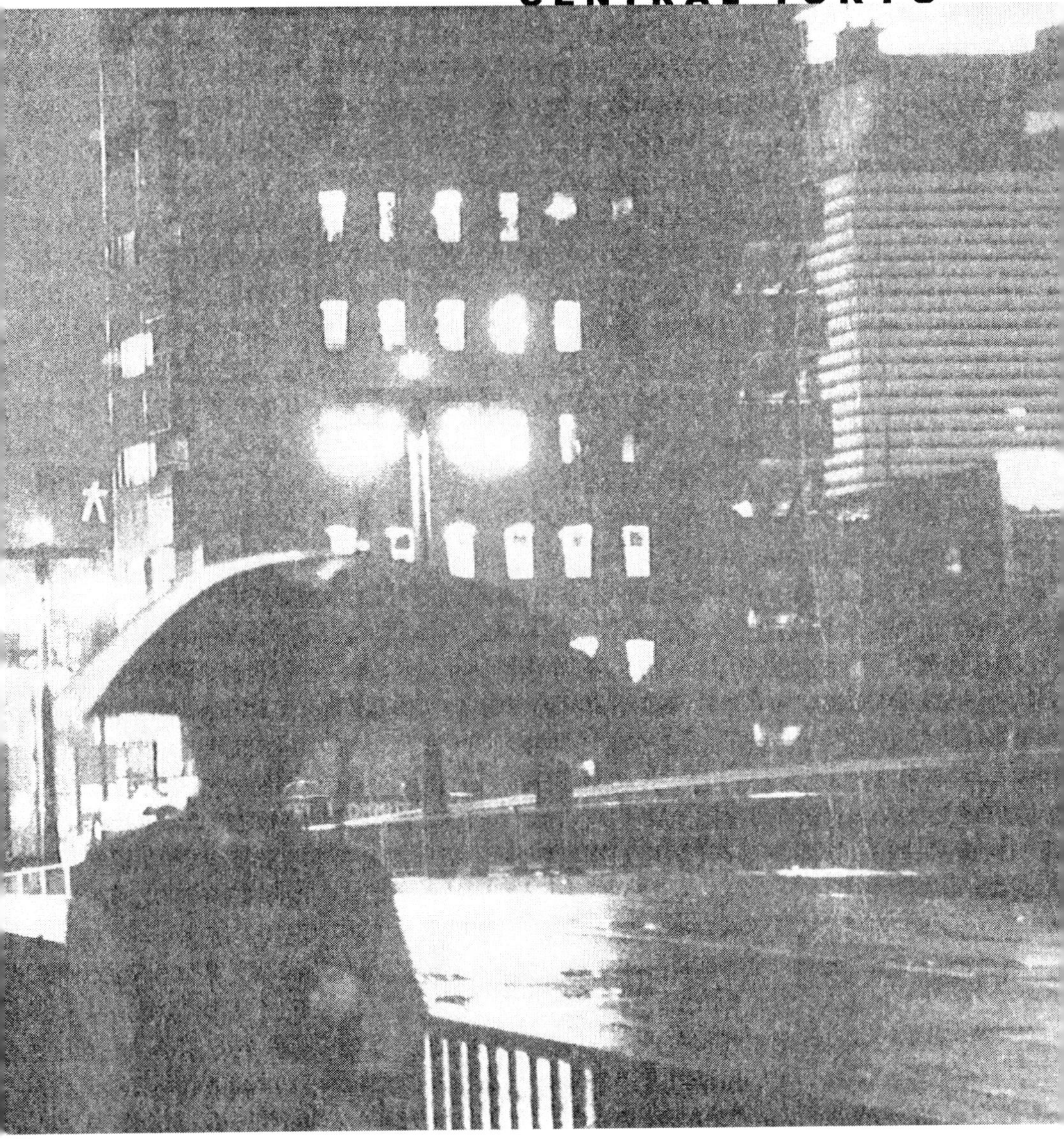

Mire

KAJII MOTOJIRŌ

The short story Deinei *(Mire) by the frail and febrile Kajii Motojirō (1901–32)*
begins as what seems to be a run-of-the-mill I-novel, proceeding seemingly to
no point and in exquisitely trivial detail: "I" has received a second money order
from home — the first was invalid for some unexplained reason — and decides to
"kill two birds with one stone," a strategy allowing him to cash the order and
divert himself with a visit to the Hongō district of Tokyo. As the story languidly
unfolds, we come to realize that the intricate, yet labored cogitation underlying
each decision suggests that the narrator's temporizing is pathological. The nar-
rator of "Mire" is anxious, distracted, and obviously depressed. Fortunately for
our purposes his Poe-like self-absorption is still less than total; he is able to
situate his dark ruminations in — and make his way through — the streets of
Tokyo.
The ever revising Kajii, who received little recognition for his short stories

during his brief and unhappy life, left behind a small body of well-crafted work that is an uncommon and felicitous combination of intense I-novel self-observation and vivid imagining in which the self serves as a point of departure into a psyche as extravagantly creative as it is ill at ease in the world. "Mire" and his other short stories reflect the isolation imposed on him by his personality and by the tuberculosis that eventually killed him at the age of thirty-one.

Kajii wrote "Mire" in 1925, a time when the Ginza district was the undisputed center of Tokyo. The Lion Beer Hall where the narrator gets mildly tipsy is still at one corner of what is generally considered the main intersection in the Ginza district. Built originally at street level and dropped into the basement after the war, it is now part of a chain and remains a popular place for beer and refection, if somewhat yuppified now with dark wood paneling and abstract art on its walls.

· I ·

It happened one day.

The money order from home that I'd been waiting for arrived, so I decided to kill two birds with one stone: visit the Hongō district and cash it. I lived in the suburbs, and the thaw after a snowfall is tiresome to deal with, but this was money I had been waiting for, so I set off in spite of the snow on the ground.

Some time before, a piece I had written with the expenditure of considerable energy turned out to be a failure. Aside from the fact of its failure, the oddly morbid nature of *how* this occurred had a baleful effect on me thereafter. Thus it was that I was looking for some sort of diversion. Since I'd run out of money, it had been impossible for me to get out and about. To make matters worse, for some reason the money order they had sent from home was invalid and I had to send it back, a reality that, during the four days I had to wait for it, made me all the more miserable. The money order I received this particular day was the second one.

I would guess it had been over a week since I gave up trying to write. My life during this period was transformed into something utterly sapped of vitality and bereft of equilibrium. As I've already said, the failure already had the taint of disease about it. It was then that my desire to write first faltered. During this period I found, for example, that the instant I would be about to write down what had come into my mind, I was, curiously, unable to remember what it was. And I was no longer able to reread something and revise it. How should I change it? There was no way I could recapture the feeling I had had when I first wrote it. I began to sense dimly that it was no good getting entangled in something like this. Yet I'm a tenacious sort and did not give up. I was unable to give up.

My condition after I stopped writing was, as I had feared, not good. I was in something of a daze. This state of indolence went beyond the bizarre that I normally experienced. Disposing of a vase with flowers that had withered, even though the water had turned putrid and was extremely unpleasant, was just too much trouble, and I did nothing. My displeasure grew each time I laid eyes on it yet never evolved into a desire to dispose of the flowers. Rather than merely being confronted with what was troublesome, I felt I had been bewitched. I detected the scent of this bewitchment somewhere within my indolence.

I would start to do something, then inevitably at some point find myself abstracted. Though I might snap out of it and turn back to what I had been doing, having observed my stupor, my feelings toward my task would now turn strangely empty. No matter what I began, I found myself thus endlessly repeating this stopping in midstream, this unfinishing of things. And as this happened again and again, the thrust of my daily life spontaneously and inevitably marshaled these aborted attempts against me. Thus it was that, like a swamp forbidden movement, I was utterly unable to flow freely out of my stagnation. And something akin to marsh gas was bubbling up from the bottom of the bog. These were my unpleasant fantasies. Fantasies that one of my blood relatives was about to meet with misfortune, or that I had been betrayed by a friend, suddenly came to the fore.

It was just at that time when there were many fires. I made it a habit to stroll through a nearby field a good deal. New houses were under construction everywhere there. I looked at wood shavings lying all about and noticed that I was none too carefully tossing away my lighted cigarettes. Quite dangerous, I concluded. There had been two fires nearby, and each time I had been assailed by the nebulous unease that I was about to be arrested, doubtless because the memory of my heedlessness had stayed with me. I felt that if someone had said "You were walking around here, were you not? The fires started from the cigarette you threw away," I would have been completely unable to refute him. And I hated to see the telegram delivery boy running along with his messages of dread. My fantasies made me weak and wretched. Absurdly, I would then continue on in this truly weak and wretched state. The awareness of which was unbearable.

With no desire to do anything, I would vacantly gaze at my mirror or a ceramic water pitcher with roses painted on it. Though I did not sense within me a place where my heart could find rest, I did discover there brief moments when my heart was at peace. Often in the past I had experienced this feeling in an open field. It had been an extremely unfocused feeling, yet as I was staring at the grass blown by the wind, I sensed at one point that there was something in me trembling just like the blades of grass around me. It was not something sure and certain. It was a faint sign yet, curiously, I did experience the sensation of grasses rustling before the autumn wind. I felt as though I had been plied with drink, and afterwards my heart would inevitably be invigorated.

Facing the mirror or the water pitcher, it was natural I would recall that sensation. I thought fervently on more than one occasion how nice it would be if one's feelings could be diverted as easily. Yet whether I might think so or not, I often stared in vacant fascination at such things. The charming pitcher, accommodating a pinpoint reflection of the room light on its cold white surface, held for me, incapable of any act as I was, a truly bizarre fascination. The clock struck two, then three, but I did not go to bed.

Peering into the mirror late at night could be, depending on the hour, a terrifying thing. My face would appear to me the face of a stranger, and as I stared hard at it—perhaps because my eyes were tiring—it would change into a mask that looked exactly like the hideous Dropsy Mask of the Gigaku ballad drama. The face in the mirror would abruptly disappear, then reappear like invisible ink put to the heat. Often only one eye would be visible, and this would glare at me. Yet fear, by its nature, is something that to some extent one can manifest and withdraw at will. I was in terror of the Gigaku mask in the mirror, and at the same time I was driven by an urge to amuse myself with it, like a child playing at the seashore, chasing and being chased by the waves as they surge upon the shore and recede.

My sense of immobility, however, was still with me. The feeling I experienced of having been bizarrely transported to a strange place when I looked into the mirror or at the water pitcher seemed, on the contrary, to be foully entangled with my sense of stagnation. And even if that were not the case, I would sleep until noon, dreaming every minute, and often had afternoons when I was no longer able to distinguish between dream and reality, when I was unpleasantly tired. I had at some point gone on to have moments when I felt the world I was experiencing was uncanny. Instances when, walking in town, I could startle myself simply by suspecting someone might see me and say as they hurried away, "Where did that jerk come from?" I also wondered if the face of a girl taking care of a child would show itself to be a monstrosity were she to raise her face to look at me.

The money order I'd been waiting for had finally come, however. For the first time in a good while, I headed down the snow-covered street to catch a train.

· 2 ·

By the time I got to Hongō from Ochanomizu I had seen three people slip in the snow. When I got to the bank I myself was in a rather foul mood. I waited for the clerk to call my name, putting my geta, now wet and heavy, on top of a gas stove, glowing red from the heat. A shop apprentice was positioned directly across from me. A little while after I took my geta off the stove, I somehow concluded the shop boy was watching me. I had been looking at the floor, dirtied with the mud tramped in with the snow. Now my eyes, bizarrely, had no place to go.

I knew I was fighting a demon entirely of my own making, yet I nonetheless found myself imprisoned in the lad's imagined scrutiny. I recalled my habit of blushing beet red in such situations. Have I not gotten a little red already? At that instant I felt my face flushing.

It was a long while before the clerk called my name. He was a little too lackadaisical. To mount a demonstration of my impatience I twice walked up to the clerk I had given the check to. In the end I finally talked to him. The draft was in the hands of a second clerk, who was sitting there with a vacant look on his face.

I left and went toward the front entrance. Two policemen were on either side of a young woman, supporting her as they went along; perhaps she had dropped dead in the street or had passed out and fallen. Passersby had stopped and were watching. I entered a barbershop without stopping to look. The barber's water heater had broken down. I asked the barber to wash my hair, so he washed it with soap, then only wiped it with a wet cloth. I suspected this was not a new style, but I felt curiously taciturn and said nothing at first. Yet I couldn't bear the discomfort of soap still in my hair. When I asked the barber about it, he told me the water heater was broken. He then ran the wet towel over my head again. I paid and took back my hat, touching my head as I did so. As I feared, there was still soap in my hair. I felt that I would be thought a fool if I didn't say something, but I gave up the idea and went outside. I was absurdly angry when I thought of how I had begun to enjoy the pleasant feeling of a cleanly washed head, only to be deprived of the sensation. I went to a friend's lodgings and rinsed off the soap. We then engaged in small talk for a while.

As we were talking I felt my friend's face become strangely distant. And what I was saying seemed to have nothing to do with the point I was trying to make. I even had the feeling that the person I was talking to was someone else, not my friend. And I was certain he sensed that I was a bit strange. He was not inhospitable, but I wondered if he himself was afraid to mention this strangeness and so sat there saying nothing about it. However, I didn't feel I could just ask him, isn't there something odd about me? I didn't so much fear that he would say "Now that you mention it, you are odd," as that my asking him if I were odd would amount to acknowledgment on my part of my strangeness. Were I to make that acknowledgment, it would be the end of everything. The fear of that was there. It was in my mind, yet my mouth was chattering away.

"You shouldn't shut yourself away so," my friend said, seeing me to the door. "You should get out more."

I wanted to respond to that too, but I merely nodded and left. I felt like a man released from jail.

Snow was still fluttering down on the city. I walked through the secondhand bookstore district. They might have had books I wanted to buy, but I'd been short of money so long my tight fist now would not let me buy anything. I would go from one bookstore to the next, then regret not having bought a book I had seen at the previous shop: *If you're going to buy this, you should've bought the book at the other store.*

This endless dithering left me exhausted. I bought postcards at the post office and wrote a thank-you note home for the money and an apology to a friend for not writing him. What I had found impossible to write at my desk now flowed with relative ease from my pen.

One shop I entered thinking it was a used bookstore had only new books. There was no one in the front of the shop, but someone came out from the back when he heard me walk in. Left with no choice, I bought the cheapest literary magazine they had. I knew the night would be unendurable if I didn't return with something. I felt my inability to endure to be strangely exaggerated. I knew it was exaggerated, yet I did not feel I could escape it. I once again walked back to the secondhand bookstore I had visited earlier. I was, however, still unable to make a purchase. I tried telling myself I was acting like a skinflint, but it was no use. I returned again to another shop, now for the last time. It had begun to snow in earnest and they were putting inside the book tables from out front. This time I was determined to buy the secondhand magazine I had asked the price of the last time I was here and decided against buying. It struck me as inane that this magazine, whose price was the very first I asked about in the very first shop I had visited, would become, in the end, my final choice. A shop boy from another bookstore had come to throw snowballs, so the lad in the shop was distracted. I couldn't find the magazine where I was sure it had been. I certainly couldn't believe I'd come to the wrong store, but I felt uneasy and asked the shop boy.

"Did you forget something, sir?" he asked halfheartedly, for he was eager to get at his attacker. "We don't have anything like that."

It was nowhere to be found. I was, as usual, defeated. I bought a pair of *tabi* socks and hurried to Ochanomizu. It was evening now.

I bought a rail pass at Ochanomizu. On the train I tried to figure in my head how much it would cost to go back and forth per day, since I would be going to classes every day now. I couldn't calculate it no matter how I tried. The answer I kept getting was that the pass had cost me as much as buying a ticket each time I took the train. I didn't ride to my stop but got off at Yūraku-chō, walked to the Ginza district and bought tea and sugar, and bread and butter. There were few people about. Here, too, several shop clerks were having a snowball fight. The snowballs looked hard and must have hurt. Oddly enough, I found this annoying. I was also dead tired. For one thing, my failure at calculating today was too much to bear, so I was now defiant. I felt I constantly had to flaunt this defiance, buying, for example, a single 8-sen roll, then waiting for my miserable 2 sen in change. If a store didn't have what I asked for, I fussed and fretted.

I went into the Lion Beer Hall and ate. I warmed myself in the hall as I drank my beer. I watched the bartender make cocktails. He would put various kinds of liquor into a container, put the lid on, and shake it. At first the bartender was shaking it, but in the end it looked to me as though it was the container that was doing the shaking. He would pour the drink into a glass, decorate it with fruit, and put it on a tray. It amused me to watch such agility *cum* precision.

I was feeling the effects of the beer a bit as I looked at the bottles of liquor all in a row.

Lined up like that you guys look like Arabian soldiers.

Righto. Like a festival in Baghdad.

I'm hungry, more than anything else.

· 3 ·

After I left the Lion I bought soap at a shop dealing in imported goods. Before I realized it, the sense of confusion returned once again. Having bought the soap, I began to think that my purchase was somehow strange. I simply could not remember whether or not I had had a clear-cut desire to buy it. I felt helpless, like a man treading the void.

My mother had often scolded me when I blundered:

"You can't do something while you're daydreaming!"

I suddenly realized those words were at the heart of what I had done just now. The soap had been absurdly expensive. I thought about my mother. I called out my own name.

"Keikichi! Keikichi!"

In my mind's eye I could clearly see the sorrowful expression on my mother's face.

One night three years ago I came home drunk from too much saké. I had lost all sense of shame. A friend had brought me home, and he told me I had been really disgusting. I turn lachrymose every time I think of how my mother must have felt. Later my friend told me what my mother had said when she scolded me, imitating her voice. He mimicked her so skillfully I would have sworn it was her. Even the import of what she said would have been enough to upset me, but the voice my friend re-created had the power to set me to weeping.

Mimicry is really odd. Now I was imitating my friend's imitation. Paradoxically, I had to hear the voice of the person closest to me from someone outside the family. Just by saying "Keikichi!"—without even repeating the words that had followed it—I was able to bring back to vivid reality the feelings my mother must have felt at the time. Uttering my name was the most direct stratagem, more so than any other. My mother's face, reproachful and encouraging, rose before me.

The moon had risen in a clear sky.

As I walked the pavement from the Owari-chō area to Yūraku-chō, I called out my name over and over: "Keikichi! Keikichi!" I felt a thrill of terror. My mother's expression, summoned by my calling out my name, had, before I knew it, been transformed into something else. The one who presides over the inauspicious—that's what it was—was now calling to me. I heard a voice I did not want to hear.

It takes some time to get to my stop from Yūraku-chō, and it's at least ten more minutes after I leave the station. I walked on utterly exhausted along this road of the deepening night that rose through a cutout in a hill. I could hear my skirtlike *hakama* rustling. Halfway up the slope a streetlight with a reflector on it illuminated the road. With this shining on my back, my shadow, long and distinct, crept along the ground. Under my cape I carried my bundle of purchases, and now by turns the lights on both sides of the street cast down my slightly bulging shadow. It would rise behind me, shift forward, stretch ahead, my head quite suddenly raised up to a door. As I pursued the helter-skelter permutations of my shadow, my eye fell on a shadow that changed not at all. It was an extremely truncated shadow and its starkness grew the further apart the poles became. Whenever a light asserted itself, it would abate.

That's my shadow in the moonlight.

I looked up to see the moon, perhaps midway through its phases, suspended almost directly overhead. For some reason, I felt a kinship with this shadow, and only with it.

I left the broad boulevard and started down a road where streetlights were few and far between. For the first time the light of the moon illuminated in its mystery the spectacle of the fallen snow. It was beautiful. I realized that my emotions had now settled considerably, and sensed they would settle even more. My shadow, only shifted from the left side to the right, remained quite properly before me. And now it was unfragmented and sharply defined. I walked on, doubting and yearning for the undefinable feeling of kinship I had felt earlier.

I wonder why that was.

Wearing my fedora, its shape gone, my shoulders jutting with some broadness from a neck that hints at a certain delicateness, I gradually lost sight of this *me*.

There was the suggestion of something that seemed alive emerging from the shadow. It was assuredly thinking of something; what was it thinking? What I had thought was a shadow was the real me! I shall walk on! And this me, here, looked down upon the other me from a moonlike height. The ground was limpid, as under a crystal cover; I felt a touch of vertigo.

I began to sense within me a nebulous unease: "Where do you suppose it's walking off to?"

Hot water came flowing from a public bathhouse into a culvert that ran in front of the bamboo thicket skirting the road. Steam rose up before me like a decorative screen, its smell assailing my nostrils. I was myself again, fully alive. The man in the tempura shop next to the bathhouse was still up and about. I entered the dark alleyway leading to my lodgings.

Terrifying Tokyo

YUMENO KYŪSAKU

Yumeno Kyūsaku (1889–1936) was a writer of mysteries beloved for his dark imagination and willingness to go beyond the usual bounds of the genre into fantasy. His life was almost as colorful as his writings. Yumeno was the son of a behind-the-scenes politico, a "black curtain" associated with the ultranationalist Genyōsha group. He seems to have agreed with his father about very little. Fortunately his grandfather took him under his wing and, we are told, instructed him in the Nō drama and the Chinese classics even before he started primary school. He studied at Keiō University in Tokyo, but his father made him withdraw and sent him off to manage a large farm, at which he was a failure. He became a Buddhist priest briefly, left the church and married, taught Nō drama, then became a reporter for a newspaper in Kyūshū, where he began his writing career by composing fairy tales for children. Finally, at the age of thirty-five, he began writing the mysteries upon which his reputation rests. In 1936 he suddenly collapsed and died while chatting with a caller. He was forty-seven.

Osoroshii Tōkyō (Terrifying Tokyo) was published posthumously, a year after Yumeno's death. We can see that Yumeno was also something of a satirist, who attempts the difficult trick of balancing self-mocking humor and self-righteous indignation. Using little subtlety or fine-grained description here, Yumeno adopts the pose of the simple provincial, honest to a fault and over-whelmed by the city and its devious slickers with their ready cynicism.

Whenever I go up to Tokyo after I've been away for a while, I find myself flustered and alarmed and gradually growing more terrified. When I'm out in the countryside I fancy myself something of an expert on the city, but when I'm actually in the city, I am, to my surprise, often a source of amusement for everyone.

Assuming that all trains leaving Yokohama go to Tokyo, I got on a train and was nonchalantly reading a newspaper when I suddenly noticed that the train was passing a vast forest. This was a surprise. We should have been arriving in Tokyo about then, yet—hmm—I wondered what park we were passing through and looked out the window, only to see we were on a one-track line. Now I was panic-stricken. I queried the conductor and he told me we were on our way to Hachiōji. *That can't be!* I got sent back to Kanagawa, tail between my legs.

Another time I wanted to go from Owari-chō on the Ginza to the exhibition hall in Ueno, so for the first time in my life I went down into the subway. There appeared to be department stores as far as the eye could see, and I could not tell where they were selling the tickets, on top of which, I could find nothing that looked like a station platform, so I guessed I must have come the wrong way and went up concrete steps again, to be greeted by a bustling district that was completely new to me. It struck me as quite odd; I didn't remember walking that far, but I then went down the stairs I had come up and climbed the stairs on the opposite side, emerging before a huge and magnificent clock shop[1] I'd

---

1. The shop was the Hattori, the clock tower of which remains an enduring Ginza landmark. The watch shop was later moved elsewhere to become the Seiko Watch Company, its place taken by the tony Wakō department store.

never seen before. I gawked in my bafflement, wondering if this could be Hirokōji in Ueno, but apparently it was not. Anyway, I realized I had to go back once again to where I had started, and when I climbed the stairs I had first descended, passing the shops I'd just seen, I at last realized what had happened. All three areas were part of the Ginza's Owari-chō and, not knowing that there are four entrances, I had become confused, seeing the underground crossing from different directions.[2] At the same time, I could tell from the noise that the actual subway was one more floor down. *So that's it!* Nonetheless, I was overwhelmed by it all and went straight back to the inn I was staying at.

When the Yamanote loop-line train stopped at Tamachi, the people who got off left the car door open. It was terribly cold, so I tried to close the door, but it just wouldn't shut. Minoru Kita and Setchō Itamoto,[3] who were standing right next to me, broke into side-splitting laughter. I was bewildered, but before I could fathom the reason for their mirth, the door—which, in fact, opens and closes automatically—closed and almost sent me flying.

I swore that I would never forget this affront as long as I lived.

There were two cardboard boxes next to each other on a table at a Ginza night stall, and a man was moving hard charcoal from one box to the other with a pair of iron tongs. When one box became empty, he began again to pick up charcoal from the full box and return it piece by piece to the empty box. This process was repeated over and over again. I watched with fascination, but I had absolutely no idea what was going on. From left to right, then right to left, one by one piling up the charcoal first here, then piling it there; he could well have kept it up all night. The man doing this was utterly serene. That so many people stood there watching all this struck me as bizarre. I watched intently, thinking that the purpose would become obvious any minute, but in time I began to yawn, so I gave up on the whole business and went home.

When I returned home and told everyone about what I'd seen, my

2. Yumeno is at what remains the Ginza district's principal intersection.
3. A prominent Nō performer and a scholar of the Nō drama, respectively.

sister and cousins collapsed in laughter. I finally realized that the point of the procedure was to sell the iron implement that was used to pick up the charcoal.

As this sort of experience accumulated, your correspondent gradually found Tokyo growing more terrifying. I had, at the least, come up to Tokyo fully aware that Tokyo was Japan's premier arena in the struggle for survival, yet when I looked at it from that perspective it appeared that the struggle for survival was beyond even flood tide and had evolved into a horrifically deceptive battle that was foreign both to humanity and to God. It may well be that neither the radio towers nor the Diet building that soar so loftily are genuine. Even Tokyo's blue sky and the sun and the passing clouds are possibly a kineorama-like⁴ deception. When it came to me that the sun and trees and the trains and people out in the countryside are all the real thing, I immediately wanted to go back there. The desire to look upon the smiling faces of mud-covered children burned nut-brown by the sun was irresistible.

The day before I left I paid a farewell visit to a certain prominent figure in the capital. The gentleman was of advanced years, in his early eighties, and stroked his white beard with quiet deliberation.

A man of about forty who had the look of a detective, muscular, with piercing eyes, and wearing a traditional *hakama* and *haori*, came in for an audience, prostrating himself in the adjoining room, and spoke as follows.

"This is the first time I have made your eminence's acquaintance. I am from X prefecture. My friend, one Y, volunteered as a private individual to engage in military intelligence work for our government, and entered and was active in an area under the control of the government of Z, in the process of which, and at a time when diplomatic relations were tense between Japan and the Z government, my friend and a dozen men under him were caught in a wholesale roundup. At the moment he was seized he grabbed his pistol and put a bullet in his head, achieving a glorious suicide and rendering impossible an investigation of all the facts in the

4. A diorama in which changes in lighting show the time of day.

matter, thus the situation is such that his captors cannot as yet determine the offenses of the twelve men under him. Given that my friend was, from the outset, a volunteer, it goes without saying that he cannot receive from His Majesty either a medal or a pension, and even the cause of death can never be made public."

The prominent elder gently nodded, his gaze fixed upon the man's face. Your correspondent was deeply moved by the words that poured forth with such deeply felt emotion. By now the man's eyes were red-rimmed with tears.

"My friend left a wife and three sons. We, his comrades, have come together and taken steps—feeble, to be sure—to ensure that they will not be thrown out into the street and will be able to feed themselves, but what is troubling us at this juncture is that we cannot tell the three children how their father died. Even now the little ones ask by turns their mother, and then us, his comrades: 'Where did Father die, and why?' We cannot answer, only weep. Thus, sir, if you might write a line or two, something that would indicate the reason why their father died, then, after they grow up . . ."

His voice trailed off and I could not make out what he said. Both hands on the tatami, he wept unashamedly.

The old gentleman gently pulled on his white beard and stood up. He had a mat and paper spread out in the room and wrote on it for the man the following in bold strokes.

If One Secures the Mandate of Heaven He Will Effect Loyalty and Sincerity. For Mr. Y.

The man departed, his heart filled with humble joy.

Later, when I went to a certain club and related this story, one of the men gathered there burst into laughter.

"I'll bet he sold the calligraphy for 10 yen on the way home!"

All the men laughed uproariously.

"There are plenty in Tokyo pulling that trick!"

Your correspondent was astounded. In an instant Tokyo became for me a place of fathomless terror. I declared to myself the sundering of ties for all time with the sorry lot at a certain club and left Tokyo behind me.

The Image

TAKEDA RINTARŌ

Takeda Rintarō (1904–46) focuses his "Omokage" (The image), published in 1940, on a woman's obsessive and unrequited love. That Takeda essays such a depiction is not remarkable, but his use of the first-person voice is certainly ambitious. The narrative tone is conversational, in the somewhat stilted language of a woman with pretensions to proper, middle-class life.

A subtle dynamic is at work here, one Westerners may not be aware of: courtship by patronage, a tenuous yet common mode of male-female interaction in Japan and other societies where access to the opposite sex is, or was, hemmed in by various social sanctions. Her bitter-end spitefulness may puzzle or disappoint us, but it conforms to the stereotype that traditionally warns men of a woman scorned. This dictum recycles tirelessly through Japanese popular culture, as an evening in front of the telly will confirm.

Takeda, remembered for his stories of Tokyo, was also a writer in the prole-

tarian tradition. In 1927, early in his career, the authorities banned one of Takeda's short stories as antiwar and in 1929 held him in jail for a month. Yet his sometimes grimly realistic view of working people is more Saikaku than socialist realism. This is certainly the case with "The Image."

———

You pass along this street every night late, don't you. It's always well into the evening. Your footsteps tell me you're tired, so I know you've been hard at work all day. I suppose you've been working overtime until this ungodly hour for your very large family. I know all about you.

The street runs in front of a shrine, comes to a vacant lot, and where it crosses the lot there are several rows of small rental units, tenements. Your place is at the back. I'm well acquainted with your situation, of course. I've even gone to the trouble of going there to see for myself.

Your wife must have been a beautiful woman in her day, but time takes its toll, and hardship is poison for a woman, isn't it. One wonders why so many of your children are sickly. And it's dreadful that you are burdened with an old person who can't walk.

I once saw a funeral procession leave your house. When I asked around your neighborhood who had died, they said it was a relative of yours. What a pity it is you have to take care of even those outside the immediate family. It stands to reason that you'll not have enough money no matter how much you work.

We live in the same general area, but your neighborhood and the area around me are remarkably different in character. I suppose that's the case in any suburb you look at.

Someone like me must look like a millionaire to you. I've overheard gossip on the street that I'm the widow of a millionaire or someone's mistress, which comes from the fact that I live alone. I am not a widow, and you certainly won't find a mistress anywhere who doesn't receive visits from her patron.

Shall I tell you the story of my life? But then, you wouldn't be listening to it. You simply pass in front of my house late at night, literally a passer-by and I, a woman who turns off the lights, go out onto the verandah, and watch you over the hedge as you go by. And you don't even know I'm doing this.

But once something happened. Of course, I'm sure you don't remember anymore. I had been careless. I had gone out onto the verandah, forgetting that the full light of the moon, almost as bright as day, would strike my body. You always walk along, head bowed, like a man carrying an unbearable burden of some sort. But this time for whatever reason, you suddenly looked up.

The bush clover was in lush bloom. You saw me here in a cluster of blossoms. I was startled by the gaze you directed at me and dropped my eyes and hunched my shoulders, as though shyly trying to conceal myself. Yet you did not hide your own surprise and stood before me for a moment. When I realized you were watching me, I felt my heart throb within my breast, so loudly I worried lest you hear it. You immediately began walking, however, and at a brisk gait.

Ah, but I knew right away that it made you uneasy. The instant I looked up, you turned and looked back at me, no doubt to make sure I was simply a woman sitting by herself, not an apparition of some sort. That was most certainly your intent. And as proof of this, your receding figure as you headed homeward was as it always is, your head bowed with fatigue, the very picture of a man void of emotion.

I don't suppose you had the slightest idea that I had been unable to still my pounding heart for some time after that. To the contrary, I suspect you gave no thought whatsoever to who in the world it was who appeared on the verandah, her face looking so ghostly, all by herself in the middle of the night.

But that's all right. Yet the season is gradually turning chilly, isn't it. Before long, frosts will be with us, and winter with its withering blasts not far behind. What must you think when you see a woman up and about near midnight in the bone-chilling cold, the storm windows still open?

But no, you need not give it a single thought.

I was going to tell how it had been, wasn't I? It would be no small error for you to think my rattling on by myself, nodding to myself all the while, is tiresome. No, perhaps you're right, perhaps it *is* tiresome. Shall I not bother?

I'll just talk about the time I met *him* for the first time. I was only eighteen, you know. I was so young; you might say I was a mere child and yet I was certainly capable of falling head over heels in love with a man.

Of course, I was not the proper daughter of some respectable, straight-arrow family. Which is not to say I wasn't still a virgin (and he was well aware of that).

I had been working in a restaurant. It was a relatively posh place in the Toranomon district of Tokyo. I commuted there from my home in Kamiya-chō. Actually, anyone my age should have been living at the restaurant, but they made a special exception for me, under pressure from my father. That was because my father was supremely worried about the future of his motherless daughter and had no desire to have me sleep away from home.

Which makes him sound like a fine father, but in his heart of hearts, he was merely—to put it bluntly—taking good care of his precious jewel so he could fetch as high a price as possible later. Perhaps this is a problem all daughters have, yet in my case, my father really intended to sell me to the highest bidder. He used to find out everything he could about any customer who came to the restaurant because he'd taken a liking to me, then go straightaway to the customer to sell me off. To call a spade a spade, he would agree to sell me, and—I know this sounds odd—come back with a deposit. Later, I was shocked when I found out just how many men did give him an advance. And please don't think I'm bragging about my looks.

I also learned that every bit of money my father received he threw away on drink and gambling, so for someone to be suspicious of father and daughter colluding at marriage fraud. . . . Ugh! The very thought disgusts me!

I say *someone*—but this was the man I came to love with all my heart. That fact is a humiliation I will never forget.

My father would send me off strolling with customers on days when we were closed. Beforehand he would repeat over and over again his long-winded cautions on seeing men outside work. He sometimes berated me, saying rather spitefully that since I was tall and had matured early, he had to keep an eye on me.

He would drive me to the verge of tears, and I would tell him if he was going to go on like that, then I wouldn't go. It wasn't as if I'd wanted to go out walking with these men. I was, after all, accompanying them reluctantly, at his bidding.

Flustered then, he would pull out all the stops, weeping unashamedly, and humor and bully me by turns.

"You want to disgrace your father? You're going to turn your back on your debt of gratitude to your father after I've struggled all those years, without a woman's help, to raise you?"

It was something right out of a tearjerker.

My mother died before I started school. The story was, she had worked as a maid at an inn and married my father, who worked there as a clerk. It would have been better if my mother had lived. My father, who had been a no-nonsense sort until she died, would not have run wild, and things might have gone better for me too. No. It wouldn't have mattered. It amounts to the same thing, doesn't it, assuming that cold-hearted man would have despised me in any event.

Some of the customers who went walking with me were unpleasant types. I had yet to develop a taste in men; even so, a lot of them made disagreeable comments to me. But I always danced away, childlike, out of harm's way and got home unsullied.

Sometimes my father would follow us, and yet when I returned home he would give me a fearsome stare, looking me over head to toe. His attitude was inquisitorial, suspicious that something had happened.

Let's put an end to this distasteful tale, shall we? I only need talk about the time I met *him*, wouldn't you agree?

It was the night of the festival for Kotohira, the god of the sea. That's when he first came to the restaurant.

It was a slow night in February and I was to wait on the next customers to come. He was with two other men and was quite moody, which made it awkward for me, since I was still young.

The men with him were not that lively either, but his facial expression was, by its nature, especially sour, on top of which he said next to nothing, so I found him quite hard to deal with.

When I went into the kitchen for the hors d'oeuvres one of the other waitresses sympathized with me.

"A dreadful customer, isn't he."

What do you think I answered? I had thought the same thing myself in a vague sort of way. But when she said that, I immediately contradicted her.

"No he's not. He's really nice."

Isn't it odd that when I went back to the room where they were eating, I now felt warmth, scant though it was, toward the customer who had heretofore been unsociable. *I just told someone you're a nice person,* I said to myself as I gazed at him in profile. The instant he looked down, I discovered, among other things, charm in the line of his jaw that I hadn't expected. Which had no particular importance, but there it was.

From then on he came to the restaurant from time to time. At first he was usually with someone, but at some point he began coming alone, now a regular and an excellent one at that, and no one said he was dreadful anymore. As I recall, everyone fussed over him and said he was a man of depth. I couldn't quite grasp what they meant by that, but I supposed they were right, and I was delighted they were praising him. But now *I* would say things to put him down a bit.

I heard he was the owner of a large Western furniture store in the Tamura-chō district of Tokyo. Everyone was envious and said I had gotten myself a fine customer because I was the sort men liked. Why do you suppose I burst out laughing when a middle-aged waitress told me she was sure he liked me?

"That's absurd, just absurd!" I said, my face beet red, and both hands pressed hard against my cheeks.

"Listen, that's impossible!" I coquettishly repeated the empty phrase over and over again, though it wasn't particularly absurd that he should be fond of me. That's to say perhaps I meant it would be absurd if *I* should come to like *him.* And it was absurd, because I liked him, no ifs, ands, or buts.

I was going to remind my co-worker that first there was the difference in our ages, and then that he had both a wife and a lot of cute kids, when I suddenly realized it didn't bother me at all.

How immoral I was! He *could* have accepted my feeling for him. But he cruelly frustrated it, so I look back on my rebellious thoughts with all the more shame. Just talking about it makes me break out in a cold sweat.

It's not that I consider myself something special, but I think I've already said I had a good number of customers who came to the restaurant just to see me, haven't I. As I said earlier, I was like someone delivering detailed reports of some sort, holding nothing back in response to my father's questioning.

Yet I hid from my father anything about the man I liked, though I myself was unaware I was doing it.

"That new customer's not become a regular?" my father would ask again and again, trying to discover his daughter's secret. Remember, he had been a clerk at an inn. I would shake my head nonchalantly.

"No."

As time went by I began to find myself struggling with my feelings, yet I was bewildered by what was happening to me. As a girl of eighteen, I had never been touched emotionally by young men who made all sorts of advances to me, and the idea that I would fall for a man forty-one or forty-two seemed ridiculous. The pain so oppressed me I couldn't bear it any longer. Any little thing would start me crying or laughing for no good reason I could see. It was a time when I adopted a strangely grim view of life and the wild idea that perhaps I'd be better off dead.

At which point he abruptly stopped coming to the restaurant.

My loss of composure was scandalous. I didn't care what anyone thought now. What could have happened? I asked myself over and over. Had something gone wrong, something that had made him despise me? I was in such a wretched state.

Bombarded with every manner of advice and comment, my head whirled. Some of the women in the restaurant sympathized and suggested I try sending him a letter, while others mocked me spitefully: "What a pity it's ended with your love unreturned."

Going to and from the restaurant, I would slyly try passing in front of his house. But when I got there, I would go to pieces.

How can I possibly see inside his house? Almost running, I would look like someone in flight, my face turned away from the house, close enough to tears to startle anyone on the street. After I had sped past, I was, absurdly, greatly relieved, like a person safely delivered from a place of dread. And even though I expected I might by chance come face-to-face with him—so much so my heart pounded in my chest—if I actually *had* bumped into him, I know I would have run away, face down, without uttering a word.

He'd been sick. Perhaps it is going too far to say I was delighted, but that's the only way I can put it. I felt something akin to relief: he hadn't been avoiding me, for if he was sick it was only natural he wouldn't come to the restaurant. But then I was assailed by an even greater worry.

I went to a half-dozen shrines and had them say prayers for him. He had a liver ailment, and I had heard of a tatami maker in the Senju district who was willing to share a miracle cure that had been in his family for generations, so I went searching for the shop in that outlying area, quite strange and new to me. I had them send it to him, but without my name on the package. I felt that he would soon be well, and that I'd be able to see him again.

At last, after two months, he was released from the hospital. He had to be careful about the foods he ate, and saké would be especially out of bounds, so I'd already resigned myself to the fact that he would not be coming to the restaurant anytime soon, yet he came, and how happy I was when he did! I did not go to his room immediately, intentionally taking my time in another room. I drank some saké, which I normally never touched, and then, my trembling body steadied, welcomed him to the restaurant, a casual expression on my face. My voice, however, was husky, and inaudible. My eyes were filled with tears.

He thanked me for my concern. Perhaps it was my imagination, but there was a hint of hardness in his pale, gaunt face and his eyes were severe, betraying his single-minded nature.

After that he always asked for me just as he had before, but there was now nothing between us. I don't mean to be conceited, but we were kindred spirits, yet it never went beyond that. He continued to steer clear of the essential point.

I don't have to tell you how irritable I became. I made up my mind to act boldly. An audacious idea came into my head: I would confront him. I resolved that the next time he came I would get it off my chest, regardless of how difficult it might be for me, as soon as he walked in.

"Listen, I have a request to make of you. Would you let me be your mistress?"

I gave myself courage by reasoning that if I didn't come right out with it like that, I would miss my chance and never be able to say anything about it again.

But the fact is I'm a timid soul and was fearful that when the moment came, I wouldn't be able to execute my plan. I might have borrowed some strength from a bottle, but I decided that would be dishonest, and that I would be sober when I spoke to him.

He stood in the entry to the restaurant. I greeted him and led him in. We went up the stairs and I escorted him into the Nightingale Room, his favorite. Was I really walking? I kept my eyes on the tips of my white *tabi* socks as they moved back and forth mechanically.

Midway down the hall I attempted to speak.

"Uh . . ."

My thoughts were scrambled, as in a dream, and my body swayed from one side to the other.

He said nothing. He stopped for the briefest moment and seemed to look at my face, but I couldn't be sure.

By the time I led him into the room I was already too tense to say a word. The awkward silence was unbearable. I had another waitress come. I could become quite animated if there was someone else around. To offset the business in the hall a little earlier, I was now all bubbly, as if I had forgotten all about it.

I wonder what he thought of it all.

He called me the next day. Could I get off work early and come see him? His tone was formal, businesslike. I could, I said, also using correctly polite language.

We were to meet in a coffee shop in the Ginza district. I remember it was summer and the windows were thrown open; the glare of the lights reflected off them. I had the feeling somehow that the many handsome men and women sitting there in their chairs were looking out at me. I am the sort of person who could never go into such a place by myself. He apparently saw me in my confusion and immediately came out.

He asked if I wanted something cold to drink, and I shook my head. How could I possibly drink at a time like this?

We crossed the main boulevard running through the Ginza district, coming to the Sanjukken canal, where it was dark. It wasn't until we were crossing Izumo Bridge that he started talking.

"I've been thinking about a number of things."

I nodded wordlessly, though I didn't know if he could see me. He once again fell silent.

Hurry up! Please say something! The silence drove me to near madness, I'll tell you. His melancholy tone told me I would not like what I was about to hear, even though I knew he always talked like that. And that's exactly how it turned out.

He told me he had absolutely no intention of taking responsibility for anyone. His manner was indifferent, as though the matter concerned him not at all. He said the reason there were so many women working as waitresses at the restaurant was because unlike me, who was young, they were women who had gotten married and their marriages had fallen apart for various reasons.

"You're still an inexperienced young woman. I know it's meddling on my part, but I intend to find a good husband for you before you become contaminated by the business you're in now. Listen, why don't we sit down with your father and talk so that you can soon be a respectable young woman. We can't have you talking so imprudently."

He took me to task. He really did.

"Let me tell you, I'm saying this because I'm suppressing my own feelings for you and honestly thinking about your future."

Yes, he went on talking. But in my heart I wept and cried out, *That's enough! I understand!* I had been publicly humiliated. Could anything be more shameful? Yet I wasn't crushed. In fact, at that point I launched a spirited attack on him.

"Well then, when my marriage has fallen apart or whatever," I rattled on, the words coming fast and furious, "when I'm no longer able to get properly married, you promise me you'll take me as your mistress, right? That's your promise, is it?"

He didn't know what to say now.

"Uh, I . . ."

Now the shoe's on the other foot! And I wouldn't let the matter drop.

"So what are you telling me?"

What would my face have looked like, I wonder, if there had been light enough to see?

"No, listen," he began, "in any case, a woman's happiness lies in getting married straightaway and living an uneventful life. That's her real joy."

I didn't want to hear this. I was angry. I had no intention of having the man I loved lecture me like some schoolteacher.

I retorted that I had no desire to marry like that and railed at him again.

"I ask you, how can I marry someone when I love another man?"

I suspect the reason I was so tenacious was to salvage my self-respect, since I was unable, so to speak, to make a graceful retreat.

Passersby, bemused, would stop in their tracks and look back at us. We had come as far as the Tsukiji district. By now I cared nothing for what anybody thought. I was getting a bit unmanageable, and he tried to humor me.

"Well now, we'd better get back home before it gets too late. Let's talk this over when you've calmed down."

My response to his soothing words was petulant.

"Listen. It's still early, earlier than usual—don't worry about the time. What we've been talking about, you made a solemn promise, didn't you? I'm really going to do it."

I shook off his hand and broke away from him. I heard him behind me calling out to stop. For the first time, tears came.

And what do you think the fool I was did after that? I attempted to turn myself into the ruined woman he had warned against. Which is to say, I decided I didn't care if I became someone else's mistress, a woman who could no longer get married "straightaway" because she was not a virgin.

I quit the restaurant that very night. My father was completely against my plans, and said I couldn't expect him to countenance the marrying off of his precious jewel in such a shabby fashion. And yet I pushed aside his objection and married someone. After which, just as I had planned, I divorced my husband and fled my marriage.

I am astounded when I think that what I intended was to throw myself at him, as though to say "Well, now you'll accept me, won't you?" And yet I look back on the intense young woman I was then with nostalgia. I am touched by the passion that was able to impel such a direct and bizarre act without the hint of a blush. I suppose it sounds quite odd for me to say that, doesn't it.

And *he* was surprised in spite of himself.

I was now full of spite, or rather, pretended to be. I was unrelenting. "Honor your promise to me!"

I wanted to be near him, I tell you, no matter what that meant I had to do. Were that wish to be granted, I would have done anything, committed any crime.

In the end he thrust me aside. All my efforts came to nothing. Perhaps the way I went about it was wrong. Yet any misapprehension . . . no, I'll tell you, what it comes down to is that he didn't care for me. This is what his reading of the situation seemed to be: I was in cahoots with my father to extort money from him. He said he'd give us some money, and that we shouldn't accuse him of anything.

"Are you afraid?" I asked.

"Oh yes, I am."

I suspect he also misunderstood my question, which I had asked to suggest that he had been defeated by fear of a woman's feelings.

I don't know if he had heard about my father from someone. In any case, he extricated himself by using as his defense my father's despicable deeds that even I'd had no knowledge of, claiming intimidation.

Was there no way to clear up the misunderstanding? I think there was. Yet things having come to such a pass, I merely said, "Oh, you don't say?" My nature is such that I can maintain an exceedingly indifferent expression on my face, quite the opposite of what I really feel, which was to try to cling to him more tightly than ever. Perhaps you could also say the whole business had become tiresome. I felt no remorse now, having been defeated after giving my emotions free rein and letting events take their course. In any case, indifference was the impression I intended to create.

"I see," I said. "Well, good-bye then."

"Please take this, at least," he said, holding out to me money as though warding off an evil spirit. It was only this offering that I despised and wept over.

Years went by. Quite by accident I moved into this neighborhood. My father is dead and I live in idleness on the meager bequest another man left me.

I suppose you'd like to hear how I had made my way through the world during those years. I don't think I'll tell you. It's yesterday's news, so I'll end my story here. Because *I* certainly don't want to hear the details of how over the years you lost your big Western furniture business, became a blue-collar worker, and now have to support a large family by working until late at night in an ironworks.

You're very tired, aren't you. You had a bad cough yesterday, I think. The weather will be turning cold, so please take care. Please do, for my sake. Every night I quietly pray as I watch you return home through the darkness. I see your image vividly before me, no matter how dark the night.

On second thought, it'd be better if you took sick soon and died.

Fountains in the Rain

MISHIMA YUKIO

That two short stories of the prolific novelist, playwright, essayist, nationalist, and bon vivant Mishima Yukio (1925–70) are included in this collection is not an accurate index of his popularity in Japan today, where his readership is no longer at the dizzying heights of a generation ago at the time of his spectacular suicide. Rather, the stories here are very much tales of Tokyo. His Ame no naka no funsui *(Fountains in the rain), published in 1963 and set in the Marunouchi business district and Wadakura Fountain Park, focuses on an unappealing young man who would see himself about to grandly cast aside—simply as a ritualistic validation of his manhood—a young woman who apparently, inexplicably, loves him. "Apparently" is a necessary qualification, since the delineation of her as a character is as vague as the youth's is strong. But the narrative flaw is not fatal because the self-absorbed boy and his thoughts are the natural pivot around which the story revolves.*

Physical change comes to the world's business districts, but usually not on the wings of whimsy or ephemeral trendiness, and the Marunouchi business district is no exception. It has naturally changed since this short story was written in the sixties, but the change tends to reflect the conservative—though certainly not conservationist—tendencies of the financial powers that hold sway there.

The Marunouchi building, the setting for the manipulative young man's declaration of separation, has recently been demolished to make way for another structure. In terms of size it was an office building of modest pretensions, but a nostalgic repository of collective and disparate Tokyoite memory. The Tokyo Bankers' Club building, a magnificent red-brick example of the elegant old Londontown style immediately across from the park of Mishima's story, was likewise torn down recently, this in spite of considerable opposition by citizen groups. The office building that replaced it has a replica of the old building's facade awkwardly skirting its lower floors.

Even Wadakura Fountain Park and its fountains, the latter having been dedicated to the present emperor and empress on the occasion of their wedding, are not entirely beyond the reach of change; the modest arbor with its reed blinds mentioned in Mishima's story has been displaced by an imposing glass-walled structure housing a large hall and restaurant, and the fountains augmented by a cascading waterfall at the far side of the park. Still, the park remains a well-tended, pleasant refuge from the surrounding concrete, though the fountains— spectacularly refreshing of a scorching July—are not turned on if Tokyo's reservoirs run low in the summer, as they do most years.

The boy was exhausted from walking through the rain dragging about with him this girl who would not stop crying and who weighed upon him like a ponderous sack of sand.

Moments before he had told her in a coffee shop in the Marunouchi Building that it was all over. It was the first time in his life he had told a girl he was breaking up with her. This was something he had fantasized about for a very long time and now it had at last become a reality.

For that reason alone he had loved the girl—or had pretended to love her—and for that reason alone had pursued her assiduously, and had desperately sought the opportunity to sleep with her, and had gone to bed with her. And finally today, all preparations complete, and himself now fully qualified to do it, he had been able to utter the words "It's over," words that he had long and eagerly looked forward to enunciating with his own lips, as a king might a proclamation. Words that simply of their own utterance, their own power, could rend the heavens. Words with which he had passionately kept alive his dream that some day he would do it, yet all the while half resigned that this, in reality, could never come to pass. The most heroic, most brightly shining words in the world, that soar through the heavens like arrows shot from a bow, seeking their target straight and direct. Talismanic words permitted only a man amongst men, only the best sort of person: "It's over."

Yet Akio could not help regretting that he had made his statement most unclearly, with a strangled, guttural rattle, like an asthmatic with phlegm caught in his throat—the soda water he had gulped to clear his throat unavailing.

Akio at the time feared more than anything that the girl would not catch what he had said. It would be better to die than to have her ask him to repeat himself. When the goose that had been obsessed for years with laying the golden egg had finally succeeded, only to have it break before her mate saw it, you could not expect her to lay another one a minute later.

Fortunately, however, she had heard him. That she heard exactly what he had said, making repetition unnecessary, could only be considered phenomenal good fortune. Akio had at last strode, on his own two feet, through the pass at the summit of the mountain he had long gazed at from afar.

Clear proof that she had heard was given him the next instant. Like chewing gum flying out of a vending machine.

The windows had been shut tight against the rain. The voices of the other customers around them, the clatter of dishes, the cash register bell all reverberated about the room, and, held within it, resounded delicately against the humid water drops on the inside of the window panes and raised a din that befogged the mind. The instant Akio's garbled words reached Masako's ears through that din, she opened yet wider her already too large, bulging goggle eyes that seemed to overwhelm every other feature on her thin, dispirited face. It would be better to call them a kind of failure, a failure of control, rather than to say they were eyes. Suddenly tears had welled forth from them.

This is not to say that Masako had given any indication she was about to begin sobbing. Nor did she whimper. All that happened was that tears gushed forth under extraordinary water pressure; her face was expressionless.

Akio, of course, underestimated the seriousness of the situation and assumed that at such a high volume and pressure the tears would very soon stop. Watching her closely, he found himself entranced by the mint-like coolness of his own feelings. There was no doubt that this was what he had planned, created and brought to reality, and that it smacked a bit of the mechanical, but the end result was superb.

The boy told himself once again that he had made love to her precisely to see this.

I have remained free of desire throughout.

And the tear-stained face of this girl before him now was reality! Here was an authentic, genuine "abandoned woman," a woman *he* had cast aside.

And yet the flow of tears was continuing much too long, with not the least sign of subsiding; the boy had begun to feel uneasy in this public place.

Masako, still in her light-colored raincoat, had sat erect in her chair. He could see the collar of a red plaid blouse beneath the lapels of her coat. Her hands, supported by the edge of the table, appeared to be tensed hard against it, her posture unmoving and rigid.

Staring straight ahead, she had let the tears flow, and they came without surcease. She made no move to take out a handkerchief and wipe them away. And within her narrow throat her breathing was labored, making a methodical sound like the squeaking of a new shoe. Her lower lip, unadorned with lipstick in the perverse student fashion, petulantly overrode the upper lip and trembled.

The older patrons were watching them with some interest. Akio had felt he had at long last joined the ranks of adult society and yet it was these same adult eyes that now threatened that feeling.

Akio could really not help but be startled by this grand gushing forth of tears. Not for a moment did the water pressure or volume fall off. Tired, he had let his gaze drop and noticed the tip of his umbrella, which leaned against a chair. Rainwater from the tip had created a small, blackish puddle on the old-fashioned tiles that made up the mosaic floor. It seemed to Akio that this was also Masako's tears.

He had suddenly grabbed the check and stood up.

The June rains had been falling now for three days in Tokyo. When he left the Marunouchi Building and opened his umbrella, the girl followed after him, not saying a word. Masako did not have an umbrella, so Akio had no recourse but to share his with her. It was at this point that he discovered—his coldness of heart undiminished—the adult practice of concerning oneself with appearances, and it seemed now to have become fully a part of him. Having broached the matter of breaking up, he considered the traditionally romantic sharing of an umbrella as now merely a concession to form. He had left no doubt where he stood. And leaving no doubt suited Akio's nature, no matter how subtle a form it took.

The only thing the boy thought of as he walked along the broad sidewalk toward the Palace was where he could dump this bawling burden.

I wonder if they turn the fountains on even on rainy days.

He considered why the fountains had come to mind. Before he had gone another two or three steps the physical humor of what he had been thinking struck him.

As he endured the reptilian feel of her wet raincoat when he brushed coldly, roughly against her, Akio's mind was in pursuit—cheerfully, you could almost say—of a droll metaphor.

That's it! Fountains in the rain! I'll pit them against Masako's tears. Even Masako has got to come in second best. First of all, they're recirculating, so Masako can't keep up with them; the tears she sheds are all lost. She's sure no match for a recirculating fountain, no way. The little twit'll give up and stop crying, you can bet on it. And I'll get rid of this baggage somehow. The only question is: do they keep the fountains running even when it rains?

Akio walked on wordlessly. Masako doggedly accompanied him, sharing his umbrella and still crying. Shaking her off would be difficult, but taking her wherever he wanted would be simple enough.

Akio had the feeling that his whole body was damp from the rain and the tears. Masako was dry in her white boots, but to the loafer-shod Akio, his socks were like wet seaweed.

There was still some time before all the offices closed. The foot traffic along the sidewalk was unhurried and random. They crossed the street in a crosswalk and walked toward Wadakura Bridge leading to the Palace. Standing at the foot of the bridge with its old-fashioned railings and ornamental newels, he could see through the rain swans gliding in the Palace moat to his left, and to the right, across the moat, the rows of red chairs and white tablecloths of the Palace Hotel's dining room through rain-clouded window glass. They went over the bridge. Passing between high stone walls, they turned left, coming to a park with fountains.

Masako, uttering not a single word, continued her crying.

There is a large arbor at the entrance to the park with reed blinds hanging from its roof. The benches underneath offered some protection from the rain, so Akio sat down, his umbrella still raised. Masako, still crying, sat half-turned away from him, so that all he could see was the shoulder of her white raincoat under his nose and her wet hair. Delicate white droplets of pomade-repelled rain sprinkled her hair. It seemed to Akio that the weeping Masako had descended, wide-eyed, into a kind of stupor, and he suddenly felt the urge to yank that hair and bring her to her senses.

Masako's silent weeping went on. It was obvious to him that she was waiting for him to say something to her, and it was precisely this knowledge that nettled him and kept him from speaking. It occurred to him that he had said absolutely nothing since he uttered his brief pronouncement.

In the distance the fountains were furiously blowing water into the air, but Masako took no notice of them.

From where the couple sat three fountains of differing size looked as though each stood atop the other. The sound of the water, drowned out by the rain, was faint and distant. Streams of water shooting out in all directions looked for all the world like curved tubes of glass as the spray lost definition viewed from afar. There was not a soul to be seen in any direction. The green of the grass this side of the fountains and the azalea-covered wattle fence were rain-drenched and vivid.

On the other side of the park, however, the wet canopies of trucks and the roofs of buses—red, white, yellow—ran back and forth end-lessly. He could see clearly the red light at the intersection, but when the green light beneath it went on, it disappeared directly behind the spray of the fountains' gushers.

Sitting there, the boy, steadfastly silent, was assailed by an ineffable rage. The joke that had amused him moments before was gone.

He was not sure what he was angry at. A little while before he had savored a sense of high-soaring invincibility, but now he was deploring indefinable failure. That the ever crying Masako had not been disposed of was not the entirety of his failure.

His thoughts about her were as haughty as ever.

If I had a mind to, I'd push her into the fountain pond, beat a quick retreat, and that'd be the end of it.

Yet confronted with this rain that wrapped itself around him, with these tears, and this wall-like, rain-filled sky, his sense of failure was absolute. It pressed tenfold upon him and transformed his freedom into something utterly useless.

The now angry youth was merely peevish in the extreme. He would not be satisfied until he had gotten Masako wet in the rain and filled her eyes with the sight of the fountains.

He suddenly stood up and broke into a run without a backward glance, running quickly along the raised gravel path that skirted the walk surrounding the fountains and coming to a stop where the three foun-tains could be viewed full on.

The girl came running through the rain. She was barely able to stop without bumping into him, grabbing the handle of the umbrella, which he held aloft. Her face, wet with tears and rain, looked chalk-white. Her breathing was labored.

"Where are you going?"

Akio might not have been expected to give her an answer, but the words came tumbling out as though he had been eagerly awaiting just this question from her.

"You're gonna look at the fountains. Take a look. You're no match for them, no matter how much you cry."

Then the two of them, umbrella atilt, with the peace of mind that comes from not having to look each other in the eye, gazed at the three fountains, the middle one markedly larger than the two on either side, which were somewhat smaller, like two bodhisattvas flanking a statue of the Buddha.

Because the fountains and pool were in constant turmoil, it was almost impossible to see the torrent of rain actually falling into the water. All that they could hear standing there, paradoxically, was the occasional, fitful roar of distant automobiles, and because the sound of the water in the fountains was so delicately interwoven in the air it seemed almost as though it was locked tight within a total silence, though it was to be heard if you strained to hear it.

The water first erupted low and scattered in the massive black granite basin, and then, passing over the black rim, fell in a *kasuri*-like splash pattern.

Guarded by six long, arcing spouts of water jetting out radially, a giant geyser of water shot straight up from the center of the basin.

Watching carefully, the boy could see that the fountaining did not maintain a constant height. There was practically no wind, so the water was expelled high and straight and undisturbed into the gray, rainy sky, yet this did not mean that the apex of the water was always the same height. Sometimes a snatch of water was hurled unexpectedly high, breaking into droplets at its peak and falling back down into the pool.

The water near the apex thinly veiled the rain-filled sky behind it, and, pregnant with reflection, took on a gray-*cum*-whitewash cast, looking more like powder than water, and drawing tightly around it the powdery water at its periphery. Around the spouting water spray the size of large white snowflakes lushly danced, seeming for all the world like a storm of snow and rain.

Akio, however, was fascinated not so much by the three fountains' main geysers as by the sight of the water around them describing arcs as it jetted out in spokelike radii.

In particular, those of the large fountain in the middle shook their white, watery manes in all directions, leapt high across the black granite rim, hurling themselves heroically, relentlessly upon the surface of the pool. Watching the indefatigable, helter-skelter rush of the water, his heart was almost lost to it. The heart that had been safely within him was, before he knew it, bewitched by the water, set astride these torrents, and sent flying though the air.

His response was the same when he looked at the columns of water.

At first glance, each big geyser seemed almost static, like a clay model fashioned out of water, not an atom out of place. A careful look, however, disclosed a pellucid soul of movement rushing endlessly upward within the column. It filled up the cylindrical void with frantic speed, starting at the base and instantaneously replenishing any lack, maintaining constant repletion. He knew it would be frustrated by the loftiness of the heavens, yet how superb the persistence of the power sustaining this perpetual frustration!

The boy had brought the girl here to show her the fountains, but it was the lad who was thoroughly mesmerized by the sound and found it so magnificent. And as this was happening, his eyes were led yet higher, to the sky that was letting fall sheets of rain.

His eyelashes were wet with rain.

The sky was sealed off by dense clouds directly overhead and the heavy rains continued without respite. There was rain everywhere, as far as the eye could see. The rain on his face was exactly the same as the rain on the rooftops of the red brick buildings and the hotel in the distance, and his as-yet sparsely bearded, shiny face and the rough concrete floors of the deserted rooftops of buildings off somewhere, wherever, were no more than unresisting surfaces exposed to the very same rain. Under the rain, at least, his cheeks and dirty concrete floors were of a piece.

The image of the fountain right in front of Akio was forcefully wiped from his consciousness. Now he could only think of the fountains in the rain as repeating over and over again a kind of trivial futility.

As this thought occurred to him, he forgot the earlier joke and the anger that had followed it; the boy sensed that his own heart was rapidly emptying.

Only rain fell in his empty heart.

Lost in thought, the boy began to walk.

"Where are you going?" the girl asked. She kept pace with him in her white boots, this time holding on tightly to the handle of the umbrella.

"Where I go is my business. I made that clear earlier, didn't I?"

"What do you mean?" she asked.

The boy looked at his interlocutor's face with a chill in his heart; her face was drenched, but the rain had washed away her tears, and though traces of tears remained in her bloodshot, watery eyes, the voice no longer quavered.

"What do I mean? I made that clear earlier, didn't I? I told you it was over."

Beyond her profile moving through the rain the boy could now see tiny crimson azaleas blooming fastidiously here and there on the grass.

"Really? You said that? I didn't hear you."

She spoke in a normal tone of voice.

The boy was almost felled by the shock. After taking several faltering steps, protest came to him at last.

"But—then—," he stammered, "why were you crying? How do you explain that?"

The girl did not answer for a while. Her small wet hand still held fast to the umbrella handle.

"The tears just came. There was no *reason*."

Outraged, the boy was about to shout something at her when his voice gave way to a sudden and massive sneeze, and it occurred to him that he would catch cold if he did not get out of this rain.

Meeting Again

MUKŌDA KUNIKO

Mukōda Kuniko (1929–81) turned out hundreds of radio and television dramas before she rose to prominence as a writer of short stories. Her broadcast dramas, largely domestic pieces, were relatively free of sentimentality, a fact that sets them apart from the run-of-the-mill plays in an ephemeral, yet hardy, sector of Japan's popular culture. This willingness to look reality in its blemished face was even more characteristic of Mukōda's print fiction, which she wrote only during the last half-dozen years of her life — a sadly brief and harried, deadline-plagued, if profitable, existence as a Japanese author with an appreciative readership.

Although she lived through the war she has virtually nothing to say about it. The tight focus of her work is on relationships. Mukōda is an equal-opportunity storyteller who peoples her fiction with credible workaday characters, sympathetic and unsympathetic, thick-waisted and thin, devious and decent, individuals blessed by fate or, rather more likely, cursed by their own machinations. Combined with inventive yet plausible plots, the cast of characters

42

makes her fiction a reliable, often memorable, reflection of contemporary life in Japan. A recurring figure is the archetypal Japanese father of the prewar era: inflexible, dominating, though usually caring.

In the short piece Saikai *(Meeting again) we watch as Fuyuko attempts to resolve her conflicted feelings about the Ginza, Tokyo's pricey shopping and entertainment district. The story was published in 1980, the year Mukōda was awarded the Naoki Literary Prize. She was killed in an air crash in Taiwan the following year.*

It had been easy enough when she finally went back. She wondered why she had been so put off by the idea. Fuyuko had to laugh at herself. She had been carrying Mayumi when she decided to make her way in the world without ever setting foot in the Ginza again, so it had been seventeen years.

She had thus been reluctant when Mayumi suggested they meet there. Her daughter, now in high school, was rather proud of her mother, certainly a svelte beauty for a woman of thirty-eight. Whenever there was open house at school her daughter would nag her.

"At least get a manicure like the other mothers. And wear something that stands out a bit more."

Her tone, however, suggested pride in a mother who was obviously so pretty.

Fuyuko had responded that if it were shoes and a sweater to take to tennis camp she wanted, she could buy them at a store by their train station, but Mayumi was uncommonly determined.

"Come on, Mother, let's give ourselves a treat! We can meet in the Ginza, have some ice cream, then go shopping for a sweater together."

It appeared that Mayumi would be dragging one or two friends along. Fuyuko looked at her daughter, who had grown taller than her mother last year.

Seventeen years have gone by, a span as long as this child is old. It would be all right now.

Fuyuko agreed to meet her daughter that afternoon.

.　　.　　.

Fuyuko had worked at a nightclub in the Ginza district for not quite two years. Hers had been a home without a father, besides which, she had not been able to get a job where she had hoped to. She had the stereotypical ailing mother, and, faced with having to move, their need for money only grew. She chose employment that would bring in cash the fastest.

She considered her lifestyle then as having been on the prudent side. She wasn't teaching in a kindergarten, after all, so she would admit to two or three love affairs or, for that matter, four or five, but if she were unable to convince herself that she loved a man, she would not let him have his way. As for someone she disliked, she would not give him the nod, no matter how much he might importune her.

She had met her husband at the club. His parents lived in Kanazawa. When the two of them decided to marry, he had her quit the club and spend three months as an office worker in a small company, thereby gulling his parents and having a proper wedding. At the time Fuyuko was in her fifth month with Mayumi, who—no doubt in high spirits— kicked her mother during the wedding march.

The face of the Ginza, which she had not seen for so many years, had changed utterly. The nightclub where Fuyuko had worked had been torn down and replaced with a building devoted to the latest fashion in clothes. A husband and wife had operated a fruit and vegetable shop right next to the club, but this was now a foreign-owned fast-food restaurant. The neighborhood was different, but the people were also different. More people passed along the street now. Women's makeup was more pronounced. There was more music. Sounds were louder and more intense.

Fuyuko's mind was at ease as she walked from 4-chōme, the main Ginza intersection, toward the Shiseido building. The people she had known no longer walked here. There was certainly no one now to tap her on the shoulder and call her by the name she had used at the club: "Well, if it isn't Kaoru!" When she realized this, she told herself she should have come back sooner. The years she had lived so cautiously, doggedly restraining the desire to go to the Ginza and her longing for it, struck her as absurd.

When her husband had named the baby Mayumi, her mother-in-law had said it sounded like the name for a nightclub hostess. Fuyuko felt her cheeks tensing, but the expression on her husband's face was nonchalant, and he would not back down.

"Ending a girl's name with *ko* is not going to be the fashion anymore."

Fuyuko had had her daughter call her *o-kaasan*, the traditional word for Mother. When the child started kindergarten she complained that all the other children called their mothers *Mama*, using the English word.

"*O-kaasan* is better for us Japanese."

Fuyuko did not like the word *Mama*.[1] It reminded her of her past.

Seventeen years before, Fuyuko had frequented the place where they were to meet, a posh tearoom. Fuyuko had often met her husband there. And she had met other men there as well.

Mayumi arrived. As expected, she had several friends in tow. Fuyuko realized the check would set her back a bit, but such occasions as this were few and far between, so she resigned herself to the situation.

It was then that Fuyuko noticed toward the back of the tearoom a middle-aged man sitting across from a woman who appeared to be the proprietor of a bar. He acknowledged her with a look of surprise. It was Takei, a man she had dated before she met her husband. His hair was gray now, but there was no doubt it was him. He had been an up-and-coming department head. Fuyuko wondered if he were now an executive. She felt her heart racing.

"Who's that?" Mayumi asked, glancing at the man.

"Someone I have a nodding acquaintance with."

"Really?" Mayumi responded with interest, then: "He looks like Father somehow, doesn't he."

---

1. A term of address for a woman who owns or manages a bar or nightclub.

Jacob's Tokyo Ladder

HINO KEIZŌ

A recent short story by Hino Keizō is an apt selection for a collection about Tokyo, since the author often makes his physical environment the focus of his literary imagination. He does so here in Hashigo no tatsu machi *(Jacob's Tokyo ladder). Hino's fascination with urban and natural space, often unpeopled, has led some critics to label him antihumanist, but human relationships are not entirely absent from his fiction. Nonetheless, his study of "the mineral spectacle about me," as his narrator puts it in "Jacob's Tokyo Ladder," belongs to a subgenre of literature that elevates mere backdrop to compelling protagonist.*

Hino Keizō was born in Tokyo in 1929 but spent much of his youth in Korea, then a Japanese colony, where his father worked for a bank. He has acknowledged the lasting impact of the desolation he saw as a youth when he was repatriated to Japan at the end of the war. Hino experienced firsthand the bleak scorched earth and rubble of Tokyo, and he remembers what the city looked like, how it smelled and felt underfoot.

After graduating from Tokyo University, Hino went to work for the Yomiuri, Japan's—and the world's—largest daily commercial newspaper, living a number of years overseas as a foreign correspondent. He first gained notice as a writer of fiction when one of his short stories won the Hirabayashi Taiko Literary Prize in 1973. "Jacob's Tokyo Ladder" was first published in the literary magazine Gunzō in 1996.

Tokyo's new city hall that Hino takes us to—officially, Tokyo Metropolitan Government Offices—is more than a mere city hall. It is a complex of buildings, the grandest of which is the second tallest office building in Japan and the tallest in Tokyo, its twin towers rising 243 meters and 48 stories. The complex, designed by Tange Kenzō, surrounds a commodious courtyard of 5,000 square meters, a lavish dedication of space to the public weal in crowded Japan. The structure has already become an important tourist attraction. In the year following its completion in 1991 more than 8 million people were said to have visited it.[1]

Ever since the newspaper where I work moved from the Yūraku-chō district to Ōtemachi near the Imperial Palace in Tokyo, I'd gotten well acquainted with the area. Whatever subway exit stairs I might climb, I could expect to know exactly where I would come out on the street, and in the basement level of what building I could get a meal or have a cup of coffee, and until what time.

One night almost twenty years after the move, I left the newspaper building that faces the broad main street at a little before nine. It was the rainy season, but the rain had stopped by nightfall; it was warm, yet a dampness, almost a chill mist, rose in the street from the wet pavement under my feet.

Until early evening there had been plenty of traffic on the street and pedestrians on the sidewalk. However, almost all the people who make

1. Ōhama Tetsuya et al., *Edo Tōkyō nempyō* (Edo and Tokyo: a chronology) Tokyo: Shō-gakukan, Tokyo, 1993), 244.

use of the subway and walk the sidewalks of the district, with its many head offices of banks and buildings of large companies and newspapers, are employees who work in the tall buildings that stand cheek by jowl along the street. No shops or restaurants or office buildings front on the street, so there were no shoppers or sightseers. No trucks were to be seen.

After eight at night employees' foot traffic and the passing back and forth of black executive limos or regular cruising taxis ended and the street fell silent. I knew this from years of experience.

It's just like it always is.

I crossed over to the sidewalk across from the newspaper.

I was to meet someone in a hotel less than five minutes away, next to the Imperial Palace moat.

Some particularly grand skyscrapers gloomily lined that side of the street. These buildings were built from the latter half of the sixties and into the seventies, during the flood tide of rapid growth, and are nothing less than massive parallelepipeds, constructed with absolutely straight lines and planes, utterly without embellishment or a light touch. The steel shells of these buildings are massive and the walls thick as fortress walls, and even the relatively small rectangular windows, fitted with tempered glass from top to bottom, are set in perfect alignment vertically and horizontally.

One building in particular, the head office of a bank, has massive walls, all a dark taupe, making it look as if the whole edifice had been carved out of a mountain of volcanic rock. This night particularly, its dampish walls were almost black. They were far darker than the night sky—purple-tinged with a blush of pink—over the heart of the city.

In each building roughly half of the windows were lighted. I wondered if people could be working this late. All the light in the windows came from cold, bluish fluorescent lamps; my senses could not immediately comprehend the scene of people working late under it. The display lighting for the flowerbeds and trees planted near the main entrance was bright enough, but the fluorescent-style light mercilessly exposed the artificiality of what it illuminated. And this was true of the street as well. Every single leaf was so vividly new and fresh I could see the veins in them; they looked as though they were crafted of fine vinyl.

Nonetheless, to call them artificial does not mean they were like a tacky stage set you might find in some two-by-four theater. There was an omnipresence there that cannot be easily described: the tranquility that engulfs the street after a taxi has sped away at full speed toward the Ginza, leaving only the streetlights shining on the chill, brightly lighted sidewalk, the majestic silence of skyscrapers that seem to be cleaved out of cliffs.

That night, especially, the indications of this all-encompassing omnipresence were overwhelming, painfully so. Innumerable tiny sharp needles, unseen to the eye, seemed to prick the depths of my consciousness, and its substance, now riddled with pinpricks, began to shudder. Then I suddenly became aware of what I had not been particularly conscious of for almost twenty years: there were no telephone poles on the street, and not a single company sign.

The moment I realized this fact, the street I was walking loosed its moorings in time, becoming a street out of a picture by Chirico, then superposing itself over what I can only call an incredibly surrealistic scene of ruins by the enigmatic seventeenth-century painter Monsù Desiderio. I, myself, was abruptly overcome by a vertigo that was part terror, part ecstasy, and part dread; I had noticed moments before a person walking silently some two meters ahead of me.

I still had some time until my appointment at the hotel, so I scanned the deserted road in both directions, looked up at each and every slab of skyscraper rock to the top of the buildings (stopping and counting the stories by the rows of windows), then peered intently at the underside of the leaves on the trees along the sidewalk illuminated by the streetlights. I was walking along as at a picnic, like an inebriate, like a figure in a dream, yet the other pedestrian also continued all the while to walk along the sidewalk at my pace, ahead of me several steps.

A part of my consciousness recovered from its vertigo.

Who the hell is that?

He (or she) was wearing a raincoat with a hood that completely covered the head. Color of coat: black. It was a very long raincoat. So much so that it reached the ankles (such a long coat was in fashion several years back). The shoes were black, too, but the heels were not high. Which is to say, from the rear I could not tell the person's sex or age. The figure appeared to be taller than me, but these days young women who are taller than me are a dime a dozen. And men also use the quite common dark handbag.

The dominant impression was the person's bearing. It was neither masculine nor feminine. If I had to describe it, I would say it had, precisely, a bizarre sense of that street at night, a feeling particularly akin to me as I am now. Tall buildings with their perfectly flat planes and straight lines not a second out of true, fluorescent light shining on the wet asphalt, the all-encompassing, tempered tranquility. Yet behind or deep within it the preposterously absurd grows like wildfire, a teeming mass of blackness. And I sensed something ominous in the long black raincoated figure before me, the back ramrod-straight, and the stride of the too-lithe legs.

I imagined a competent female employee of a large enterprise somewhere around there in her midthirties, living alone on the top floor in her condominium with a spacious balcony, but there also flickered in my imagination a company executive, an eccentric man in his late forties with long service abroad. In both cases the sense I got of their lives was extremely weak, but this didn't mean its reality was diluted. If we take the coming together and melding of the deepest stratum of the conscious and the darkest recess of the human body as the domain of the "soul," one finds a forbidding sense of reality touches one directly.

As I walked after this strange traveling companion, my nerves, which had been pleasantly overwhelmed by the mineral spectacle about me, began gradually to tremble, cell by cell. It's nothing, I told myself, and nonchalantly quickened my pace to overtake the person striding ahead of me. The gap between us, however, shrank not at all. Was my companion lengthening his stride? Were my legs not heeding me? The other person seemed unaware of me. He was simply walking along, occasionally almost coming to a halt. It was as though he was casually trying to entice me to go somewhere.

Where? To one of the buildings on this street? Or was it somewhere outside Ōtemachi? No, it wasn't. She—or he—was not walking in a particular direction. At least I could say the person was in no hurry. The road through Ōtemachi was short. If you hurried, you'd be outside this distinctive area in no time.

Still no cars passed by, and no people emerged from in or around the buildings. A drizzling rain fell silently in the cold fluorescence of the streetlights, and the high-rise buildings, which all rose stolidly—though their shapes differed slightly—collapsed in on my upward gaze from both sides, reducing the indistinct night sky to a narrow slice of space. There were no stars.

I began to think that he was headed toward no specific place, that this character was inviting me to go to the far side of a Chirico or Monsù Desiderio painting, to the heart of this street scene's tranquility. He was not moving further ahead along the sidewalk. He was trying to take me vertically—whether up or down I don't know—from "reality." The black, overly long coat swayed, inducing yet more dizziness.

It was more like walking circles in the caldera of a dormant cone volcano than on a valley floor surrounded by rugged mountain peaks. Under my feet magma simmered beneath a thin layer of sidewalk. In the twenty years I'd been coming to work along this street I hadn't once noticed the absence of telephone poles and company signs. A unique place indeed. Surely a device for measuring the earth's magnetism or the pull of gravity would fluctuate wildly here. At least during the evening.

I passed by the main entrance of any number of high-rise buildings, each of which solidifies stalwart and simple forms. The roll-down steel shutters covering the front of the buildings had been lowered. Flood-lights on the structures threw the shutters into furrowed high relief. They looked as though they would be unmoved by typhoon or earthquake. Really? This strip of land most certainly had been mudflats until several hundred years ago.

My sidewalk companion's buoyant stride beckoned me with apparent significance as, increasingly, his (or her) shoulders swayed and the hem of the long raincoat swung back and forth. The fluorescent streetlighting became ever more lucid, and from time to time the raincoat appeared almost transparent. I followed my companion, all the more enthralled.

Fortunately, it seemed as though my cowalker, turning right at the intersection, was also headed for the hotel. Ahead of us after we turned was the boulevard that skirts the Imperial Palace moat, then the moat and the grove of trees on the palace grounds. The grove was thick, dense, and dark, and the taillights of cars streaming from Kudan to Hibiya and the Ginza were a vivid red. I was beginning to make out what appeared to be the figures of people going in and out of the hotel. If my companion was also going to the hotel, I would soon be able to find out who he or she was, or at least see the face.

As I turned right at the intersection, at last able to catch my breath, I turned and looked behind me. The way I had come was still without any sign of life; the ridgeline of the buildings, absent the slightest tremor, and the flat surface of the street and the ubiquitous blue fluorescent light were all surreal, as though frozen, their crystalline lure beginning to permeate my body anew.

I told myself that this was nothing special, that for the briefest moment the membrane around my consciousness had merely thinned a bit, leaving me feeling a little strange. The tautness of my nerves eased and so my pace slackened accordingly, widening the distance between me and the person walking ahead of me. A bit further apart now, I could see that, though out of fashion, the too-long black raincoat was not outlandish.

I came to the boulevard that skirts the palace moat. When you cross the T-shaped intersection there, going to the left, you come right to the hotel on the corner. The signal was green. My co-walker was already starting across the street. There was no breeze, yet the hem of the long raincoat gently billowed out. I scrutinized the figure in front of me—it was, after all, going to the same hotel I was—and when I suddenly raised my gaze somewhat, I heaved an audible sigh of relief.

Further along, where the boulevard skirts the moat and cuts through the plaza in front of the palace, running straight as an arrow, Tokyo Tower soared shining and brilliant into the sky, superimposing itself over the figure in the black, billowing raincoat. I had been here dozens of times during the day and often enough at night, yet never realized that you can see almost the entire tower, so seemingly close. The night sky near Shimbashi was murky and turbid, yet within it the tower, emitting a graceful light of silver and flame, stood steadfast and utterly vertical. Beyond the waves of raucous sound and reflected neon from the backstreets of the Ginza and the Shimbashi district, the lighted tower took on an almost holy cast. Silently it linked heaven and earth.

The instant I began to think about all this, I saw out of the corner of my eye that the pedestrian signal was beginning to flash caution. Awakening from my reverie, I quickened my step to cross the street, then noticed that the person who had been walking ahead of me had vanished.

Perhaps he's already crossed the street.

I scanned the road from the intersection to the entrance to the hotel, but a black raincoat was nowhere to be seen.

I had been enchanted with the sight of Tokyo Tower for only a moment. In that time it would not have been possible for her, or him, to hail a taxi, for example, and get into it. At this time of night there was no building he could have entered save the hotel. I muttered to myself that it was not possible; my senses would not immediately accept what had happened, and happened on a street where, several meters in front of me, there were no other pedestrians.

Before me as I stood there stock-still and baffled, within my field of vision, I saw a silver Tokyo Tower rising up straight and true—yet quite illusively—the abrupt intrusion of a separate "reality."

Exactly one week later they discovered cancer in me, using an ultrahigh frequency diagnostic device at the newspaper's clinic. I had had absolutely no symptoms. The doctor took one look at the image of my kidney, which had swollen abnormally before I realized anything was wrong, and grunted.

"This is not good."

Having been told the bad news, I went out the building's main entrance in a daze, and I retain no recollection at all of what Ōtemachi looked like that day. Thereafter, however, essentially unable to do any work or sleep at night, I turned over in my mind again and again that night's curious experience: the bizarre state in which I had been so vulnerable, the strange character in the black raincoat—I never knew its sex—and its abrupt disappearance. I wondered if it had been a surreptitious warning. Perhaps the mysterious dark figure that continued to walk several paces ahead of me was an accommodating harbinger of my impending fate.

I was unexpectedly reunited with Tokyo Tower in my room on the sixth floor of the hospital in Shinanomachi that I entered soon afterward. It was almost in the center of my field of vision when I looked out the window of my room, and as night fell the tower would begin to glow. It was a bit further away and smaller than when I had seen it from the road by the palace moat but, vertical, still gleamed placidly, silver and flame.

I was beset by severe hallucinations, auditory and visual, as I was coming out of the anesthesia after the operation. Even when uncanny, chaotically shifting hallucinatory images dominated my conscious vision—eyes open or closed—Tokyo Tower alone continued to look the same as always and continued to talk to me: *Only a vertical shaft running from the heavens to earth will remain unchanged, no matter how much everything else falls into mad chaos.*

I know that to some extent it kept my increasingly dissonant consciousness from final collapse. And I kept recalling a passage I'd forgotten from an ancient work, from Genesis in the Old Testament: *And he dreamed, and behold a ladder set up on the earth, and the top of it reached to heaven: and behold the angels of God ascending and descending on it.*

Six years later, again during the rainy season, I headed for the first time to Tokyo city hall in Shinjuku to get a new passport, my old one having expired; I was going abroad in connection with my work, the first time since my surgery.

I had seen the recently built city hall countless times from afar, but gazing up as I stood directly in front of it, I saw that it was indeed tall. And on all sides nothing but hotels and major firms in buildings of at least thirty stories. And on none of the building walls were there company signs or advertising. The colors differed from building to building, but they all had the same thick walls and rows of tiny windows lined up like so many embrasures in a fortress wall. And I saw no telephone poles.

It's the same as Ōtemachi! I felt myself on the verge of being drawn into another world, one unlike the everyday world I know.

I got to the place where the passport work was done by going down an escalator on the first-floor hall to an area that was like a sunken plaza, then taking another escalator in the corner to the floor below that. Plenty of people had come for passports, but because it was a spacious area I had the feeling I had lost myself in a vast, gigantic maze. The ceiling, the floor, the walls, were the color of the sky: ash gray. My skin was now abnormally sensitive, not so much because I was in a crowd, but rather because I was in a great open space. It was not unpleasant. The unseen stimulation, however, drained me of my vitality.

I don't know whether or not I took the escalator up after I finished with the passport, but I found myself in the sunken plaza. The plaza was indeed sunken, but overhead it was open and spacious, the two extraordinarily tall city hall building towers rising so high they seemed about to topple over on me. The walls were inlaid with a delicate, precise mosaic pattern, making it difficult to see the windows. The face of the building was not a smooth metal surface. It reminded me of a stain-covered tower of stone that was beginning to erode away, or perhaps a gigantic old tree caught in the embrace of withered vines. I could see no one in the plaza. Clouds hung low and threatening in a monsoonish sky. The top of the city hall towers seemed almost to touch the clouds.

On both sides of the main building were structures that, ring-like, surrounded the plaza to form a horseshoe. I recalled the square in front of Saint Peter's basilica in the Vatican. The row of statues of the saints on the roofs of the looping, cloister-style architecture that girdles the square. Gradually the city hall building took on a religious aspect, beginning to look at its top like the spires of a gothic cathedral. I descended into a state of perception in which I saw holy statues standing in a row atop the cloister that encircled the square.

The saints had most assuredly been martyrs, but I had not lived such a sublime, near-demented life. This would doubtless still be true the day I died.

I went into a cafeteria-style restaurant I had discovered off in a corner, still with the bizarre sense of imminent enthrallment. The place was not crowded. I sat down in a seat that faced the plaza behind a large plate-glass window. The grease the french-fried potatoes had been cooked in had been stale and the ice coffee tasted like muddy water. I vacantly gazed out on my "cathedral square." It remained, as before, almost deserted. Its ashen paving stones began to gently undulate.

I had applied for a passport that would be valid for ten years. Which is to say, this was my last passport application, of that I was sure. I would not come here again; there would be no need to commit to memory the place where I had picked it up. This fact was a bit frightening and a bit depressing. A damp wind blew down on the square, then through it, as though moving on to other things.

I remembered a good friend, now dead—he may have killed himself—and a love from long ago who died young from uterine cancer. (I neither visited her when she was sick nor went to her funeral.)

It strikes me as curious indeed that I alone am still alive. The series of events six years ago, from notification to surgery and discharge from the hospital, was like something that had happened to a stranger decades earlier. How am I to live the rest of my life? How many years do I have?

It was then that I became aware of someone walking toward me across the square from the front of the city hall building. In spite of the fact that no one had been there just moments before.

What the devil!

The figure of a man was approaching me. In a gray suit, and wearing a necktie. A leather briefcase. He was a little taller than me and heavier. I could see his face. He was an academic who for some years had been on the newspaper's book review committee with me. We'd been good friends, although our fields of expertise were quite unrelated. He was also a bit younger than me. He was on quite firm ground both intellectually and emotionally. He was almost the direct opposite of me.

What're you up to? In a place like this?

Without thinking, I got to my feet, left the cafeteria, and ran to the edge of the plaza. I was suddenly very happy. My companion was startled, but unlike me, was not agitated.

"I had something I wanted to check out at city hall," I said, laughing with absolute naturalness.

Our houses were in the same direction from the paper, so after the biweekly meetings of the book review committee we would find ourselves in the same car taking us home. He was an honest, open sort, raising his kids as they should be raised and taking care of his elderly parents. Why would a person like him turn up, out of the blue, at this deserted plaza?

"I also have coffee here whenever I come to city hall," he said calmly. We had returned to the cafeteria and were sitting across from each other at the same table I'd been sitting at.

"When I sit here and look up," I said, speaking rapidly and still exhilarated, "the city hall building looks like towers rising up to the heavens."

"I get that sense, too."

"You look just as though you descended those towers."

He smiled without answering. He did not know what I had been thinking, what I had retrieved from memory, as I had sat there by myself. Though we were good friends on the surface, our relationship was not such that I could tell him what was in my heart.

"I was surprised, too. To see you standing, all of a sudden, in front of that glass door."

I concluded it was good. Good—as I was out and about when my senses had suddenly become disordered—that this had unexpectedly happened and the one who had appeared was not just anybody, but a person I now considered to be the most human person I knew.

I had the feeling I could hear what sounded like a voice in the distance: Live your life with strength, without flinching or confusion.

I passed my gaze along the mosaic wall of the towering city hall building and looked beyond it to the clouds, which were once again hanging low over the city.

The Death Register

AKUTAGAWA RYŪNOSUKE

Akutagawa Ryūnosuke's (1892–1927) autobiographical sketch Tenkibo *(The death register) has been well received in Japan for decades precisely because it is factual and affords a private glimpse of its inscrutable and immensely gifted creator, who killed himself at the age of thirty-five at the apex of his popularity because of, as every Japanese schoolchild learns, "a vague angst." The fact that he wrote this piece in 1926, less than a year before his death, adds a cachet of imminent doom to an otherwise straightforward, if somewhat morose, literary sketch from his childhood.*

Akutagawa's emotional distance from his father in this piece is striking. In contrast to his recollections of his mother, he clearly has trouble remembering much about the man, even the important things. He tells us "I can't recall the date of my father's death or his posthumous name," and the old man's funeral is essentially a blank, save for the moon shining on the roof of the hearse. When his father is on the brink of death, Akutagawa goes off to amuse himself with geisha: "I set off for the teahouse, leaving my father back in the hospital hanging on to life by a thread." Given these remarks, we are not surprised to find that Akutagawa never says "Father," chichi, in the short story "Death Register" but inevitably uses the distancing, objectifying "my father," boku no chichi. Although largely undiscernible in translation, Akutagawa's frequently un-Japanese diction—his abundant use of pronouns in particular—betrays the sway of English literature, his major in college and a continuing influence.

· I ·

My mother was a madwoman.

Not once did I feel the warmth for her that a child feels for its mother. She would sit by herself in the family home in the Shiba district of Tokyo and puff away on her old-fashioned long-stemmed pipe, her hair rolled in a chignon and held by a comb. Her face was tiny, as was her body. And her face, for some reason, had a gray pallor, without the slightest hint of vitality. Once when I read the old Chinese play *The Romance of the Western Chamber* and came across the phrase "the smell of dirt, the taste of mud," I immediately thought of my mother's face, that gaunt, emaciated profile.

Thus it was that my mother never looked after me as a mother should. I remember once going to pay my respects—I'm pretty sure I was with my foster mother—going up to the second floor and quite suddenly being hit on the head with that long-stemmed pipe. By and large, however, my mother was a remarkably placid lunatic. When I or my elder sister would press her to draw a picture for us, she did it on a sheet of rice paper folded to quarter size, but not just with India ink. She would use my sister's watercolors and paint pictures of young women on an outing and their clothes, or plants and trees in bloom. Unfortunately, all the people in the pictures had the faces of foxes.

My mother died in the autumn of my eleventh year. The cause of death seems to have been general debility rather than a particular illness. Only recollections of her around the time of her death remain relatively clear in my mind.

I think it began with the arrival of a telegram telling us she was gravely ill. Late one windless night my foster mother and I rushed in a ricksha from the Honjo district to Shiba. To this day I have never again worn a scarf, but I remember that night wrapping around my neck a thin silk kerchief on which was painted some sort of Southern Sung landscape. And I remember the fragrance of the perfume called Iris that clung to the kerchief.

My mother lay in an eight-mat room on the ground floor. I sat with my sister, four years my senior, at my mother's bedside, the two of us sobbing continuously. I felt all the more sharply the pangs of sorrow when someone behind me said: "Her time has come, her time has come." My mother, however, who had lain eyes closed and still as death, abruptly opened her eyes and said something. In the midst of our sorrow my sister and I tittered softly.

The next night I again sat at my mother's bedside until almost dawn. And yet, unaccountably, unlike the night before, the tears would not come. I felt ashamed because my sister had been crying almost nonstop, so I faked it and wept for all I was worth. At the same time, I believed there was no way my mother could die as long as I was unable to cry for her.

My mother died essentially without pain on the third night. Before she died she seemed to regain consciousness. She gazed into our faces, the tears running down her cheeks. As always, however, she said nothing.

Even after we placed her in the coffin I found from time to time that I could not keep myself from crying. Whereupon a distant relative, an elderly woman known to us as "the aunt from Ōji," said, "How admirable!" But my only thought was that here was someone who admired odd things.

The day of the funeral my sister and I, she carrying the mortuary tablet, me, behind her, a censer, set off in rickshas. From time to time I would doze off, awakening each time with a start to find the censer slipping from my grasp. It was taking us forever to reach the cemetery in the Yanaka district. The rather long funeral procession wended its way with deliberation through the streets of Tokyo on one of those crisp autumn days that follow one after the other.

I can remember that November 28 was the date my mother died, and the long and archaic Buddhist name given her posthumously. And yet I can't recall the date of my father's death or his posthumous name. Perhaps this is because remembering my mother's date and name was the sort of thing an eleven-year-old would be proud of.

· 2 ·

I have one older sister now. She is, in spite of her poor health, the mother of two children. What I would like to add to my own private "death register" is, of course, not this elder sister. It is an elder sister of mine who suddenly died young just before I was born, a sister who was said to be the brightest of the three siblings.

This first daughter was called Hatsuko. We still have a photo of Hat-*chan* in a small frame on our Buddhist altar at home. She was not at all a fragile child. Her dimpled cheeks were as plump as ripe apricots. I have to say that it was little Hatsuko whom my mother and father especially cherished. Hat-*chan* went all the way from Shinsenza in Shiba to, I believe, Mrs. Summers' kindergarten in the Tsukiji district. However, she would always come back to stay at my mother's home, the Akutagawa house in Honjō, on Saturday and Sunday. During these times away from home she doubtless wore fashionable Western clothes, though it was still the 1880s. I remember that when I was in elementary school I would dress a rubber doll I had in remnants from Hatsuko's kimonos. These scraps of cloth were all imported calico prints inevitably covered with delicate flowers and musical instruments.

One Sunday afternoon early in spring Hat-*chan*, walking in the garden, called out to her aunt in the sitting room. (Of course, I visualize my sister as wearing Western dress then too.)

"Auntie, what do you call this bush?"

"Which bush?"

"The one with the buds."

A single low *boke* tree stood in the garden of my mother's family home, its branches drooping over an old well.[1] Little Hatsuko, her hair in braids, and perhaps her eyes wide in wonder, was looking at the plant with its prickly branches.

"That bush is what you are, dear."

Unfortunately, Hatsuko didn't understand her aunt's little word play.

"Then it's called a fool's bush, right?"

Any time someone mentions Hatsuko, my aunt repeats the exchange, even now. Actually, I talk of Hatsuko stories, but there are no more about her. It was perhaps only a few days later that Hat-*chan* lay in her coffin. I don't remember the Buddhist name that was inscribed on her little mortuary tablet. But, curiously, I recall clearly that it said she died on April 5.

For some reason I feel a sense of closeness with this elder sister, an elder sister I'd never seen. Were Hatsuko still alive, she'd be over forty. A forty-year-old Hatsuko would probably have looked like my mother, who vacantly smoked her long-stemmed pipe upstairs in the family home in Shiba. I sometimes sense the wraithlike presence of a woman of forty or so—whether my mother or my sister I cannot tell—watching over me from somewhere. Is this merely my nerves at work, enervated by coffee and cigarettes? Or is it the power of the supernatural showing itself to the real world when given the opportunity?

· 3 ·

Since I was brought to my foster parents—the home of my mother's elder brother—soon after I was born because my mother had gone mad, I likewise felt indifferent to my father. He was in the dairy business and apparently a minor success of sorts. My father introduced me to what were then novel fruits and beverages in Japan: bananas, ice cream, pineapples, rum (and there were doubtless more). I remember drinking rum in the shade of an oak tree outside what was then a pasture in Shinjuku. The rum was an amber-colored drink very low in alcohol.

---

1. The *boke* is a deciduous shrub of the rose family. *Boke* also means senile, dotty.

My father pressed such rarities on me, still a young lad, to get me back from my adopted parents. I recall how one night as he plied me with ice cream in the restaurant Uoei in the Ōmori district of Tokyo he openly urged me to decamp and return home with him. On these occasions my father was extremely "able in word and ingratiating in manner," as the *Analects of Confucius* says. Unfortunately, however, his attempts at persuasion never bore fruit. That was because I loved my foster parents, and especially my aunt.

And my father was a short-tempered man. He would get into arguments with people all the time. When I was in the third year of middle school, we wrestled, and I threw him down nicely with my specialty, the outside thigh sweep. As soon as he got up he squared off against me.

"One more time," he said.

I easily threw him down again.

"One more time!"

He came flying at me, his face flushed. An aunt who had been watching us wrestle—she was my mother's younger sister and my father's second wife—gave me a meaningful look several times. After grappling with my father I intentionally fell on my back. If I hadn't lost to him, he most certainly would have laid hold of me yet again.

When I was twenty-eight—I was still teaching then—I received a telegram: "Father hospitalized," and immediately left Kamakura for Tokyo. He was being treated for influenza in Tokyo Hospital. For three days or so I slept with my two aunts, one from either household, in a corner of the hospital sickroom. In due time I found myself getting bored, at which point an Irish newspaper reporter I was acquainted with telephoned to invite me to a geisha teahouse in the Tsukiji district. Using the journalist's imminent departure for America as a pretext, I set off for the teahouse, leaving my father back in the hospital hanging on to life by a thread.

We had a traditional Japanese meal in the pleasant company of four or five geisha. I'm sure we were finished around ten. I left the journalist, and as I started down the narrow stairs, I heard someone call my name, or rather—as is the custom of geisha—the first syllable of it. I stopped midway down and looked back up the stairway. A geisha who had happened along was staring down at me. I said nothing and descended the stairs, getting into a taxi waiting at the entrance. It immediately drove off. I then thought, however, not of my father, but of the woman's fresh young face—her hair was set in a Western style—and especially her eyes.

When I returned to the hospital I found my father was waiting impatiently for me. That was not all. He sent everyone else behind a two-panel decorative screen and began to tell me about the years he had been married to my mother, things out of the past I knew nothing about, clasping and stroking my hand as he did so. These were trivial stories: the time when he and my mother went to buy a tansu, and when they ordered sushi somewhere. Nonetheless, as he talked I felt my eyes fill with tears. And, of course, tears ran down my father's emaciated cheeks.

My father died the next morning without much pain, though he was apparently delirious.

"Here comes a warship, and with so many flags! Everyone shout banzai!"

I don't remember much about my father's funeral. I do recall, however, that when his body was being carried from the hospital to his house, a full spring moon shone on the roof of the hearse.

· 4 ·

This year for the first time in a while I visited the cemetery with my wife; it was mid-March and still cold enough for me to use my pocket warmer. It's true it was the first visit in a while, but the red pine that spreads its branches over the little grave and, of course, the grave itself, had not changed.

The remains of the three who had been added to the temple death register are all buried in a corner of that Yanaka cemetery, and, in fact, lie under the same gravestone. I recalled the time my mother's coffin had been quietly lowered into the grave. Little Hatsuko's burial was doubtless much the same. Only in my father's case do I remember gold teeth mixed in with his finely pulverized, stark white bones.

I'm not fond of cemetery visits. Were I able, I would prefer to forget my parents and my elder sister. That day, however—perhaps out of physical exhaustion—as I gazed at the dun-colored gravestone in the sunlight of an early spring afternoon, I wondered to myself just who of those three had been happy.

> The spring air shimmers:
> I merely go on living
> this side of the grave

In truth, never had I felt Jōsō's[2] haiku so oppress me as it did that day.

2. Naitō Jōsō (1662–1704), one of the poet Matsuo Bashō's ten principal disciples.

Kid Ume, the Silver Cat

KAWABATA YASUNARI

Doubtless in years past Kawabata Yasunari (1899–1972) was one of the two or three writers who had a faithful, if small, following outside Japan. Even before he was awarded the Nobel Prize in literature for 1968 he was one of the Holy Trinity of midcentury Japanese literature, the other two being Mishima Yukio and Tanizaki Jun'ichirō. Today his non-Japanese admirers are certainly proportionally fewer than before, owing to the erosive effects of time, but also certainly to the simple availability of more writers and the export abroad of literary sorts more compatible with contemporary Anglophone tastes, especially younger authors such as Murakami Haruki and Yoshimoto Banana. The fascination that Kawabata held for the auslanders was, in part, that he conformed to their expectations of Japaneseness. This perception, however, is a double-edged katana; what to one reader — or generation — is engagingly exotic tradition may to another seem merely bewildering fustiness.

Asakusa no kurenai-dan (*The crimson gang of Asakusa*), *published serially in 1929–30 in the evening edition of the* Asahi *newspaper, is a literary ramble through proletarian Tokyo, an essentially plotless exploration of interwar To-kyo's shitamachi, which, to oversimplify somewhat, is the older, less favored, poorer section of town, proud of its plebeian traditions but losing, bit by bit — even today — its identity to the modish, modern, powerful movers and shakers who live in the Yamanote area, the higher ground in all senses save, perhaps, pride of place. Kawabata has seized upon this pride and, energizing it with his own keen sense of place, has drawn an unsentimental, unsparing, yet poignant portrayal of this special time, now past, and place, so greatly changed. Many Japanese literary critics place Kawabata in the expressionistic Neo-sensualist school of Japanese literature, and even if North Americans tend to reject such categorizing as mere pigeonholing, most will agree that Kawabata's literature stands in contradistinction to the so-called proletarian writers of the period and that this distinction applies to the greater part of his work. Yet we clearly see in the following excerpt from* Crimson, *written during the Great Depression, that Kawabata was willing to confront festering social ills, and to write sympathet-ically of Umekichi, one of Tokyo's plentiful homeless children of the interwar era. Kawabata does not simply describe; he condemns. It is ironic that at one point he uses the voice of arguably the most apolitical novelist of the twentieth century, Tanizaki Jun'ichirō, to indict the whole of Japanese society. Kawabata's narrative voice in* Crimson *is also out of character. He attempts direct engage-ment of the reader through adoption of the address "Dear Readers" and a gen-erally more relaxed, conversational style than in his later, better known works such as* Snow Country *and* The Sound of the Mountain.

He began a sequel several years after The Crimson Gang of Asakusa *but, as was the case with a number of his other narratives, never finished it.*

Umekichi had not fallen haplessly into the clutches of the Crimson Gang. Rather, they had come to his rescue and awakened him from a nightmare of many years. I shall, Dear Readers, introduce you to Umekichi, a text-book example of the lawless youths who make Asakusa their lair, and what he has owned up to. First, his love life.

Instance one. His sixth year. He is made the plaything of a woman over forty.

Instance two. His thirteenth year. He befriends a girl a year older than himself as he is hanging out in front of the stationery store across from his school. Her father works in a large corporation. She invites him to her house. No one else is at home. Neither of them is timid. He goes back three or four more times. The family moves away after word gets about.

Instance three. His fourteenth year. He gets to know the daughter of a notions dealer on a bench outside a candy store. The two of them go to Ueno Park and temple fairs and hole-in-the-wall eateries more than twenty times.

Instance four. His fifteenth year. Two girls sit next to him in a motion picture theater in Asakusa Park.[1] He meets one of them in another theater. And where she then takes him is to a house with two entrances, both of which have glass shoji.

Instance five. The same age. He goes to a bigger house. As Umekichi feigns sleep, a fair hand takes a silver 50-sen coin from his coin purse and puts it in a single-stalk flower basket hanging on the alcove post. Umekichi looks into the flower basket when the girl is out of the room and finds 8½ yen in silver 50-sen coins. He takes the money home with him.

Instance six. The same age. A young woman of seventeen or eighteen takes her sister of twelve or thirteen to see a play in Asakusa. The younger girl, noticing what the nearby Umekichi is doing to her sister, drags the latter out of the theater. He follows them. They are the daughters of a book lender. He starts going to the store to borrow historical tales. He takes out the elder daughter a half dozen or so times. Her mother puts an end to these outings.

Instance seven. The same age. He disports himself about Asakusa with a waitress from a Chinese restaurant for four months and becomes an older youth's "punk" to earn the money he needs to do it.

Instance eight. The same age. He fleeces one of the young women who live in the house with two entrances of a total of some 150 yen. She herself had willingly come to him. Her father habitually plays the horses.

---

1. Originally part of the Sensōji temple complex, most of the park was sold off for commercial use in the immediate postwar period.

Umekichi was aware that from time to time there were sizable sums of money about.

Umekichi's love life finally takes on a deeper tinge of illegality at the age of fifteen. I shall refrain, Dear Readers, from revealing these incidents to you here, lest I rudely awaken you from your dreams in your warm and cozy beds.

Dear Readers, who have your own warm beds, were I to call him Praying Mantis Urchin you would conjure up a can-do fellow, one of Asakusa's *gure*, or homeless youths. It is said he knew nothing about storing cushions or putting away futons. They say if he were told to put them away, he would roll up the cushions and futons together into a ball, for he had no recollection of using such things.

Praying Mantis Urchin, however, was not a dunce like the green-grocer's daughter O-Shichi.[2] He knew the juvenile penal code (author's note: the one before the current juvenile law) backwards and forwards. He had been collared by the police a couple of dozen times and even sent off to Iwojima; he would tell the district attorney point-blank: "Hey, I ain't gonna stop doin' bad things 'til I turn fifteen."

And he was as good as his word. It was only after he was sent off to the island at fifteen that he first did honest labor. I'm told he sent a sack of beautiful shells the size of a grain of rice to a protector who had looked after him in Asakusa.

Try this sometime. Buttonhole one of the younger Asakusa *gure*, the homeless lads, and ask him about his parents. It is possible, Dear Readers, his rather too outlandish answer may surprise you.

"I don't have any yet."

"Not *yet?*"

"Right. My buddy Shin got himself a 'dad'[3] the other day, but I haven't yet because I'm too young."

---

2. A young woman of Edo who in 1682, having met a man who became her lover after taking refuge from a fire in a temple, is said to have set a fire so that she might return to the temple and be reunited with her love. Apprehended, her punishment was death by fire. O-Shichi is "a dunce" here because if she had told the authorities she was fourteen instead of fifteen, her life would have been spared.

3. That is, head of a gang, or someone who provides protection in return for loyalty.

And yet be aware, Dear Readers, that educating and supervising a child is an extravagance today, even for parents who can provide a futon for the child to sleep on.

You, Dear Readers, are aware that the vagrants of Asakusa live off the leftovers of eateries, yet did you know that the poor and laborers go to the vagrants to buy what they have been given, that is, leftovers of leftovers, for 2 or 3 sen a meal? Is it any wonder that in a world such as this, one should find forty or fifty thousand juvenile delinquents under the control of the Metropolitan Police alone? And so many among these are those who have been in service: errand boys, shop employees, blue-collar apprentices, waiters, child workers.

To give you an idea, listen in for some thirty minutes or so to the conversation of girls working as nursemaids as they relax in Asakusa Park.

"But if that's the case," wrote the novelist Tanizaki Jun'ichirō, "what does that make Japan today? What is the city of Tokyo today? Is not the whole of Japanese society today, and of Tokyo, a kind of *senile* delinquent? And amongst all this senile delinquency we find only in Asakusa Park juvenile delinquency. Though it be delinquent, in its youth we see vivacity, progress, love and respect."

And according to an article in the *Asahi* newspaper, the radio station JOAK will set up two microphones on the precincts of the Asakusa Kannon temple on New Year's Eve and will broadcast the night's festivities to us from 11:50: the footfalls of those making their pilgrimage, the sound of the bell, the clattering of coins into the collection box, the sound of worshipers clapping their hands, the 108 peals of the bell, the cock's crow, and so on.

And I'm toying with the idea of having the members of the Crimson Gang gather in front of the microphone and shout in the new year: "1930! Banzai!" Be that as it may, they're broadcasting there because Asakusa, the heartbeat of Tokyo, represents the spirit of New Year's Eve even at the very depths of the depression.

They say there's a tavern for beggars in Asakusa. They put a half-naked girl on a table and the lot of them drink themselves into a stupor as they spin her around and around.

And let's assume there is really a Kiyomoto ballad recital taking place in a house near Komagata Bridge. Those who have gathered there are all dubious-looking pimps. A girl of sixteen or seventeen makes her appearance.

"I solicit your patronage," she says yet in the end provides no samisen, only saké.

On rainy nights men bring large oil-paper umbrellas from flophouses in the Honjo area and come pimping, looking for vagrants along the earthen walls of the temple or from under the eaves of the theaters. Juvenile delinquents stealthily tail women entertainers going to meet their clients.

Yet what is to be feared about Asakusa lies not in this sort of thing or the likes of its Okuyama entertainment district in the dead of night. Autumn or winter, it is to be found in the confused swirl of people at Yoshiwara's Cock Fair or the Kannon's year-end fair or New Year's Eve. How was it that Umekichi was trapped in this whirlpool and fell at last to the depths to become Kid Ume, the Silver Cat?

Umekichi never talks about his parents. Doubtless he is illegitimate or an orphan. Or it might be that they are the sort of parents one is better off without.

At thirteen he went as a shop boy to a Western-style umbrella maker in Ryūsenji-machi in the Shitaya district. This is the neighborhood the respected author Higuchi Ichiyō writes about in her story *Growing Up.* The mistress of the umbrella maker's household was bedridden, having long been sick. Umekichi hated seeing the woman, so frail and wan. On top of which, her seven children kept him running. Umekichi fled after three days there.

He was then apprenticed to a saké merchant. (I have already written that at fourteen he had taken as his second girlfriend the daughter of a notions dealer.) The saké dealer sent him packing for pocketing money to spend on the girl.

One day when he was hanging around Asakusa Park, a newsboy started a conversation with him and then let him join his group. Before three months had gone by Umekichi had gotten into a knock-down-dragout fight with one of the older newsies. He was beaten up and sent on his way.

A beggar in the park took Umekichi under his wing and let him stay for three nights at the big garbage dump on the riverbank at Komagata—what they called the Azuma Hotel—after which he drifted as far as Chiba prefecture, starting from the Honjo and Fukagawa areas.

"That half year living as a beggar and as carefree as a crow I was as innocent as a newborn babe. It was fun, I'll tell you. That'll never happen again." That's what Umekichi always says.

He then made his way back to Asakusa. He became a shill for an Indian selling rings on the street, someone who pretends to be a customer buying a ring. The man loved him as one would a little girl. Yet when the moment of truth arrived Umekichi left the man from India.

"You son of a bitch! Paint your body another color if you're gonna make love to a Japanese!"

Once when he was absentmindedly sitting in Asakusa Station, a kindly looking old man came and took Umekichi home with him. The old fellow was a notorious cat-catcher. He was soon taken away by the police. When that happened Umekichi was taken under the wing of the cat-catcher's buddy. He roamed Asakusa as the apprentice of the cat-catcher.

When a cat-catcher comes across a cat, he tosses out a sparrow tied to a string. The bird flutters about. The cat pounces. He draws in the string little by little. The cat is lured closer and closer. At which point the cat-catcher grabs it. Quick handwork is the key.

Any cat Umekichi and the cat-catcher caught would be immediately beaten to death. They would skin it in a dark part of the park or in the cover along the riverbank. The cat-catcher then wrapped the skin around his waist, where it was hidden under his clothes. He was able to get a good price from samisen makers.

The two had no home but stayed in cheap lodgings, wherever they found themselves at night.

It was at this time that Umekichi joined an Asakusa gang of young delinquents. He was in his fifteenth year. Before long the two cat-catchers were hauled into the Nihonzutsumi police station in Yoshiwara. Umekichi, however, still a child, was seen as more or less blameless.

When he turned up again in Asakusa, he sensed that the police would be keeping an eye out for him for the foreseeable future, so he joined a group selling one thing or another for a fictitious orphanage. While he was doing this, going about pretending to be an orphan and pressuring people into buying stationery supplies, he met another high-pressure salesman, a student selling medicines. Umekichi decided he would make more money peddling those, so he quickly metamorphosed into a student supporting himself by selling medicine. His purse grew fatter and how useful his middle-school uniform was in snaring women!

Thus came the enhancement of his sobriquet as well. He was no longer Kid Ume, the Cat-catcher. He had suddenly risen in stature to become Kid Ume, the Silver Cat.

These days, when he's a member of Yumiko's Crimson Gang, Umekichi is now the age of a faux college student, but in fact his calling has come quite close to being legitimate: an apprentice to a barber. Yumiko had gotten him the job there. How he met her is a story in itself.

We have an instance of Umekichi employing on a particular young woman one of the gang's time-tested Techniques for Leading Women Astray: Squeezing. Touching. Talking. The program. You're going to drop it. Total devotion. Baby. Now you've gone and done it, haven't you. Stumbling. Walking her home. Paying visits. Hem-rolling. Pursuit. Thanks. The thrown towel.

He was at the Tamaki Theater, known for its Yasugi-bushi, a folk song from Shimane prefecture. The young woman was unmoved.

However, when they started singing the finale, "The Ballad of Ginza": "Ginza, Ginza, beloved Ginza!" to the accompaniment of a meld of Western and Japanese jazz and eight dancers in long-sleeve kimonos, she bit her lip, eyes downcast. Umekichi could see that her eyelashes were wet.

"What an innocent! Happy day!" he said to himself, as he tried furtively to put his arm around her shoulder.

The girl leaped from her chair in an instant, leaving the theater without so much as a backward glance at Umekichi.

But according to the reckoning of the ever confident Umekichi, she was already his. In his *hakama* and school cap with its dubious badge, he was passing himself off as a college student.

They say that the young women of Tahiti wear a white flower over the right ear when they want a lover. In Asakusa, though certainly not an island in the distant South Seas, an artificial rose stuck in the hair can display a girl's susceptibility. And the same rose, red, can also signify a girl gone wrong.

Of course, even in Asakusa Park the era of the die-hard, so-called Righteous Band[4] has passed, yet if your son, Dear Readers, were to walk about with his cap insouciantly rumpled out of shape, then someone would stop him in his stroll.

"Hey! You there! Whose punk are you?"

And who's to say they wouldn't squeeze some money from him? "Punk" here means follower.

Well, this young woman was wearing a muslin kimono that had seen better days and a soiled obi; only her imitation silk undersash, red and generously exposed to view above the obi, was new. And her thick makeup had the unintended effect of making her look absurdly sad. And thus we see that her psychology was likewise flawed. All Umekichi needed do was exploit it.

So he took a woman's handkerchief from his pocket, caught up with the girl, and said unceremoniously: "Didn't you drop this, dear?"

"Right. Thanks."

"Say, aren't you the girl who was sitting next to me in the Tamaki just now?"

The young woman crumpled up the handkerchief, put it in the sleeve of her kimono, and walked briskly off. Umekichi appeared a bit surprised but persevered.

"Your eyes filled with tears in the theater, didn't they. I was watching you. You must have a reason to be sad. You dropped the handkerchief when you came out and were wiping away the tears. I'll bet it's a little damp from your tears."

"And just out of kindness you thought you'd ask me what I'm sad about, eh, pal?"

"Huh?"

4. A reference to the shōgitai, the Manifestly Righteous Force, peacekeeping retainers of the Tokugawa Bakufu who resisted the Meiji restoration and were defeated in the Battle of Ueno in 1868.

"I'm one step ahead of you, am I?"

"Hey, listen!"

"I suppose you want the handkerchief back. But you don't mind if I keep it, do you? I'm sure you still got three or four at the ready in your pocket. Show me a new line, one that makes being taken in worth my while."

Umekichi laughed.

"What a bonehead move! I should've recognized you! What a laugh! Anyway, a handkerchief is good for wiping away tears."

"Sure is," the young woman said as she pulled out the handkerchief and pretended to wipe tears away with it. "I'll tell you, it was odd the way the tears came as I listened to 'The Ballad of Ginza.'"

"You're suffering from Ginza-itis too, eh?"

"Listen, at the Tamaki, whether it's Yasugi-bushi, Ohara-bushi,[5] or even the cheer 'Banzai!,' the audience acts as though they're being entertained at a geisha house, raising a happy ruckus, singing along, a real feast for factory workers and ditchdiggers. But then what? When they start singing that jazz version—'Ginza, Ginza, Beloved Ginza'—the audience falls dead silent, as docile as beggars before their lord. What's the big deal about the Ginza? What have the patrons of the Tamaki got to do with the Ginza? I'll bet there are plenty of them who haven't even seen it. Just as there are fine young ladies who go to the Ginza all the time and know nothing about Asakusa. It was more than I could bear."

"Well then, that shows you're a bit of an ideologue, I'd say."

"You're Silver Cat. Am I right?"

"I see I'm not as sharp as I used to be. I can't believe I didn't recognize you. Your hair, it's a wig, right? And your clothes, they're rented? I came to catch a fish and got hooked myself."

"Listen, I'm on my way to return these clothes I rented. Want to come with me? And will you really try to seduce me now, knowing who I am?"

"Well, if it's certain you're a woman."

"Find that out for yourself."

5. A Kagoshima folk song.

The First Day of the Fair

TAKEDA RINTARŌ

The short story "Ichi no tori" (The first day of the fair) by Takeda Rintarō, like his "Image," also in this collection, has as its central character a young woman, though she does not narrate the story. Like the unnamed narrator of "The Image," O-Shige works in a traditional Japanese-style restaurant, in this case the intrigue-ridden Tamura in Asakusa. But O-Shige is a not of a piece with the other woman. The entirely likeable seventeen-year-old is capable, after significant vacillation, of turning her back on her predatory boss, having already turned down an unreasonable request from her importuning mother and the woman's sleazy consort. We can suppose that such rebellion will have serious consequences, but we know that the maturing O-Shige will be able to deal with any eventuality. The Japanese reading public was much taken with O-Shige when this short story first appeared in the journal Kaizō *in 1935, so much so that Takeda presided over what can only be called an "O-Shige boom," writing a number of short stories revolving around the fictional young woman.*

The fairs in question are the two or three Rooster Fairs held in November at the Ōtori Shrine in the Senzoku district of Tokyo. Their main attraction is the sale of ornamental bamboo rakes that, according to tradition, will help their new owners rake in good fortune in the coming year. And the fairs offer their patrons a last occasion to stroll about outdoors at a festival, eating and drinking, before the onset of winter.

O-Kiyo, her sash and toiletries in one hand, was looking into the wall mirror as she combed her hair. Her kimono was fastened with only a cord.

"Shige, there's something I want to talk to you about later."

The seriousness of her tone was unexpected, but even more curious was her peering into O-Shige's face with such a friendly look in her eyes as she spoke, given that she normally never smiled, assuming instead a self-important air that favored neither the aforementioned O-Shige and the other employees—which might be expected—nor even her younger sister O-Toshi and her elder brother's wife, O-Tsune.

"What's up?"

O-Shige had been taken to task before for her congenitally blunt language and told she was not suited to an establishment that had dealings with the public, but O-Shige's response even now was quite abrupt, notwithstanding the fact that she was speaking to a woman who was related to her boss.

O-Kiyo glanced at her younger sister and the other women, who were unhurriedly applying white makeup to the napes of their necks as the male bath attendant went about scouring the tile floor and putting away the *furo* pails.

"Come on, let's not wait for the others." O-Kiyo said, pressing the other woman.

O-Shige, somewhat bewildered at this turn of events, was quickly shepherded out of the bathhouse and into the street. It would soon be winter, and the first of the fall fairs was just around the corner, yet this year it was warmer than usual, and the breeze was pleasant against their cheeks, ruddy from the bath. There was a small restaurant that had Chinese noodles and a 10-sen plate of curry and rice still open on the main street of the Umamichi district.[1]

"It's my treat," O-Kiyo said as she opened the glass-paned door. She seated herself at a table that had not yet been cleaned and regarded a menu, giving a cursory glance at the girls who had returned from their jobs in the park and taxi drivers having a late meal.

"What'll you have?"

"Let me see now," O-Shige said, looking up at the names of dishes posted along the wall, "I'll have toast, toast with jam, if I may."

This was a special treat for O-Shige, so her answer was politely framed. O-Kiyo, elbows on the table, fixed her gaze on O-Shige.

"Come on! Stop staring at me!"

O-Shige touched the inner corner of her eye with her finger. O-Kiyo always took advantage of the fact that she was the sister of the owner even though they all worked in the same place and dealt with the same customers. Yet no matter how much she disgusted O-Shige, she was the elder, besides which, O-Shige was a bit intimidated by the other's renown when sitting face-to-face like this.

O-Shige was apprehensive and pressed the other woman: "The matter you wanted to talk about, what was it?"

"You're awfully stylish these days, aren't you."

To her surprise, O-Shige felt herself blush at this comment.

"I'm not so sure about that. I doubt I'm overdoing it." O-Shige sensed that the malicious O-Kiyo was mocking her, suggesting that there was no point in painting a house whose foundation is cracked.

"It's natural enough. You're seventeen." O-Kiyo smiled, her lower lip protruding.

"You know, my mother's forever telling me I'm like a man. She asks me, 'Isn't it about time for you to act your age?' "

"She's right. You're an adult now."

---

1. An area in Asakusa north of the Sensōji Temple complex, the main street of which is also called Umamichi, that is, "Horse Boulevard."

"Goodness," O-Shige said, blushing beet red again. She had begun to sweat and picked up her bath cloth, now thoroughly chilled.

"Listen, Shige, I'm on your side. Do what you have to do." O-Kiyo gave a sympathetic tilt to a face that tended toward the traditional oval shape.

O-Shige said nothing. She wasn't sure what the other woman was talking about.

"There's absolutely no reason for you to defer to my sister-in-law. I'll talk it over with my brother and help you get things sorted out. I certainly will."

"Sorry to keep you waiting," the waiter said, bringing their orders. His arrival was ill timed. It was all O-Shige could do to conceal her confusion.

"That's hers," O-Kiyo told the waiter as she took her noodles from him. She split her chopsticks: "Go ahead and eat."

O-Shige's heart was thumping. She was instinctively on guard.

Does she know about it? But she couldn't possibly. Maybe she has only an inkling and is trying to pump me by pretending to be on my side with a rare show of kindness. And after she gets what she wanted, watch out! I can't afford to be careless.

"Excuse me! Water, please."

O-Shige got her water and ate her toast.

"I'm not kidding. I'd really like to get the better of my sister-in-law. She lords it over everyone. It's so disgusting. She's so conceited she thinks every single customer comes because he's taken by her looks."

O-Shige was amused to hear O-Kiyo talk like that. Yesterday morning at breakfast she had screamed at O-Shige in near hysteria—so that everyone was sure to hear—that two men were her customers and that O-Shige was not to try to take them away from her. O-Shige suspected that O-Kiyo wanted to imagine that even now a customer might have his eye on her, O-Kiyo.

Hah! Alas, not so!

Yet O-Shige did realize that, depending on how you looked at it, it was only natural for O-Kiyo to be irritated. But it wasn't simply a matter of their working in a watering hole, where, naturally, every woman had to be vain enough to think that a particular customer was hers and hers alone. O-Kiyo certainly had to have her own memories from the past. O-Shige had heard a lot about O-Kiyo while she was still attending Ryū-senji Elementary School. She would often hear men talking about "young Kiyo at the Tamura." At one time she was counted among the two or three Famous Young Beauties of Asakusa, and little O-Shige and other young girls harbored a vague sort of infatuation for her. When they came to the park to play, they would conspire to loiter outside the Tamura, which at the time was not as big as it is now, in order to get a look at O-Kiyo, to catch even a glimpse. Some of Shige's friends even told her they had followed O-Kiyo, or that she had looked at them and smiled. O-Shige and her friends imagined O-Kiyo to be attending to a leisurely mulling of the saké every night, a beautiful woman in her gorgeous kimono, as men contended for her attention. In fact, customers *had* come to win O-Kiyo's affection. Some had patronized the restaurant simply because of her reputation as a famous beauty, and others persisted night after night in an attempt to ingratiate themselves with her. Inevitibly, on occasions when she poured saké for a man only once or twice—and that only out of duty—he would be seen clumsily telling the usual jokes to keep her attention and then laughing with unseemly delight. O-Kiyo was in the habit of staring somewhere off into space, her elongated eyes fixed effortlessly on a point in the distance, to let the lighting in the room highlight all the more her white forehead and well-sculpted nose. Even when she was haughty the customers had seemed to find her fascinating. But those days were now gone.

O-Shige had been in service at an inn last year. When she heard she was to work at the Tamura how happy she had been! She was thrilled at the very idea of living under the same roof as the renowned O-Kiyo and so pleased with herself she wanted to write and let her old friends know about her good fortune. And she had not been overly concerned when her mother received an advance payment—with disadvantageous conditions attached—from the Tamura. When she came there on probation she had greeted O-Kiyo with special politeness, gazing at her in awe. But afterward she gradually became disillusioned and even had the curious feeling of doubting whether this was the same O-Kiyo who had caused her heart to dance. It was one thing to hold one's head high as the owner's younger sister, but O-Kiyo was more than a nuisance: indolent, tight-fisted, crude of speech, and ever complaining. She hurled fearfully cruel language at the servants and the merchants who enjoyed the Tamura's patronage. They were driven to tears by her ingrained maliciousness. But what surprised O-Shige more than this was how O-Kiyo's popularity at the restaurant was waning. O-Kiyo's younger sister O-Toshi had replaced her as the one everyone pampered. And her brother's wife, the seductive O-Tsune, was also well received. Even O-Shige was liked for her disposition and found that not a few men made advances to her using one stratagem or another. Formerly it had been for O-Kiyo that each and every customer had ordered high-priced saké, but recently it was the other women men clamored for, leaving O-Kiyo on the sidelines, an increasingly severe expression on her face. She was twenty-five, but because of an unhealthy lifestyle, her skin had coarsened and her features, now careworn, no longer captivated men. But beyond that, the twisted nature of her personality seemed to come more and more to the fore now, to become all the more disagreeable. Nonetheless, it goes without saying that she did not stop working at the restaurant. She wanted to believe that she could forever remain the Tamura's premier attraction. She attempted to play the part again, thereby drawing attention to its impossibility and reaping, simultaneously, animosity and ridicule.

And yet in certain situations a suggestion of sadness would cloud her expression for an instant. In a chaotic mix of drunken voices and feminine laughter, O-Shige—she herself in a jolly mood—got up to get another bottle of saké and found O-Kiyo at the entrance to the kitchen; her face was pale and she was looking wistfully in the direction of the merrymaking. O-Shige started as though she had bumped into something, but by then O-Kiyo had already regained her usual feigned indifference. We can assume from her going to the customers with a new attitude, smiles for all, that she was desperate to retrieve once again her former popularity. Should a regular customer from the old days—one who had fancied her but had at some pointed drifted away because he was ignored—return out of nostalgia, she would be thoroughly cheered, her voice rising in animation.

"My goodness! What a rare treat!"

And although she had never been so coquettish previously, she would now stay close by his side and exclaim loudly for all to hear that the customer had not forgotten her after all. She would then ask about someone they had both known.

"Whatever happened to that fellow, what was his name, the one who always used to rattle on and make everyone laugh so, you know, and yet he himself would act as though what he was saying not the least bit amusing, and after he'd had us rolling on the floor, would scowl sourly."

O-Kiyo would make a point of persisting: "And there was that art teacher with the bad leg who sent me love letters."

"Ah, him," the man would begin, looking about the room and commenting with nostalgia and apparent regret how much the Tamura had changed. O-Kiyo, warming to the subject, would customarily have something to say in agreement.

"Yes, you're absolutely right. You can see how vulgar it's gotten. It was better before. But for some reason they say that when you don't change it *this* way—if you don't give it mass appeal—people won't come near the place. So the policy, management policy, has changed since my father's day. It's a problem. We keep getting more and more provincials, you know."

O-Kiyo inevitably took this tack both with those customers who had been interested in her and those who had not maintained a long-standing interest.

Since O-Kiyo was no longer attractive enough, the customer's feelings for her would evaporate right before her eyes: *Was I really infatuated with this woman?* Then his gaze would quickly settle on her younger sister making small talk with a customer at another table.

"Say, isn't that little Toshi?"

O-Kiyo would reluctantly glance over at the young woman, jealousy in her heart.

"It is. She's a big girl now, isn't she."

"She certainly is! She used to come here all the time, still in her elementary school uniform, and ask me to show her how to do her math homework. Toshi, honey, could you come over here?"

After which O-Kiyo's longtime customer, entranced by the naive,

pure beauty of her younger sister, who was O-Shige's age, would ignore
O-Kiyo completely.

This was not something that happened only once or twice. And if it
were not O-Toshi, it would be someone else: "Wow! Is that the young
master's wife?" or "Say, O-Tsune! . . ." or, sometimes, to O-Shige: "You're
quite the Asakusa girl, aren't you! It's a pleasure to see such a feisty
spirit!"

The customers thus shifted their affections to the other women.
O-Kiyo was left to fend for herself, and in her isolation her perverseness
only worsened.

"You never, ever hear of someone in Asakusa stealing another's customer away!" she would scream, "It just isn't done!"

Yet it wasn't simply her loss of popularity that made O-Kiyo resent
her sister-in-law. O-Tsune, the daughter of a man who ran—with considerable panache and a sense of style—a large and prospering restaurant in the Shinagawa district of Tokyo, was a year older than O-Kiyo,
but as a woman she was just now hitting her stride: her roundish face
and pleasingly plump body were certainly equal to the task of provoking
in men at least the idea of going astray. On top of which, compared to
O-Kiyo, she was not prim or rigid, and her attitude was open: when she
saw someone she would lean gently and coquettishly against him, say
something provocative, and in response to requests would sing old dit-
ties and traditional love songs, so men clamored for O-Tsune in spite of
O-Kiyo's backbiting.

"She's not some rice cake–peddling slut or a girl working in a cheap
bawdy house. I'm surprised she has no qualms about acting in such a
vulgar way!"

O-Kiyo would make a point of wondering out loud around her brother
Toyotarō if her sister-in-law wasn't being too familiar with a certain customer, then taunt him, "Brother, you'd best be on your guard."

The couple's marriage had been a love match. Notwithstanding the
fact that he had had a formidable rival for her affections—the master of
a sushi restaurant in Asakusa Park—O-Tsune had rejected the other man
and married Toyotarō and had been the very model of the good wife.
Toyotarō was quite the philanderer. It was not just a matter of wondering

what he was doing and where he was doing it; she would infrequently hear disagreeable stories. Yet O-Tsune's devotion to Toyotarō was none-theless unwavering. O-Kiyo did not want to acknowledge their mutual affection; the fact was, it exasperated her. After her father had died, the Tamura—like a structure eaten from within by termites—was lost to her, and now belonged to another. This unease inexorably filled her entire being and left a tight knot of anxiety sitting in the pit of her stomach. And this she would complain about when she had someone who would listen to her: the Tamura's unique, as she would put it, "Old Edo" atmo-sphere had disappeared. This had come about when the restaurant ran up a sizable debt it couldn't pay off and O-Tsune's family had put a massive amount of money into the operation. The Tamura was then obliged to consider their investors' ideas, turning the establishment into, in O-Kiyo's spiteful phrase, "something akin to a roadside teahouse you'd find in a post town." Which is to say, they ripped out the stylish fixtures and the tatami flooring, changing it to entirely Western seating, then posted the prices of items on the wall, creating, all in all, a tasteless mess. O-Kiyo's father had always had an utterly old-fashioned way of doing things. He provided his patrons high-quality food, fresh and from the most reputable sources, and he was not one to simply rely on saké barrels and labels. He hypercritically scrutinized each barrel, giving saké to his customers only after taste-testing it himself. Customers he took a dislike to were abruptly ejected, and if he couldn't get the cooking in-gredients he wanted when he went to his suppliers, he would put up the sign Sold Out Today and accept only drinking customers. He was the cook, so he would then promptly stop work and head for the Kin-shatei,[2] to take his ease on the tatami and watch the matinee. One could even say this attitude survived even after O-Kiyo's father died and Toy-otarō succeeded him, and that expenses had exceeded income. O-Tsune's father, who could scarcely credit such a lack of business acumen, was not sparing of advice as he put money into the enterprise.

"With the customers we get these days, feeding them fine food is like casting pearls before swine. If it's cheap and looks okay, second-rate stuff

2. A *yose*, or vaudeville theater, in the Rokku, or sixth district, in Asakusa.

will do just fine. Even in the case of saké, I don't give a damn what's in it if it's a brand that's been well advertised."

He started providing the Tamura with the same items as his Shinagawa restaurant. His ambition was to rename the Tamura and have it be the Asakusa branch of his restaurant, but, of course, he couldn't come right out and say that. He could only comment that if the name Tamura was popular and drew customers, they would have to live with it, but if that were not the case, it would be to their advantage to give the restaurant a catchy name, one that would bring good luck. Little by little the Tamura was paying back the money it had borrowed as it got back on its feet, during which time O-Tsune's father did not let them forget where the money had come from.

"See, it's just like I've been telling you."

This did not sit well with O-Kiyo either, and she had nothing good to say about him.

"The damn fool acts like he's done us a big favor, like he's *given* us the money, but pretty soon, you watch, he'll be coming to collect interest."

"Now, now, don't talk like that," her brother Toyotarō said, assuming the role of conciliator. "He said he'd be willing to take care of your trousseau."

"You can forget it," she retorted. "I'm not marrying a hick gambler."

O-Kiyo refused to speak to O-Tsune at all, and when they happened to meet she would quickly look away. O-Tsune, for her part, would frown and put this down to the disagreeable nature of sisters-in-law in general. If something important arose between them, something that had to be dealt with, they would argue the matter through Toyotarō.

"There's no reason to hide anything from me, right, Shige?"

"I'm not hiding a thing," O-Shige responded, wiping jam off her lip.

"Then come out with it. My brother seems to be quite fond of you."

"Why do you say that?"

O-Kiyo threw her head back and laughed.

"Stop it, now, this pretending not to know what I'm talking about. Would you like some more to eat? I'll have a piece of cake. What about you?"

The glass-paned door rolled open with a clatter. It was a customer with an order for delivery: "Pork cutlets for three, okay?"

"I've had enough."

"You needn't be shy. Have some donuts."

"Okay then, I'll have milk. But I'm really imposing."

With that, O-Shige giggled. She had just recalled one of her regular customers, the young owner of a dairy who was too shy to come to the restaurant alone, so he always brought along a gaggle of friends. They would tease him and he would end up treating them and running up a hefty bill.

"That's awful, laughing to yourself about something."

"No, no, I was just thinking of the milk fellow."

"Oh," O-Kiyo said, her expression losing its warmth slightly. She was not interested and immediately returned to the topic at hand.

"I saw you two the other day."

O-Shige could scarcely bear the mocking look in O-Kiyo's eyes.

"My brother was taking quite a chance, taking you in his arms at the back door, and in broad daylight."

O-Kiyo, mindful of where they were, had whispered, but for the seventeen-year-old O-Shige, it was all she could do to stay in her seat. She looked down at the table. When she realized she might have been observed, she was suddenly, and uncharacteristically, nervous, as though it had been all her fault.

"Listen, I'm not angry with you. Maybe it's going too far to say I'm praising you, but anyway, you can probably understand how I feel. O-Tsune fancies herself a bit too much, so I want to let her feel some real pain. Do you understand?"

O-Kiyo had begun her incitement of the younger woman.

"You want sugar in your milk? Hurry up and drink it. Depending on the circumstances, Shige, it would be okay to get him back if you really have a mind to."

O-Shige had taken a serious misstep some two weeks earlier. It was vivid in her memory but at the same time seemed so abstract to her it might as well have happened to someone else. All she was sure of was that it *was* reality; she could not grasp her own forbearance and behavior at the time, no matter how often she replayed it in her mind. Remorse that she had done something awful lasted only as long as the physical discomfort that seemed to be detached from her own body stayed with her, and when time passed and that disappeared, it no longer meant anything to her. And the remorse, too, barely made itself known the next day. She had flown to Toyotarō's arms because she was oppressed by sour, sad emotions that demanded revenge.

At least O-Shige had known who she wanted to get back at. There was no doubt the focus of her anger was her mother and her latest husband, Shinkichi, a man she was loath to call her stepfather.

A dilatory autumn rain had been falling since morning. The maid O-Fuji, who worked in the kitchen, had told O-Shige to go to the back door. There was O-Hama, her mother, standing and shaking the rain off her umbrella.

Not again!

O-Shige guessed what it was that had brought her mother there, yet her response was a purposefully annoyed "Yeah?"

"Can you get off today?"

"Nope. It's the fifteenth, you know. Besides, the mistress went back to Shinagawa last night."

"What a mess! What am I to do?" her mother said, making a show of her despondency.

"I took off work last month because I was sick, so I can't take any time off for a while yet. Is that all?"

With apparent impatience O-Shige fiddled with the cleaning rag she had been using.

"I wonder if I couldn't ask the young master a special favor in that regard?"

"You know, you're a real pain!"

"I don't care about myself, but I can't bring shame on Shinkichi-*san*."

O-Shige fell into a sullen silence. Her mother's use of the polite *san* made her want to scream like a spoiled child: *Right, Mother! Your husband means more to you than I do! Of course!*

"Really? If it benefits Shinkichi, then what do you care happens to me!"

"You can't mean—"

"I don't give a damn. Borrow as much as you damn please from my wages!"

Choked with emotion, O-Shige could not say another word. It was all she could do to keep from crying.

"He's your father. You owe him that much. You've no right to talk like that."

O-Hama was only thirty-seven. She had gone with various men since she had lost O-Shige's father. It was late summer last year when she got together with Shinohara Shinkichi, a man who did who knows what in the park; he was younger than she was. He was short and squat. His features were not particularly fearsome, yet he had cold eyes that did not miss a trick, and his hair was cropped so close to his melon head you could see his scalp. It would not be off the mark to say the overall impression he created was one of menace.

"He's not my father! I owe that shiftless bum nothing!"

O-Hama herself worked as a waitress in a restaurant specializing in horsemeat that fronted Yoshiwara. She and her daughter were supporting Shinkichi.

Then O-Hama began her long-winded entreaty: Shinkichi had made a solemn promise to the master of the Tomizushi restaurant. The master was fond of O-Shige, and that being the case, he wanted her to quit the Tamura and come over to his place. Yet this was merely O-Hama's smooth and superficial way of describing the situation. In fact, the master of the Tomizushi had competed for O-Tsune's hand with Toyotarō, with whom he had been on bad terms ever since they were children, and he had lost. He was still single and hoped to openly make O-Shige his mistress. O-Shige could well imagine that Shinkichi, who had dealings with the Tomizushi, had readily agreed to that. And O-Shige's mother told her that the Tomizushi's master had said he was going to the Tokyo Theater today, so Shinkichi had taken it upon himself to get O-Shige to go with him and had already bought two tickets.

"I beg you," O-Hama importuned her daughter. "Do whatever you have to do to get off! If you don't, Shinkichi will be an utter laughing stock."

"You're only concerned about yourself. It's got nothing to do with me."

O-Hama was left to her own devices. O-Shige was blunt: "I'm busy now. Go home."

Then she added: "Think what you are saying. Do you really think my boss will give me time off if I tell him I'm going out with the master of the Tomizushi?"

O-Shige's mother made her way home in the rain, now falling harder than ever. O-Shige got perverse satisfaction from her mother's discomfort: *Let it rain, and the harder, the better!*

Nonetheless, she immediately began to worry that Shinkichi would be railing at O-Hama again. O-Shige loved O-Hama very much and had a habit of sprinkling her conversations with *my mother this* and *my mother that.* This situation at last focused her hatred on Shinkichi. She now wanted her mother entirely to herself. How was it, she wondered, that a fine woman like that falls in love with such a loser? All she had to do was leave him. How proud she could be if her mother were with a person at least a bit more worthy of being called Father! O-Shige indulged in a little self-pity. If Shinkichi weren't there when the customary day off came around, O-Shige could go to the room O-Hama was renting above a *tabi*-maker in Kisakata-chō and relax without a care in the world, letting herself be spoiled by her mother. There had to be a way, she reasoned, to get her to leave Shinkichi.

On Saturday, the fifteenth, the restaurant had been a frenetic whirl of activity, and to make matters worse, they were short-handed because O-Tsune was away. O-Shige was standing abstractedly in the kitchen a little after nine eating a late dinner when Toyotarō, who was in his office, gave her a look that urged her to quickly get up to the second floor.

"How's that?" she asked, then started. From the dining area of the restaurant come the sound of abusive language. It was Shinkichi.

"This is bad," her boss said. "Hide!"

She put the rice bowl she had been eating from on the shelf and climbed the stairs, taking care not to make a sound. Upstairs was where the women slept.

O-Shige's response to Shinkichi's angry shouts thundering up the stairs was that of a young girl: *Oh, no! This is awful!* And, she lamented to herself, there was no woman on earth as luckless as she was. Mortified beyond description and beside herself in her agitation, she wondered if she would be better off going downstairs and shouting right back at him: *Who the hell are you to come in here and make a nuisance of yourself on whatever pretext suits you?* Yet she realized that would cause more trouble for the restaurant, so she was forced to restrain the considerable urge to fly out of the room and down the stairs in a rage.

The sound of rain beating down fiercely on the roof had a soothing effect on O-Shige. She opened the window to a not-unexpected flow of chill air. In the distance the Five-Story Pagoda cast a dark and melancholy shadow in the light of a faintly smoking arc lamp.

A cheerlessness had enveloped O-Shige since morning. Shinkichi certainly didn't frighten her, she thought to herself as she leaned against the windowsill, dozing off only briefly.

O-Shige waited a reasonable length of time, then assessed the situation downstairs. Shinkichi was apparently no longer in the restaurant, so she quietly descended the stairs. It pained her to apologize again and again, first to her boss, and then to the other employees. O-Kiyo and O-Toshi were not sparing with their sarcasm.

"Your mother's got quite a husband there, hasn't she."

The women closed up the restaurant and went off to the public bath. O-Shige had a splitting headache, so she decided not to go and busied herself straightening things up.

"O-Shige!" the boss called to her, "there's something I want to talk to you about. Come see me later."

His and his wife's room were in a separate building. O-Shige walked quickly through the rain as fast as her kimono would allow.

"May I come in?" she asked, opening the shoji after she had touched her hair to see if how wet it was. Toyotarō's wife had phoned to say she would not be coming back from Shinagawa tonight. Toyotarō was alone, warming his hands over the hibachi, a samisen and knickknacks behind him.

"Come in."

He was smiling a wry, inscrutable smile. He told O-Shige to sit down in front of the hibachi.

"So the Tomizushi fellow wants you, does he?"

"Well, I'm afraid I don't know about that."

"Really?" Toyotarō said, taking out a cigarette. "I suppose you'd be willing to go along with whatever he might propose."

O-Shige's denial was so earnest she forgot the formal language she normally used with him.

"I sure wouldn't!"

Toyotarō nodded, then softened his tone.

"Please listen to what I have to say and don't laugh. To be completely honest, I've been fond of you for quite some time. It would have grieved me, however, if you'd thought I was trying to woo you by using my position as your boss, so I suppressed my feelings and said not a word."

Telling risqué jokes when bantering with customers had never bothered O-Shige, but she had never had the experience of being alone with Toyotarō like this where, completely serious, he was all but taking hold of her hand. She hadn't the foggiest idea what she should do. She was utterly stunned, her mind in turmoil.

"I intended never to tell you, but then I found out about the Tomizushi fellow tonight. You can't expect me just to withdraw meekly from the scene. There's been bad blood between me and the Tomizushi fellow for years. I, too, have my pride."

O-Shige had been listening, her head bowed, feeling only excitement, but when she heard the word "pride," her heart sank and her emotions turned bittersweet.

"Understand how I feel," Toyotarō said with even greater gentleness in his voice.

O-Shige let him have his way, holding fast in her mind's eye the figure of Shinkichi and her mother, reviling them bitterly: *Let whatever is to happen, happen! It's the fault of you both that I am seduced by this womanizing boss of mine! Let my debasement be complete!*

O-Shige did not particularly like Toyotarō. She was not attracted by his overly refined nature and a face wanting definition, his thinning hair, a complexion feminine in its paleness. And in O-Shige's eyes his flirting with his wife and other women was unmanly and certainly a shortcoming. In normal circumstances she probably would not have given herself to him no matter how ardently he courted her.

In the wake of this episode, O-Shige was startled to suddenly discover herself harboring affection for Toyotarō. O-Tsune had returned, so there was no opportunity for the two of them to meet alone. O-Shige was unsettled whenever their eyes happened to meet and felt herself being strongly drawn to him. She sensed that her looks at him were too keen and needy. O-Shige felt a twinge of jealousy to see O-Tsune apparently conducting herself as a good wife should, yet she hated herself for feeling that way. From the first moment O-Shige had naturally resigned herself: it had been merely an impromptu dalliance to be expected of a man with Toyotarō's reputation for amorousness, her feelings for him were not deep-rooted, and the day-to-day routine often deflected them.

One day early in November Toyotarō was washing his face, having just got up and come from his bungalow. O-Shige had come to the kitchen door to dispose of trash.

"Hey O-Shige, hold my sleeves up a bit, would you?"

O-Shige looked about to see what his wife might be doing, then did as he asked. When he was finished, he handed her his toothbrush and powder, told her to put them away, and began oiling his hair, looking into the mirror in the half-light of the kitchen as he did so. There was little room to pass, so O-Shige turned sideways to squeeze by. When she did, Toyotarō suddenly turned around and took her in his arms, pressing O-Shige, whose body had instinctively stiffened, hard against him.

"I'll take you to the first fair the night of the fourth," he whispered. "Wait for me next to the Hanayashiki Amusement Park after we close the restaurant."

O-Shige went back to into the dining room and dusted the tables, but she felt as though Toyotarō's chest was still pressing against her breast; she touched the front of her kimono, wondering if the warmth of his body might still be clinging to it. She was, after all, thoroughly delighted. Yet though her boss had asked her to meet him, she wanted both to talk to him about whether she should really go or not and to push the whole thing out of her mind.

Next to her stood the plump O-Fuji.

"You and the other girls are lucky," she said, then to herself: "It must be fun to be able to talk with the drinking guests. Oh, I wish I could work in the dining room!"

She was an unattractive woman, so they had her in back helping the cook, and she was quite unhappy about it.

O-Shige had lost her train of thought.

"What are you talking about?" she asked querulously.

What had happened that morning must have been what O-Kiyo said she had observed. She goaded O-Shige: "There's no reason why you can't see him outside the restaurant. I'll do what I can so that you'll have some free time."

In the end, O-Shige had let the other woman know nothing, had laughed it away.

"Well anyway," O-Kiyo said, making the point one more time, "this little chat is between you and me. In any case, that's how I intend to keep it, and you will too, right?"

O-Kiyo took out her money.

"How much is it?"

Had O-Shige been provoked by O-Kiyo and forgotten herself, she could well have told her everything, but her deep dislike of the older woman had ultimately proved a barrier.

A light rain fell yet again the afternoon of the fourth. O-Shige hoped for a heavier rain, rain by the bucketful. In her indecision she was looking to the weather to decide the matter. The rain would give her an excuse. She saw in her mind's eye the deserted amusement park, not a soul in sight.

Early that evening when there was a bit less to do, the lad named Shūichi—everyone called him Shū—came in. O-Shige suddenly realized she had forgotten about him and felt the need to turn to him.

He was the son of the *tabi*-maker where O-Shige's mother was renting a room. He had graduated from a private college and was doing nothing in particular, amusing himself about town and helping out with the family business only when he got around to it. He drank like a fish, and once he started he was inseparable from his saké cup until daybreak.

O-Shige sat down next to him, a relieved expression on her face, as though a snarl of knotty entanglements had begun to unravel itself.

"What's the matter?" she asked.

"With what?"

"What do you mean 'with what'?" she responded, her voice raising coquettishly in her embarrassment. She realized she had really been asking herself what was wrong.

"Remember, about my mother?"

The taciturn Shūichi stared hard at O-Shige. The other day when he was so drunk you could scarcely credit anything he said, he let slip that he was in love with O-Shige's mother.

"What in the world are you saying?!" she had laughed derisively, "In love with that old girl?"

And then she had had second thoughts and pressed him further.

"You're joking, aren't you?"

"Listen, I'm not joking." His tone had been emphatic, his expression serious.

"Best not to overdo it," she had told him. He had nonetheless held up and shaken one empty saké bottle after the other, demanding replacements.

Afterward she began to indulge in a rather far-fetched fantasy: if Shū took her mother away from Shinkichi, it would be the answer to her prayers. Every time he came to the Tamura she would ask what he had talked to her mother about that day or urge him to take her to the movies, all the while trying to gauge the nature of his relationship with O-Hama.

"And Ma likes you, you can bet on it. I can tell."

"There's no way you can tell."

It was also from him that O-Shige heard Shinkichi had gone on a trip to Osaka at the beginning of the month with a bunch of fly-by-night hucksters who worked the temple fairs around the country. O-Shige had stopped dropping by her mother's place.

"Really? Well, as they say, when the cat's away, the mice will play."

"Uh-huh."

This "uh-huh" that O-Shige casually took no obvious notice of was something of a surprise. And it moved her to action. Bright and early the next day she told them at the restaurant she would be back in an hour, then went off to visit Kisakata-chō for the first time in a long while. Upstairs, O-Hama, who worked nights, was in bed, but O-Shige queried her as soon as she saw her face.

"Shū's not here today?"

"What's that? Oh, it's you," O-Hama responded, getting up. "You gave me a start."

O-Shige asked her mother more than once if Shūichi had been talking to her. Her eyes not leaving her mother's face for a second, O-Shige tried to ascertain how things were between her and Shūichi. The daughter knew her mother like the back of her hand: she was a woman who had never walked the straight and narrow. O-Shige was uncharacteristically uneasy about what her mother might do if Shinkichi were not around, regardless of how O-Hama might act when Shinkichi was with her.

Although she had at first wanted to bring her mother and Shūichi together, before she knew it her thinking had changed, a change that was not unrelated to her first experience with a man, yet she had not seriously thought about this paradox.

"Your mother? Your mother's gone to work."

"Has she now."

O-Shige made no effort to conceal her testiness. Suddenly distant, she went to another patron's table. Nonetheless, she came back again to talk with Shūichi, the provision of a saké bottle as her cover.

"Shūichi," she began but found nothing more to say. Then: "I wonder if it's stopped raining."

She ran out the entrance.

"Oh dear! It's stopped." She remembered her promise to her boss.

"You're awfully gloomy tonight, aren't you."

"I'm depressed," O-Shige told him.

"Really? Depressed? Even you, eh?"

"You don't understand me at all."

Shūichi was drunk before long, which meant he gradually lost his color. It seemed to O-Shige that his drunkenness would infect her as well tonight.

"Have some more."

"Didn't you tell me before I'd best not overdo it? Okay, I'll have some more."

"You pour me some. Shūichi," she began again, "Shūichi, I think my mother is a tart."

"A tart?" He was amused: "How can you say something like that?"

"It's no laughing matter! Don't you lose your head over Ma."

"Don't lose my head?" he echoed.

"I'm not kidding," she said firmly, her patience clearly wearing thin, "so . . ."

"So . . . what?"

"So . . . listen . . . when I say 'so' . . ."

O-Shige began to cry in her frustration.

"You shouldn't do that, Shū," O-Tsune said, standing next to them. "We can't have you giving our girl a hard time. Come now, make up with her."

O-Shige withdrew to the kitchen and was crying uncontrollably. She felt a hand gently tap her shoulder and looked up, her tear-stained cheeks notwithstanding. It was her boss. He laid his hand on the nape of her neck.

"I'll be good to you later, so stop crying like a child."

"Stop it!" O-Shige said, pulling away from his grasp. She wiped at her tears with her sleeve and stood there stock-still, essaying an actor's smile, and when she was confident of her smile, she went back into the dining room, wearing it like a mask.

"I'm sorry," she said, apologizing formally to Shū. "Sorry. Say something."

"Uh-huh."

It dawned on O-Shige that she could go to the fair with Shū. That would put both O-Kiyo and Toyotarō in their place.

"You're staying until closing, right?"

"Yeah, sure."

"And afterward, would you wait for me at Niō Gate?"

"I can, but why?"

"The fair."

"Oh. This year there are three fair days in the month. Business down-turns and lots of fires, eh?"[3]

"You don't want to wait?"

"Nobody said anything about not waiting."

The night sky was crystal clear. O-Shige got permission from Toyotarō to leave early, changed clothes and quickly got out her new, holiday-best geta.

"In front of the Hanayashiki. Okay?" Toyotarō, ever persistent, said under his breath.

O-Shige nodded, then ran to Niō Gate. Shūichi, feeling no pain now, was engaged in a shoving match with one of the gate's pillars.

"Funny, huh. I've been wrestling."

"Right."

When they came to Yonekyū Boulevard, O-Shige leaned forward slightly and looked in the direction of the Hanayashiki Amusement Park, as though she might be able to see something in the dark.

"What're you doing?"

"I suspect someone I know is down there."

It was a little past midnight. The Ōtori Shrine was so jammed with people come to get a charm on the first day of the fair they could scarcely move. The two young people were swallowed up by the huge mob. Shūichi grabbed O-Shige's hand.

"Hang on tight and follow me!"

The great mass of humanity, undulating like a giant snake, threatened to carry O-Shige away with it.

"Shū, I've lost one of my geta!"

"You'll never find it in this crowd!"

---

3. There are normally two *tori,* or rooster, days in a month. Three such days falling in November were thought to augur bad luck, principally in the form of fires.

Elegy

SATA INEKO

Unlike most of those who gained recognition as proletarian writers in Japan, Sata Ineko, born in Nagasaki in 1904, came to her subject having experienced poverty firsthand. Although her family had been solidly middle class, she was the love child of teenage parents—her father was still in middle school when she was born and her mother was fifteen—so Sato did not have a stable home during her formative years. A precocious child, she regretfully left school when she was eleven to work in a candy factory, after which she supported herself with menial jobs in various restaurants. Literary types who frequented a café in the Hongō district of Tokyo where she worked as a waitress helped her gain entrée to the literary world, or at least publication in a small journal; they also exposed her to the ideology of the left. She joined the Communist Party in 1932, taking part in political—including feminist—activity, which led to her arrest in 1935 and detention for two months. Her turbulent private life included two failed marriages and several unsuccessful suicide attempts. Sata drifted away from the proletarian movement and took part in military-sponsored tours of China and Southeast Asia during the war, activity later criticized as cooperation with the militarists.

Sata said that a sense of nostalgia for the old Tokyo that burned in the American fire-raids of 1945 motivated her to put down on paper her recollections of the city in her impressive Watashi no Tōkyō chizu *(My map of Tokyo), an excerpt of which, "Banka," is included here as "Elegy." "Elegy," which first appeared in print as a short story in 1946, is a largely autobiographical vignette of the author at the time of the great Tokyo earthquake of 1923, when she was working at the Maruzen bookstore in the Nihombashi district of the city. Today the name Nihombashi is linked with banking, large department stores, and the historic bridge itself. But as "Elegy" reminds us, before it was a modern commercial and financial center, it was a residential district, and by the onset of the Shōwa era in the mid-1920s, one mostly of artisans and merchants, large and small. To say that Maruzen, where Sata sold foreign luxury goods, was a bookstore is to say that the* New York Times *is a newspaper; the fashionable store had functioned since the Meiji era as the premier purveyor of higher culture from abroad, selling, besides Western books, a wide range of imported luxuries and Occidental exotica to customers who included the well-to-do, as well as the elite of the scribbling classes. Maruzen still flourishes, but Sata Ineko died in 1998.*

It was fall, the end of October, so by five o'clock it was already night in the streets and you couldn't make out the faces of passersby, yet the afterglow of dusk seemed to linger in the darkness of early evening, the electric streetlights not yet able to make their presence fully felt. Thus it seemed even darker for the hour than it really was. People going about their business, especially hereabout, where things were regulated by the clock, manifested the tumult proper to the hour. Here in the streets, paved with wood bricks, rose the sound of shoes and clogs, and the grate of fair-weather geta. In the refracted light people moved on obscurely like figures in an India-ink painting. Only the streetcars went by raucously, casting noise and the light within them out into the darkness. Faces resigned to silence could be seen cheek by jowl under the light.

From time to time the wind would rise and sweep broadly over the ground, as though suddenly remembering that's what it was supposed to do, and plaintively penetrate to the inner being of people and remind each person walking along the street and those clumped darkly at intersections waiting for the trolley that the heart of the city where they now stood was far distant from their own home. When that happened, each would feel the anxiety—as everyone drew nearer to the person in front or in back of him—of one who had been abandoned to his own devices in the very center of the city.

At the time—this was before the big quake—there were some small watch and notions shops along the main street from 3-chōme[1] to the Nihombashi bridge, next to Yamamotoyama, the venerable tea sellers, and across from Maruzen, but for the most part you had large enterprises that in the evening would lower their steel shutters, giving the commercial district quite a modern look, yet somehow in keeping with things traditional. There were many Western-style buildings, but even the Maruzen building, whose service entrance I now emerged from, gave, in its color, the allover impression of rusted iron, and the offices of the Nozawa Association as well, catty-corner from Maruzen, were in a red brick building, a Western building style that had already become old-fashioned here in Nihombashi. And it was not just that the buildings were old. The tenacious, musty traditions of old Edo had spread their roots throughout the whole of Nihombashi, so that you had shops like the Yamamotoyama, with its mammoth tile roof and broad, open entrance and tatami-laid floors. And its clerks, of course, wearing striped-pattern kimonos and aprons. This was not the case only at the tea sellers Yamamotoyama. Even at the Maruzen Bookstore, which most certainly felt a degree of pride and pleasure in being the sole importer of foreign books into the country and in drawing to the store the elite of Japan's intelligentsia, the great majority of the clerks could be seen wearing their striped kimonos and aprons. And many of the customers wore geta. Thus at the Maruzen entrance two elderly men worked as footwear checkers. Both men were the placid, self-effacing sort that made you marvel at Maruzen's good fortune in finding such people. Which does not mean,

1. A several-square-block area south of the Maruzen bookstore.

however, that they were servile. One had a head of white hair that he always kept trimmed, his features those of a refined elder. The other man was a little younger and shorter. There was a hint of weakness in his flat face, but one would normally not notice this. Both walked like men who had never worn shoes, back slightly bent and stride measured. On either side of the entrance to Maruzen as you went inside were rows of hemp-soled straw sandals with red thongs. Customers wearing geta would put these on before entering the store and get a claim check from the old men. Customers wearing shoes would have tan shoe covers put on their shoes. The streets of Tokyo still made that sort of thing a necessity.

The sound of the high-bladed geta that intermingled with the other footfalls along the main street through Nihombashi right after five o'clock came from the feet of male salesclerks in striped kimonos. Women clerks wore the lower-bladed fair-weather geta. At the time a woman who could type English was someone to be reckoned with; as for the rest, female salesclerks dominated the category known as career women. This was perhaps because Mitsukoshi, Matsuzakaya, and the other department stores employed large numbers of them. You could identify them at a glance. Even at Maruzen, where female clerks had begun to be hired some time later, they attempted to force them into this female salesclerk mold. The women put their hair up in a foreign, fluffed-out, rounded style and, by and large, wore muslin obi higher up on the waist. Behind the counter they wore a purple muslin smock over this, with a numbered badge pinned at the chest.

I'm on my way home from work now, so I'm not wearing my smock. I wear a lined, machine-woven kimono with a red splash pattern secured by a tie-dyed muslin obi. My companion wears pretty much what I do. To people on the street we can be taken for nothing more than two women clerks now off work and homeward bound. We are merely figures from an end-of-the-workday vignette that passes dimly before your eyes in the autumn wind as night falls in the city. Just as the two of us emerge into the light shining brightly into the street from within the Yanagiya on the corner with its colorful displays of floral hairpins, tie-dyed chignon bands, and fancy neck bands—only available there—several male employees catch up with us, then pass us by, throwing a teasing "We'll go first, if you don't mind." That's all that happens. No one notices in the light cast on my retreating figure from the notions shop that my obi is tied rather lower than custom demands for a woman who works as a clerk. Only I am aware of this. Even my companion is unaware that my map of Tokyo extends from Ikenohata in the Ueno district to Nihombashi, that I have played the quick-change artist, going from waitress in a small traditional restaurant to salesclerk in the prestigious Maruzen.

It was an ad of several lines in a newspaper that linked me to Nihombashi, yet the groundwork that made it possible for me to make such a quick change lies in my childhood. The daughter of a low-level company employee, I felt more comfortable being a salesclerk than a waitress in a restaurant. Nonetheless, the spirit of *shitamachi*, the plebeian section of Tokyo where I lived my early years, had a part in forming my character and quite naturally colors my likes and dislikes. Perhaps I have within me a complexity of a kind. To others I was just another insignificant salesclerk; to myself I was a young woman with her own proclivities.

On close observation we can see that surely everyone has their own proclivities. It makes one realize that human beings may well live quite disparate lives, according to the needs of those lives. Even Satō Kimi, who was walking with me, was somehow different. She was the daughter of a lumber dealer whose business had seen better days, and having had what you might call a Fukagawa lumberyard daughter's upbringing on the river, she had at least taken lessons in traditional *nagauta* singing. Nonetheless, she had nothing of the temperament of the lumberyard family about her, nor in her—a strapping woman compared to me—was there any affectation of bearing. She had a face as round as the moon, though the way she did her hair was simplicity itself, making her look to be no more than a good-natured soul. Nonetheless, there was no doubt that she was, after all, a woman I had met in Nihombashi, a woman I had most certainly met at the Maruzen Bookstore.

She was the woman who excitedly told me she had seen Ōsugi Sakae[2] come down from the foreign books department on the second floor.

2. Ōsugi (1885–1923) was an anarchist and left-wing leader who, together with his wife

"His eyes are fantastic! They absolutely flash! You could be captivated by his eyes alone!"

The very excitement she felt at having seen Ōsugi, her singular feelings of the moment, radiated from her. She talked to me about all sorts of things. She told me things no one else had told me: that corruption was at the heart of Nihombashi. She said that society was rotten to the core, so it had to be smashed. Her expression as she told me these grim things was not the least bit grim.

We usually had such conversations on the way home from work, when we would go to the Hatsune in the Ningyō-chō district for a bowl of zenzai, bean jam with rice cakes. The Suiten Shrine was surrounded by a stone wall right by the main street where the trolleys ran, and you could always see tiny flames from its lanterns flickering within a sea of worshipers. Hanging lanterns ringed the shrine, which shimmered red and yellow and black, projecting an uncommon vitality beyond its walls. We would enter the Hatsune on Ningyō-chō Boulevard, indifferent to all this on our right. Inside the restaurant with its elaborate latticework sliding doors there was tatami flooring.

Kimi also talked about her love life. Her anarchism had come from her lover and was not merely inspired by Ōsugi Sakae's fiery eyes. She had accepted her lover's ideology as her own and given herself, with her diseased lungs, to the cause, a commitment so strong she had felt self-satisfaction in doing so. In truth, one could tell from a glance at her body, which tended to plumpness, that she was not healthy. She walked with a pronounced shuffle, her shoulders hunched, and coughed whenever she laughed.

"So, you know, I told him I wanted our relationship to be like brother and sister. At which point, his eyes insistent, this is what he says: 'I don't want a sister. I want your flesh!' A man's eyes are frightening at a time like that."

She said this with a gleam in her own eyes, then laughed, coughing lightly. The blunt word "flesh" had for some time had a kind of literary

---

and nephew, was beaten to death by military police in the chaos following the great earthquake of 1923.

ring to it. Admittedly, it had already become a bit passé by then, but to come right out and say, "I want your flesh," without resorting to the word "love," certainly demonstrates an audacious attitude.

I just listened, saying little more than "Wow!" This was not like the *shitamachi* way of resorting to indirection, saying of even the man you loved simply that he was "a good person." It was not the *shitamachi* custom to boldly go where others feared to tread, so I was not about to ask her: "And then what happened?" And she, for her part, seemed to take pleasure in telling me only as much as she had told me.

Some time after this Kimi invited me to his house in the Koishikawa district. Her lover was fair-skinned with narrow eyes. He and his mother lived together in the small house. He was disheveled in an unlined kimono with a splash-patterned *meisen* weave, but with his bony shoulders thrown well back. I did not sense, however, the intensity of a man who would say: "I want your flesh."

"Don't get any ideas," Kimi said to him to forestall any move he might have made toward me. "She's purity itself."

Her lover, who had not said anything along those lines, just smiled faintly. I had sensed no particular need for her to head off anything. And to be called pure certainly was not a source of pride for me. Certainly I thought so because I had already observed much about the private lives of others.

As was true of Kimi, her lover also was consumptive.

I had not seen too much of Nihombashi in the daytime in the two-and-a-half years I had been there. I would stand behind my case of merchandise and look out and see only that part of the broad boulevard that was framed by the store's large entrance, the summer sun shining down at high noon. At the time the location directly across the street from Maruzen, where the large Takashimaya building now stands, was a vacant lot left to the weeds. The Takashimaya stood then more toward Kyōbashi and had a display window that was impressive enough, but it looked like an old-fashioned dry goods store. The second floor of Maruzen sold foreign books and the floor below was divided into sections selling stationery, Japanese books, and foreign luxury goods. I was in the cosmetics department, next to the main entrance. Behind me there were high, long display shelves for perfume backed by a large mirror. The bottles of perfume, arranged on several levels of glass shelving, stood in double image, reflected in the mirror behind them and shimmering in every shape and size.

I learned to recognize the Western alphabet there and learned, together with abbreviations for the words "company" and "limited," the names of foreign cosmetic firms and the names of perfumes. Nihombashi geisha would come in to buy Amour made by the firm Roger. The geisha who came to Maruzen to buy foreign perfume wore white rough unlined silk obis over their kimonos. Under Maruzen's high ceiling even those somewhat haughty geisha looked short-legged.

"I'll take the red-box perfume," one would say, looking up at a shelf as she fanned herself with a snow-white linen handkerchief. To highlight the name, a flying Cupid, bow drawn, was embossed on a golden label affixed to the square Amour bottle. The perfume came in a red box, so everyone called it the red-box perfume, just as Race Horse Soap, wrapped in magenta-colored satin cloth, was known in Japan by the picture on its label. As for the dark-colored perfume of the English companies Yardley and Atkinson, Marchioness T always came to buy it with the marquis. A woman who owned an amusement park in Tsurumi bought up so much Colgate's White Rose we had to bring it in from our warehouse. She was a petite woman of apparently considerable influence who dressed in an uncommon fashion: a lined Ōshima kimono and a hat made of the same material. The actor Sadanji[3] and his wife were also regular customers in the foreign luxury goods department. They would buy Houbigant perfume and Binaud lotion, as well as Buckingham-weave neckties and Edgar's handwoven scarves and linen handkerchiefs. His wife walked along with Sadanji with an open bearing, her hair simply swept up atop her head, nicely complementing him in his Western clothes. Then there was a customer as beautiful as a young female impersonator in Kabuki whose movements, though, were rather too brisk for a female impersonator, who, we were told, was the head of the Ki-

3. Ichikawa Sadanji (1890–1940), an actor remembered as a modernizing force in Western-style theater and Kabuki.

neya school of *nagauta* samisen. He was pleasant with us clerks, so we were not intimidated by his beauty. The plump figure of the writer and translator Uchida Roan could often be seen making a leisurely descent in traditional Japanese attire from the second floor. Since he was an executive of Maruzen, we would bow to him. And Yoshida Genjirō, the author of *The Day the Songbird Comes*,[4] always came with his wife. It was here, too, that I first saw the author of *Nobuko*.[5] The way an individual expresses himself and his attitude remain breathtakingly constant, regardless of the passage of time.

It was from about then that Coty cosmetics became popular. I had come to feel quite comfortable with my work and would go to Mitsukoshi and Shirokiya to look at their prices. By this time Mitsukoshi no longer had customers change into store slippers. I would set off in the felt sandals I was using for work. When I was walking through Nihombashi on a work-related errand I was all business and walked along at a good clip. Even these days, when the Nihombashi area is being rebuilt, with shacks going up on the burned-out ruins, it would appear that what one still sees more than anything else are the busy gait of men carrying briefcases and the sight of women office workers walking about in their uniforms, all on commercial or company business. Even shoppers walk along with obvious purpose. Though carpenters are no longer in work aprons, one comes across them in Nihombashi even now looking very much part of the scene.[6] Not surprisingly, the main street around 3-chōme has the deeply chaotic, rust-colored tinge of burned out ruins, and there have developed gaps, their fate elusive, that leave the street squalid, yet from the intersection to the other side of the bridge even now one senses the character of the old waterside fish market that used to be there, and the aroma of fish cooking draws passersby.[7]

As for Nihombashi in the days when I would walk along on store

4. A collection of essays on the place of religion in life that enjoyed some popularity when it was published in 1921. Yoshida (1886–1956) also wrote fiction and for the theater.

5. Miyamoto Yuriko (1899–1951), a prominent left-wing writer with whom the author coedited a magazine about working women in the early 1930s. *Nobuko* is a largely autobiographical novel depicting the breakup of a marriage.

6. Nihombashi was at one time known for its lumberyards and attendant carpenters.

7. The wholesale fish market was moved after the earthquake of 1923 to the Tsukiji district, but restaurants specializing in seafood still remained.

business, the Shioze bean-jam bun shop in front of the Shirokiya department store was an extravagant presence, both Japanese and Western in style; the back of the shop was traditional, but at the front were glass shelves on which sat stemmed display jars containing *bolo* sweet balls and cookies. Next door, in the spacious show window of the Kurokiya, a lacquerware shop, there were top-of-the-line hand warmers, on display with individual gold-lacquered candy dishes and candy caskets.

The bridge Nihombashi is named for smoothly insinuated itself into my heart; I never stood there and gazed in wonder at those decorative lamps encased in iron filigree of such imposing workmanship. And the riverside buildings that rose straight and high along the water gave form to the beauty of the river that flowed the length of the city, yet I did not have the time to look upon prospects of this sort either. Since I made my living in Nihombashi, I merely walked briskly along its streets.

As I stood at the cosmetics counter in the Mitsukoshi department store I would casually check the price of their Cutecura soap. I would buy a bottle of Coty's L'Origan or the red-box perfume. If the red-box perfume at Mitsukoshi's was 5 yen 50 sen and our price at Maruzen was higher, I had to go back to the store and drop it to the same price. With the shrewdness of your average Nihombashi salesperson, I would make the rounds of the other stores, checking their merchandise and prices. I was happy that in contrast to the department stores that carried a wide range of products, we concentrated in one area, stocking only imported goods.

Since almost all of the articles we handled were foreign goods, the young men who worked at the store would return to their dormitory when they left work and take English lessons. That they were taught English by a certain peer—a son-in-law of the sixteenth shōgun—who came to the lessons driving his car himself also says something about the novelty typical of the time. And this plebeian peer of imposing lineage would come to shop at Maruzen with his wife. I suspect that the lady's doing her hair in a chignon meant for them that she had chosen a style close to that of the commoners. The young shop boys who had His Lordship teach them English wore their men's obis fetchingly over narrow-sleeved kimonos. They were called Saku-*san*, Toshi-*san*, Katsu-*san*, and Zen-*san*, and the like. After a fixed period, when they reached eighteen or nineteen, they would be allowed to wear the traditional cotton *haori*. Even then they were, for all that, former shop boys, so they were called Man-*san* or Yoshi-*san* in the manner of the old merchant houses. This convention applied even in the foreign books department on the second floor. There were clerks in foreign books who wore suits, but just one or two; those who waited on customers in the store naturally maintained the old clerk–shop boy traditions. When these shop boys made their rounds of the regular customers to settle accounts, they were sent out in rickshas.

The streets behind the Maruzen led to the Nihombashi geisha quarters. People there had resigned themselves to the fact that the main street out in front did not belong solely to their neighborhood now; it was also the heart of the metropolis of Tokyo and had become a thoroughfare. Thus they had created their own world in those backstreets. On these streets took place the most homely enterprises of the area. There were small pickle shops. And there were neighborhood fishmongers. And samisen makers and geta makers. And geisha houses with wide-lattice doors and eave-hung lanterns on which the house name was written in *kana* script also lined the side streets as far as the street that goes to the Gofukubashi intersection.

There was a ricksha stand in one of the alleyways that ran off the backstreets. It had several pullers and the shafts of two or three rickshas were always lined up in readiness on the dirt floor. The owner was an older man, amiable, heavyset, his hair receding from a ruddy forehead. Yoshiko, his only daughter, had come to Maruzen and was working with me in the foreign luxuries department, so I had occasion to stop off at this ricksha stand. This was after Satō Kimi had left Maruzen, her health, as we feared it would, having quickly worsened. The rickshas for taking the store's shop boys to collect payments from our regular customers were dispatched from her father's stand, so from the day Yoshiko started working at Maruzen she had a jump on the other women clerks, given her familiarity with this person and that one on the staff whom she already knew. Her home was so close she came to work in the sandals we wore in the store.

This young woman lived under a kind of curse: the considerable degree to which the pride of being a child of Nihombashi determines one's nature. She had been born on the second floor of a backstreet ricksha station, yet around her modern steel-reinforced concrete buildings strove, unchecked, to be the tallest, and here, of course, was the heart of the economy of Japan, not simply Tokyo, the place whence commercial prosperity on a modern scale began its expansion. As the family business was rickshas, they put up several young pullers in their home, and they had an old woman who did the cooking. Yoshiko had became an English typist when she graduated from Nihombashi Girls High School. There weren't that many English typists at the time. This says something of her mettle. And she had worked for a trading house in Nihombashi ward but had quit her job and come to Maruzen.

"A waste of talent, don't you think? Why did you give up being a typist?"

"It was a bother somehow. My house was close to work, right? I thought it would be better to quit."

Her tone of voice was always a bit high and her speech was rapid-fire and rasping.

"Then this job is a step down for you?"

Her haughty expression took no account of her questioner's feelings. Her response was matter-of-fact.

"Yes, you could say that."

Yoshiko always gave the impression of being on the defensive. Even in making a haughty response like that, she seemed to be putting up a front to keep others from treading her vulnerabilities underfoot or getting off the first shot. She walked erect, shoulders back, inevitably taking rapid, mincing steps. There was something self-consciously elegant about such a gait. When she talked about a man she liked she bubbled, like a geisha playing up to an actor in a Japanese movie. She saw nothing but foreign films, however.

If you asked her the time she would answer in English, "Just now!" then give you the time.

We got off work and were walking along the Ginza. As usual, I was walking fast to keep up with her rapid pace. We practically never looked into a store's show window. When we had gotten to the outskirts of the

Shimbashi area, she turned her head smartly like a foreign soldier to look back at me.

"Come back!" she said jokingly in English and did an abrupt about-face. Ginza at the time still had plenty of room for strollers. Although the working women of Tokyo had abandoned geta and now wore felt sandals, she—and I—were most certainly the avant-garde, simply from the fact that she lived near a thoroughfare that had been paved, and from the fact that we had changed our coiffure by taking a curling iron to our fluffed-out clerk-style hair.

This was when the Blue Bus ran from Kaminari Gate in Asakusa to Shimbashi. Yoshiko had an aunt in Mukōjima and often stayed with her after seeing a movie in the Asakusa's Rokku district. I was commuting from Hikifune, but I almost never went with her. That was because she always took the Blue Bus, a cut above the streetcar. The Blue Bus would speed on, violently shaking its way along the road, which at the time had a stretch so rough it was likened to the Genkai Channel, yet it got you to Nihombashi five minutes sooner than the streetcar and brought a sense of the new to the city.

One winter day I received a short note from Satō Kimi scrawled with a well-used brush dipped in India ink. All it said was *An important matter has suddenly come up. I beg you to come.* The wording struck me as somewhat exaggerated and affected. And I was taken aback by the phrase *I beg you to come.* Kimi, who had quit her job because she was ailing, had suddenly married out of pure whimsy, and pure whimsy is the only way to put it. Of course, this is if we accept her story at face value. She said that one day at the home of her boyfriend, the one familiar with anarchism, she had come out with the following.

"I really think it horrible for me to burden my mother with my illness. I want to throw away this ailing body of mine somewhere, anywhere."

That day there was a man at the gathering whom she had never met before. He was a middle-aged man who had returned from America and was said to be operating a ranch somewhere. The man, taking her at her word, responded: "Well then, I'll retrieve you."

She had married him and now they had a home in Kamata. I had met him—his name was Ōta something—once before when the two of them invited me somewhere on my way home from work. He was a thin-lipped man turning paunchy in his middle years. His lower lip seemed to curl up into his mouth, and he would go on and on—even to me—about the project he was about to embark on, about ranch land he had bought somewhere or other. He spoke softly and without inflection and scarcely opened his mouth. Only his thin lips fluttered excitedly.

"It would seem," Kimi whispered to me, "that if you live in America a good while you tend to embellish a bit."

Kamata was being developed then, and rental houses, their paint faded, stood in rows on land apparently reclaimed from the bay with industrial slag. I encountered Kimi in the shopping district that ran from the train station. She sauntered toward me, a thick wool shawl wrapped around her shoulders.

"My goodness! What a pleasure to see you!" she said with complete composure. As though she had forgotten what she had said in her note. I told her I'd come in my concern over the note.

"Oh, that. Well, Ōta created quite an uproar while I was back with my parents, having taken sick. He hired a housekeeper. It had to do with her. This is perfect. I can tell you on the way home. I'll get some meat."

Kimi continued to talk even at the shop she stopped at to buy beef, an amused expression on her face, as though she were telling me about someone else's problems.

The housekeeper's husband had come bursting into the house in the middle of the night and dragged Ōta, still in his nightclothes, out into the street. The housekeeper joined her husband in beating Ōta, and when the neighbors came out—their kitchen door was right next to Ōta's—he told them to go and get a policeman.

"The housekeeper and her husband would have been in trouble if the police came, so, well, that was the end of it. Ōta summoned me by tele-gram, and it was a surprise, I'll tell you. It'd be an understatement to say we stand embarrassed in the neighborhood."

So that was what *An important matter has suddenly come up. I beg you to come* was all about. She had asked me to come, and I had, but there was now absolutely nothing for me to do. Kimi herself had forgotten her pointless request.

Just as he was a man without inflection in his voice, Ōta was also a man without changes of facial expression.

"Hi, glad you could come. Oh, you got the meat, did you? That's great."

His expression was even less that of a man who had confronted "an important matter."

"Take up the bedding, would you."

"Right, I'll do it now."

Ōta began clearing away the futon Kimi had just been lying on, opening with a clatter the sliding closet door, the paper covering of which buckled as he pulled at the handle. The house was cheaply built, only three rooms, and no yard; when you opened the window you were confronted immediately with an alleyway. He looked back at me as he carried the bedding. His movements were incongruously smart for his portly frame.

"She's like this all the time, you know. So I have a wife, and at the same time, I'm forever just like a bachelor."

In the kitchen Kimi laughed loudly.

"No, really," Ōta went on, disregarding her, "I do as much for her as the average husband would."

"Drop that," she responded, interrupting. Her voice was husky. "I've already told her everything."

Ōta betrayed neither pain nor pleasure. His expression was unchanged.

"I can't help thinking they were in collusion."

This time Kimi agreed with her husband.

"It was the old badger game, clear and simple. Ōta's an easy mark, so he got taken. It was an ugly scene, to put it mildly. For a man to be dragged out in his nightclothes . . . but for a woman to do that."

"They were in it together. They had it all planned. Anyway, I've finally got the ranching project off the ground. I can't be doing dumb things like that, I'll tell you. It would be better if Kimi were in good health and could help me. I don't suppose there's someone who could. If I could get someone like you it would really be great. Right, Kimiko? What do you think? Couldn't we get Miss Tajima here to give me a hand?"

Kimi's response was, not surprisingly, halfhearted.

"Uh-huh."

That day when Kimi saw me back to the station, she told me Ōta was trying to get money from her family.

When the ferroconcrete building with its glass windows rocked violently I could hear a loud clatter, like the shaking of crated chinaware or boxes filled with beer bottles. It was right at lunchtime and there was little happening: half of the staff had gone to the cafeteria. There were few customers in the store. My coworker and I clung to each other, swaying back and forth by the display case in the middle of the room. At the back of the store white hatboxes flung themselves in quick succession off their high shelving and crashed to the floor. Bottles of perfume, toppling from their shelves, crossed my line of vision with the grace of a flock of birds flying from one branch to another. I was startled and felt almost physical pain to think of the bottles of perfume being smashed to pieces on the concrete floor. The necktie rack sitting atop the display case fell over, revealing people on the other side of the case running toward the door, backs bent in a semicrouch and arms flailing. Each time the large building would shake violently, I felt like a toy placed inside a big box. But it was a huge box, vast and towering, and these dimensions terrified me much more than the high ceiling that had been over me every day.

When the initial shaking stopped someone shouted, "Everybody out!" and I went out the entrance with the coworker I had been clinging to. The instant we emerged, the red brick building of the Nozawa Association catty-corner from us collapsed, cascading into the street. In that instant I realized for the first time what I was experiencing: *This is a major quake.* The main street was in the process of going from a moment of nightmare paralysis to the pandemonium of alarm. We gathered in the vacant lot where there had been construction going on directly across from our store. Those who had been in the cafeteria came out the main entrance. I now watched from across the street as people emerged from Maruzen.

We soon heard that the elegant restaurant Matsumoto-rō in Hibiya Park was burning, and that a large crevice had opened up in the street in front of the Takashimaya department store and that a shopper, a woman, had fallen into it. It was soon decided that Maruzen employees were to break up into groups and make our way home with no further ado. The streetcars had stopped running. I and my group had the farthest to walk. I thought I should travel a bit lighter, so I asked Yoshiko to take care of my lunch box. Frightened and nervous, and resigned to having to walk home, my body trembled ever so slightly.

"You all right?" Yoshiko asked, taking my lunch box. "Take care." She watched me leave, concern in her eyes.

I started walking. I was with three others, a woman from the foreign books department and two male coworkers. The red brick of the Nozawa Association building had collapsed into a mountain of rubble in the street. As we passed it, a lone patrolman, standing atop the hillock of brick, was waving his arms. He had set up a sign written on a scrap of wood that said in large script that a Blue Bus was buried under the bricks. The woman from the foreign books department was a quiet, fair-skinned woman who was terribly nearsighted. She commuted from South Senju, so some days we found ourselves on the same train. She was the sort who normally didn't have much to say, but one day when she was next to me she turned and looked up at me and said in a thin, almost cooing voice, and without the slightest of preliminaries: "Really, Tajima-san, your skin is as white as a lily." In fact, these words described her better than they did me.

Our group of four, including the two young men I knew only by sight, crossed Nihombashi Bridge and made its way to Hongoku-chō. As we came to the Mitsukoshi department store, we could see flames bursting one by one through the windows high up in a building on the side street where the Nimben store is.[8] The billowing flames were bright red, notwithstanding the fact that it was in the middle of the day. The bizarre spectacle of seeing no one attempting to deal with this terror provoked dread in my already shaken soul. The streets were in absolute chaos, though no one was shouting. There were a great many people on foot. When we got to Misuji-machi, having crossed Izumi Bridge, we saw a

---

8. A seller of dried bonito in Nihombashi since the Edo period.

man who had brought his valuables out of his house to the street and was sitting by the side of the road and gazing up at the sky, blackened by the smoke roiling up from the earth. As we made our way from Umaya Bridge to Azuma Bridge, the sky over Senju was already jet-black, and at the approach to Azuma Bridge we couldn't make any headway because of the people who were fleeing toward us from Senju.

"Yes, Senju is already afire," a man coming from the opposite direction responded as he went by us.

"What am I to do?!" the other woman bound for Senju said, bursting into tears. Beyond Azuma Bridge, Narihira Bridge was pouring black smoke into the air. I had to get across the bridge before I was cut off by the flames. I left the three of them and ran across Azuma Bridge.

One saw many things amongst the flow of refugees walking the tracks of the Keisei line over the next two or three intense days. A man carried on his back the limp form of an injured Kabuki actor still wearing the red costuming of a young maiden. Hideously, the white makeup that thickly coated his face as it lay against the shoulder of the man bearing him had now taken on the appearance of a mask, suggesting that he had already breathed his last. The heavy hem of the red maiden costume was tucked up, exposing a man's slender legs, which dangled limply beneath it. Corpses floating facedown in the purple water of the Hikifune canal into which drained wastewater from factories. A rumor that Koreans were poisoning water wells made the rounds. Someone said that he was pursued all night by Koreans but got away. Whereupon a married woman who lived in the same tenement, a woman who did not suffer fools gladly, spoke up.

"What on earth are you talking about?! It's the Koreans who had to run. You were just running in front of them. Anyone can see Japanese outnumber them a hundred times over. There's nothing to fear from them."

I was impressed by her assessment of the situation. Nonetheless, I kept at hand a fireman's axe my younger brother had brought home from somewhere or other. It was bright and shiny and remarkably heavy. Stripped emotionally, we now could begrudge others absolutely nothing and shared some of our padded *tanzen* kimonos with an elderly couple who had come from somewhere else and were sleeping on the rubble-strewn grounds of a factory, exposed to the dampness of the night. Still afraid to go into our house, we also slept on the factory's open field. I found out that Yoshiko had visited our house in our absence.

"Your friend dropped this off, saying that you had left it with her."

An older woman who lived in the neighborhood handed me my lightweight aluminum lunch box. The lunch box wrapped in a soy sauce–stained *furoshiki* resting lightly in my hand, I felt myself become both a bit annoyed and teary-eyed at Yoshiko's indefatigable reliability. The bridge at Nihombashi, which she normally would have taken, had to have been consumed by flames the day of the quake.

One night a month later I passed through the gate of the absurdly cavernous exposition hall building that stands like a cadaverous ruin even now in Ikenohata.[9] The streetlights that dotted the area provided little light and the empty open area within the high, pale yellow walls suggested the grimness of a prison yard. When I had worked in Ikenohata several years earlier, this structure had been in its glory as an exposition hall. I hadn't known what it had been used for subsequently, but half of it stood deserted in its jerry-built shoddiness, its ornamentation stripped away, and if that wasn't bad enough, now an unpleasant air hung over it, since in the wake of the earthquake it was serving as a free clinic. The gloom was to be expected. And it was nighttime, which added an inexplicable, willful inscrutability.

I at last found out where the room I was looking for was and went into the concrete hall. As I entered I could see the interior was dimly illuminated by electric lights. It was even worse than the miserable scene I had imagined. I went into the room and stood rooted to the ground, wondering just where I was. At the center and on both sides of the long room pallets made of floorboards rose high above the floor and were arranged to form aisles. Straw mats were spread out on the pallets and patients lay on these under utterly colorless quilts, their heads

9. A section of Ueno Park and the site of a series of industrial expositions beginning in the Meiji era.

all toward the aisles. I would have to walk along and look at each patient's face.

I heard a voice coming from somewhere in the room: "Uh, Miss Satō is over this way."

I went toward the voice, making my way through the fetid air of a ward filled wall-to-wall with TB patients. Hearing someone call out her name, Kimi raised her head up off her pillow and looked in my direction. She recognized me as I approached. An involuntary cry of surprise caught in my throat.

"My, it's good to see you!" she said, attempting at first to greet me with her usual cheerful expression on her face. Her voice was as husky as an old woman's.

In the midst of her greeting she was overwhelmed by a wave of intense emotion and burst into tears. Taking off the surgical mask that had been handed me at the door, I also began to cry as I stood at the side of her bed.

"Don't take off the mask," she said, wiping at her tears. "It's contagious." She looked up at me, her head back down on the pillow and wiped at her tears.

"It was terrible, I'll tell you. I had just gone back home to Fukagawa. I got into the pond in the park to protect myself from the fire. That was the wrong thing to do. You remember I was renting a room in a relative's house. I thought a hospital would be better for me now, being together with people in the same circumstances. So now I'm in this awful place. People die day and night. I'm terrified, wondering if I'm going to be next."

"What about Ōta?"

"He's in Kamata, but I don't think there'd be any point in going back there. He says he's looking for a house on the outskirts of the city. He thinks then we'll live there with my mother. But the truth is there's apparently already some woman with him in Kamata."

"He doesn't come to see you?"

"He comes. Now and again."

The patients' pallets, which were lined up on both sides of us—beds of board on which straw mats had been spread—creaked faintly from time to time. Bursts of vigorous conversation from the nurses intermingled with the subdued voices of the patients. These reverberated off the high ceiling and echoed with unexpected gloom about the room.

Kimi began to tell me in overblown terms that Ōta was just no good, that at bottom he had been after her family's money, which, in any case, certainly didn't exist. She was almost her old self again. It was just then that, speak of the devil, Ōta came into the room.

"You know, when I went to your mother's place she just now told me that she had sent Miss Tajima here."

Kimi, who had just been vilifying her husband as good for nothing, now badgered him.

"Did you bring me some bananas? You really annoy me. I asked you the last time you were here, didn't I? Did you find a house? Not yet? Are you really trying hard to find one?"

Ōta fielded the invalid's questions, then turned to me and said he, too, was trying to get something published.

Satō Kimi died early the next year. Her mother was a full-faced woman of the *shitamachi* who still retained much of her youth.

"I wanted her grave to be in my family's cemetery, you know," she complained tearfully when she saw me. "Ōta was adamant that he wanted Kimi to be by him. She's to be interred at a temple near his home in Kamata."

In the cemetery, shrubs with green, yellow, and crimson-colored leaves covered the compact section where the family plot was, and right in the middle of all this stood a wooden grave marker on which was written *The Grave of Ōta Kimi*. The area had a beauty very much befitting her grave.

If we assume that he had gone so far as to take Kimi's grave from her mother in order to give substance to his lies, then perhaps Ōta was a rogue of the first order. And if Ōta had designed the beautiful setting, then perhaps a part of him held fast to a vision not entirely concerned with propriety.

The Old Part of Town

HAYASHI FUMIKO

The short story Dauntaun (The old part of town) by the prolific Hayashi Fumiko (1903–51) is a tightly structured, compact tale of loneliness and loss, a classic short story that epitomizes the fragility of life and the equally fleeting moments of happiness—perceived, all too often, only in retrospect. Its heroine Riyo lives in the difficult, largely indifferent world of Japan just after the war. The pattern of serendipitous solace found and lost apparently recurred in the author's own life, which was chaotic and unconventional from beginning to tragically premature end. The story ends with the faintest suggestion of promise in the gloom as light strikes sewing needles and, perhaps, makes Riyo aware that she is not entirely alone in the devastated, hardscrabble world of Japan right after the war.

"The Old Part of Town" made its English debut in the midfifties, less than a decade after its original publication in Japanese in 1949, but the rendition was

more paraphrase than translation and did not do justice to the superbly affecting
style of its creator, also known and respected as a poet.

The translation of the title is a compromise. Hayashi writes it with the stan-
dard two sinographs for shitamachi, *literally "lower town," that is, the flat-*
lands, but she then gives them the pronunciation in kana *of* dauntaun—*down-*
town. Since the term "downtown" suggests the business district and flatlands
and lacks the proletarian élan of shitamachi, *I have rendered it as "the old part*
of town." Unfortunately, this also misses the mark somewhat, suggesting, as it
does, a run-down, neglected area, which the shitamachi *area is not, overall.*

Thanks to her considerable talent and her furor scribendi, *Hayashi emerged*
from a life of frequent homelessness and the direst poverty to become one of
the wealthiest writers in Japan. She was quite popular in the thirties, but what
is considered her better-remembered fiction was written in the immediate post-
war period just before her sudden death. This includes, of course, "The Old Part
of Town."

The wind was chill, so Riyo decided to walk on the sunny side of the
street. She went along, her eye out for the smaller houses. It was noon-
time, and she was looking for someplace where she could settle down
with a cup of tea. She skirted the front of a row of houses, then made
her way around a wooden fence of what appeared to be a construction
site, peering inside to see piles of rusting iron. There was a small shack,
and on the other side of its glass door a fire crackled. A man came up
behind her on a bicycle.

"Where's the Katsushika ward office?" he asked, one foot on the
ground. Riyo didn't know.

"I don't know. I'm just passing through myself."

The man on the bicycle went over to the shack and shouted his question. Another man with a sweat cloth tied around his head, apparently
a laborer, opened the glass door and stuck his head out.

"Go to the main street that passes through Yotsugi," he told him, "and
straight along the new road toward the station. You can't miss it."

The man with the sweat cloth struck Riyo as probably a decent sort,
so she let the bicycle go by, then approached him tentatively.

"Perhaps you'd like some tea from Shizuoka?" she hazarded softly. The man was burning firewood in a small stove on the dirt floor in the dimness inside. A large teakettle sat on a grate made of rebar.

"Tea?"

"Yes, it's Shizuoka tea," she said with a smile as she immediately began to set down her rucksack. The man said nothing and went over to a stool on the dirt floor. Riyo hoped the man would let her warm herself in front of the warm, briskly burning fire, if only for a little while.

"I've walked quite a way, and it's very cold. Do you suppose I could warm myself a bit?" she asked nervously.

"Yeah, sure you can. Close the door and warm yourself for a while." He took the stool he was about to slip between his legs and gave it to Riyo, then sat down on a rickety packing crate.

Riyo put her rucksack down in a corner on the dirt floor, squatted down diffidently, and held her hands up to the fire.

"Sit on the stool," he said, thrusting his chin at it. He then looked back at Riyo, who was feeling herself growing warm on the other side of the fire.

She had the air of one who paid no heed to her appearance, but she was more attractive, more fair-skinned than he would have expected.

"You're goin' round sellin' things?"

The kettle began to boil noisily. An absurdly large family altar with a vivid green branch from a *sakaki* tree as an offering was attached to the besooted ceiling. Beneath the window hung a chalkboard and a pair of rubber boots, full of holes, stood against the wall.

"I'd heard that business would be good around here, so I came early this morning, but I've only made a sale at one house, and I was thinking of going back home, but I thought I might eat my lunch at someone's place and was walking around looking for a likely house."

"You can eat your lunch here. There're lucky days and unlucky days when you sell. You might do right well if you went someplace where there's a few more houses."

The man took something wrapped in a newspaper sticky with grease from a shelf that looked like a misshapen bookcase. It was a piece of salmon. He removed the kettle from the iron grating and put the fish on it. A delicious aroma filled the shack.

"Well now, why don't you sit on the stool and enjoy your lunch."

Riyo stood up, took a kerchief-bundled lunch box out of her rucksack, and sat down.

"No business is easy, right? This Shizuoka tea, about whadya get for a pound?"

The man turned the salmon over with his fingers.

"I sell it for a hundred twenty or thirty yen, but there're also some leavings, and if your price is too high you have a hard time selling anything."

"I'll bet. A family with old people'll buy, but a young family's got to be a tough sell."

Riyo opened her lunch box. In the brownish barley—white rice was a luxury—were two small fish on a skewer and some pickled vegetables.

"So where d'ya live?"

"Inari-chō in the Shitaya district, but I've just come to Tokyo, so I don't know one side of town from the other."

"You mean you're rentin' a room?"

"No, someone's putting me up."

The man withdrew a large alumite lunch box from a soiled knit bag and took off the lid. It was filled to bursting with rice and sweet potatoes, more mashed than packed. He grabbed the broiled salmon and set it on the lid, put the kettle on the grate again, and thrust scraps of wood into the stove. Riyo put down her half-eaten lunch on the stool and pulled out a bag of her tea from the rucksack and measured off a portion on a sheet of tissue paper.

"Do you mind if I put this in the kettle?" she asked.

The man waved his hand from side to side in embarrassment; he didn't want to impose upon her.

"You don't mind usin' your good stuff?" he grinned. His large white teeth had a youthful brightness. Riyo plucked the lid off the kettle and quickly dropped the tea inside. The water came to a vigorous boil. The man took a tea mug and a dirty water glass from a shelf and set them on a new packing crate next to the wall.

"Tell me, what's your husband do?" He broke the salmon in two and put half on Riyo's food. Taken aback by his question, she was nonetheless delighted to receive the salmon.

"My husband is in Siberia. He's not come back yet, so here I am having to do this to put food on the table."

The man looked up, surprise in his face.

"Where in Siberia is he?"

She had received a letter from him last year from Suchin in the Baikal region, autumn had come and gone, and she somehow made it through another winter. It had become routine for Riyo to awake every morning to melancholy. Since her husband was so far away from her, his absence somehow didn't register, but she had also gotten used to this lack of feeling. The song "The Hills of a Foreign Land" was popular now, and she would have her son Tomekichi sing it for her. As she listened to him sing, a feeling of utter sadness would come over her. She felt as though the war was still hovering over her, over her alone. It was as though only she had been left behind in the mists of fading memories, set apart from the peaceful tenor of today's Japan. You can bet there's no such thing as God, Riyo was in the habit of telling herself. Every day in the broiling summer was intolerable as she waited anxiously and irritably, and as the hot weather gradually eased she found herself depressed by the oppressive approach of winter. She was angry in her solitude: *There are limits to how much a person can endure.* The image she had in her mind of Ryūji, who had now spent four winters in Siberia, little by little began to lose substance, like a ghost that was fading away.

Not once in the six years since Ryūji had gone off to war had Riyo experienced joy, the soaring of her spirits. The flow of time bypassed the ken of her life, and nothing stirred her. Nobody talked about the war anymore, and on those occasions when she told someone her husband was being held in Siberia, the sympathy extended to her was merely casual, as though he had gone there on a trip and hadn't come back. Riyo didn't know what sort of place Siberia was; she could only envision it as a vast desert of snow.

"He says he's at a place called Suchin, not far from Lake Baikal. He's not able to return yet."

"I was repatriated from Siberia myself. I was put to work cuttin' down trees for two years at Mulchi, near the Amur River. It's all a matter of luck. Your husband's got it rough, but you've got to wait for him, so it's rough for you, too."

He took off his cloth headband, wiped the tea mug and water glass with it, and poured the boiling tea into them.

"Really!? You're a returnee too? How lucky you've come back in such good shape!"

"I managed to go to Siberia an' live to tell about it."

She looked carefully at the man's face as she put away her lunch box. He struck her as unextraordinary, which was precisely why she was able to talk with him comfortably, to feel at ease with him.

"You have children, I'd guess."

"Yes, I have a boy eight," Riyo began, "but I've been having problems with his school, transferring him into it. The problem is the processing of his ration papers has been delayed, and everything depends on that, the upshot of which is he can't go to school either. Just when I'm at my busiest selling, I've got to drop it and go around to the ward office every day for the paperwork. I'll tell you, it's wearing me to a frazzle."

The man took the water glass in hand and, blowing vigorously to cool the hot tea, began drinking.

"This is great tea."

"Do you really think so? I've got better tea. These are second pickings. It wholesales for about 100 yen a pound. But my customers tell me it tastes better than you'd expect."

Riyo took the tea mug in both hands and drank, blowing on it as she did so.

The wind direction had changed at some point; a strong west wind was now blowing hard against the iron roof, and set it to rattling. Riyo had no stomach for going out, wanting only to remain by the fire, if only for a little longer.

"I better take a coupla pounds," the man said, taking 300 yen from a pocket in his work clothes.

"Oh dear! You shouldn't feel you have to buy anything. Let me give you some, just two pounds."

Riyo quickly took two one-pound bags from her rucksack and set them on top of the packing crate.

"Don't be silly! Business is business. You can't expect me to just take it."

He paused.

"If you're around here again, drop by."

"Yes, I'll certainly take you up on that. I don't suppose this is where you live?"

Riyo looked about the tiny shack. After he had put away his lunch box, the man split off a sliver of wood from the splintered end of a piece of kindling and used it as a toothpick.

"I do live here. I'm watchman for the iron there and I do the shippin'. My older sister lives nearby and brings me my meals, but that's all."

He opened the doors beneath the Shinto altar. Riyo could see a bed in a closet-like enclosure. A picture postcard with the actress Yamada Isuzu on it was tacked to the wall.

"My goodness! All the comforts of home. It's really cozy, isn't it."

Riyo wondered how old the man was.

From then on Riyo came to Yotsugi every day to sell, and would drop by the shack in the iron yard. The man's name was Tsuruishi Yoshio. Yoshio was delighted with Riyo's visits and would buy candy and the like in anticipation of her coming. Riyo now had the pleasure of being able to drop by Yoshio's, and, at the same time, she was gradually building a clientele for her tea business, which made her peddling in the area easier. On the fifth day she took Tomekichi with her to Yoshio's shack in Yotsugi. Yoshio was delighted to see the boy, and immediately took him off somewhere. When they returned a little later, Tomekichi was carrying two large caramel puffs that were still hot.

"The lad cooked them himself," Yoshio told her. Sitting Tomekichi down on a stool, he patted the boy's head.

Riyo had begun to wonder whether Yoshio had a wife or not. This was not an especially crucial concern, but as she watched Yoshio, so obviously fond of Tomekichi, the question suddenly presented itself to her. Riyo, who was thirty years old, had never thought about a man other than her husband, but as she became aware of Yoshio's easygoing disposition she was somewhat bewildered to sense her feelings toward him gradually changing.

Little by little Riyo began to pay more attention to her appearance, and put more effort into selling as she made her rounds. She had her family in Shizuoka send her dried mackerel and sardine flakes to see if she might sell those as well, and she began to see, to her surprise, that occasionally there was a greater demand for fish flakes than tea.

It was perhaps little more than a week after Riyo had started going to Yoshio's place. Riyo and Tomekichi had yet to see the Asakusa entertainment district, so Yoshio said he had a day off, and would take the two of them there and show them around. It was still too early for the cherry blossoms, but if they had time they could also stroll through Ueno Park. On the appointed day, Riyo, as Yoshio had instructed, stood waiting with Tomekichi in front of the information booth in Ueno station. The sky was leaden, neither clear nor cloudy, but it was the kind of day that would be pleasantly mild if it didn't rain. After a good ten minutes Yoshio came along in a threadbare gray suit with sleeves that were too short for him.

Riyo, Tomekichi in tow, had on a dress made of blue kimono material with a wave design over which she wore a padded tan suit jacket, all of which suggested this was a special occasion. She looked younger than she usually did, and next to the very tall Yoshio, seemed as short as a schoolgirl, thanks, perhaps, to the Western-style dress.

"Hope it doesn't rain," Yoshio said, casually scooping up Tomekichi and starting off through the crowd of people. Riyo carried a big shopping bag, into which she had put bread, seaweed sushi rolls and tangerines. They rode the subway to the end of the line at Asakusa, walked past the Matsuya department store toward the Sensōji Temple's Niten Gate, and down the shop-lined approach to the temple.

Riyo found Asakusa an unexpected disappointment. She was let down to find that the small vermilion lacquered temple building housed the renowned Asakusa Kannon, Goddess of Mercy. Yoshio explained that before the air raids there had been a huge hall so big you had to tilt your head back to see the top, but she felt no real sense of its hugeness.[1] There was nothing but wave after wave of people. A mass of jostling humanity

1. The rebuilding of the main temple was completed in 1958.

surrounded the small vermilion building. In the distance they could hear the plaintive, seductive sounds of a trumpet and a saxophone. The wind whistled through the full-budded branches of the trees in the park's burned-out center square, the trees writhing in its grip.

When they passed under the arch of the old clothes market, they could see all the jerry-built shacks of the cheap eateries that stood cheek by jowl around the pond. The smell of cooking oil and steam from kettles of *o-den* hung in the air. Tomekichi had had Yoshio buy him a yellow cotton candy generously spun around the end of a chopstick at a street stall and walked along licking it.

Theirs had been only a chance encounter, yet Riyo drew strength from it and felt as though she had been with Yoshio ten years. She was not the least bit tired. The streets were lined with movie houses and small review theaters. The three of them strolled through the ravine of large buildings, where American-style billboards bellowed and hectored them.

"It's startin' to rain," Yoshio said, holding up his hand. Riyo looked up at the sky. Large drops of rain began to fall. They concluded the outing they had been looking forward to was now ruined, and went into a small coffee shop with a lighted glass sign out in front that proclaimed it the Mary. The artificial flowers hanging from the ceiling made the place seem all the chillier. They ordered black tea. Riyo took the sushi rolls and bread from her shopping bag and gave them to Yoshio and her son to eat. Yoshio didn't smoke a cigarette, so they were soon finished with their meal, but now it was raining in earnest, and before they knew it the place was packed with refugees from the rain.

"What shall we do? It's really raining, isn't it. And it doesn't look like it's going to stop, either."

"We'll wait a while, and when it eases up I'll take you home."

Riyo wondered if by "home" Yoshio meant her place in Inari-chō. Even if she did let him see where she lived, she could hardly invite him into the house. She had asked another woman from her village to put her up until she could find her own place. She had no room of her own; she slept in the four-by-six entryway. Riyo would rather have gone to Yoshio's shack in Yotsugi, but they certainly couldn't settle down and relax at his place; there weren't even enough chairs to sit on.

Riyo checked her purse in the shopping bag, taking care that Yoshio didn't notice what she was doing. She had some 700 yen. She wondered if there might not be an inn somewhere where they could get out of the rain for that.

"I wonder if we couldn't find an inn or something where we could get out of the rain?"

A odd expression crossed Yoshio's face when he heard the words "find an inn."

Riyo then candidly and without hesitation explained the situation where she was staying.

"So I don't want to take you back there. I'd like to see a movie, and if we can find a little inn, rest a bit there, have them bring us some noodles or something, then happily go our separate ways. I wonder if I'm being extravagant?"

Yoshio had apparently been thinking along the same lines. He took off his jacket, draped it over Tomekichi's head, and went out into the rain with Riyo. They ran under the eaves of a nearby movie theater. They found no seats inside and had to stand. They were soon exhausted from standing and breathing the stuffy air. Tomekichi had drifted off into a sound sleep on Yoshio's back. They knew they would have to get to an inn soon, so after an hour or so they left the theater and began walking about, in a driving rain, looking for a place to stay. The rain beat down all about them, the din resounding in their ears like the drumming on the leaves of a banana plant. They at last found a small inn near Tawar-amachi.

The couple was shown into a tiny room at the end of a hallway whose floor was riddled with knotholes and creaked as they walked over it. The soft tatami was clammy to the touch.

Riyo took off her wet socks. Yoshio deposited Tomekichi asprawl in front of the alcove and put a dirty cushion under the boy's head for a pillow. A burgeoning torrent of water poured off the eaves in a noisy cascade. There was apparently no rain gutter. Yoshio took out a discolored handkerchief and wiped the rain off Riyo's hair. It was a natural gesture, and she casually allowed herself the luxury of accepting his simple kindness. Within the narrow focus defined by the sound of the rain joy welled up inside her. Why did his touch please her so? She had the feeling that her long-endured isolation would disappear in a burst of joyful song.

"You suppose we can get some food in a place like this?"

"I wonder," Riyo responded. "I'll go and ask."

Riyo went out into the hall and asked the maid, dressed in Western clothes, who was bringing them tea. She told Riyo they could only have Chinese noodles. Riyo ordered two bowls.

The couple sat and drank their tea, a boxed, coalless *hibachi* between them. Then Yoshio stretched out his legs and lay down by Tomekichi. Riyo looked at the threatening, gradually darkening sky through the windowpane.

"How old are you, Riyo?" Yoshio suddenly asked.

Riyo turned to him and giggled.

"I can never tell how old a woman is," he continued. "You're twenty-six or seven, are you?"

"Listen, I'm an old woman. I'm thirty."

"Wow! You're a year older than me."

"Really! You're so young!" she said, staring at Yoshio in surprise, "I assumed you were over thirty."

For the briefest instant Yoshio's gentle eyes, with his thick eyebrows, flashed and his face flushed, then he looked at his dirty feet. He had also taken off his stockings.

Night fell, but the rain continued.

Later two bowls of lukewarm noodles were brought from a Chinese restaurant. Riyo shook Tomekichi awake and had the half-asleep boy take some of the broth. Riyo and Yoshio decided to stay the night. Yoshio went to the office and paid for the room, and three sets of fresh, clean bedding—something they hadn't expected—were brought in. Riyo laid out the futons. The room seemed futons wall to wall. She removed Tomekichi's jacket, took him to the bathroom, then put him to bed right in the middle of the bedding.

"They seem to think we're husband an' wife," Yoshio commented.

"So they do. Their mistake, I'm afraid."

Riyo felt vaguely uneasy, as though she were wronging her husband, perhaps because the futons lay there before her. She didn't know what might happen later, but she wanted to believe that things had unavoidably turned out this way because it had rained, and that was the explanation she gave herself.

It was the middle of the night and Riyo was pleasantly drifting off to sleep when she heard Yoshio's voice.

"Riyo! Riyo!"

Startled, she lifted her head from her pillow.

"Riyo, can I come over by you?" Yoshio asked in a whisper. The rain had eased, and the water dropping off the eaves sounded only feebly now.

"It'd be wrong."

"It'd be wrong, would it?"

"Yes, it'd make things difficult."

Yoshio sighed.

"Yoshio, I haven't asked you, but what about your wife?"

"I don't have one now."

"You did before?"

"Right."

"What happened?"

"When I came back from the service she was livin' with another man."

"That must have infuriated you."

"Well, yeah, I was mad. But what's gone is gone, right?"

"That's true, but I'm surprised you were able to give her up so easily."

Yoshio fell silent.

"Shall we talk about something?" Riyo asked.

"Hmm. I don't have anything to talk about specially," he said, pausing. "Those Chinese noodles were awful, weren't they."

"Weren't they! And 100 yen a bowl!"

"You two should have a room of your own."

"I wonder if there's not something near you. I'd like to move somewhere near you."

"There's practically nothin'. I'll let you know as soon as there is."

He was silent for a moment.

"You know, you're really somethin', Riyo."

"Dear me, how is that?"

"You really are. Not all women are loose."

Riyo said nothing.

She wanted them to be in each other's arms, and then . . .

Riyo's breathing was labored, but she breathed in short, choppy breaths so that Yoshio wouldn't notice. Her underarms were hot and sweaty now. Trucks passed by in the street, shaking the inn.

"War turns human beings into little more than worms. I know, because I was really gung ho and did things only a madman would do. I ended up a buck private. They really slapped me around, I'll tell you. I want no more of that."

"Yoshio, tell me about your father and mother."

"They live in the country."

"Where in the country?"

"In Fukuoka."

"What does your older sister do?"

"She's on her own, like you, raisin' two kids. She's got herself a sewin' machine and she's makin' dresses. Her husband was killed early on in the fightin' in central China."

Yoshio's voice was placid now, his spirits somewhat revived.

Riyo was loath to see the night end like this. She felt a twinge of regret when she realized that Yoshio had resigned himself to the situation. If she had never laid eyes on him before, lovemaking might have meant nothing to her. Yoshio made no attempt to ask her about her husband.

"Damn! I'm wide awake. There'll be no sleepin' for me. A man should never do what he's not used to doin'."

"My goodness, Yoshio, haven't you ever played around?"

"Sure I have. I'm a man. But my partners have all been professionals."

"Men have it easy."

It had just slipped out, but no sooner had the words left her lips than Yoshio jumped up and threw himself down heavily next to her. There was a quilt between them; Riyo did not resist the force of this man pressing upon her in his passion. She remained silent, her eyes wide in the darkness. Yoshio's head pressed painfully against her cheek. A rainbow of light flashed before her. His warm lips clumsily brushed the flare of her nose. Her legs were rigid under the quilt.

"You don't want to?"

Her ears were ringing loudly.

"It's not right. I keep thinking about Siberia."

Riyo sensed she had said the wrong thing, what she had never meant to say. Yoshio held his awkward position, leaning heavily on her, and lay motionless on the quilt. His head drooped and he was dead silent, looking like a man prostrating himself before a god. Riyo instantly felt she had wronged him. She embraced Yoshi's warm neck with all her strength.

Two days later Riyo cheerfully set off with Tomekichi for Yoshio's place in Yotsugi. Yoshio would normally be found at that time of day standing in the shack by the glass door, headband around his head, but he was not there today. Riyo thought this odd, and had Tomekichi run ahead to see what was the matter.

"There're some strangers there," the boy said, running back to his mother.

Riyo was uneasy. When she got to the door of the shack and looked inside, she saw two young men taking Yoshio's bed from the closet.

"Whadya want, lady?" the one with beady eyes asked over his shoulder.

"Is Mr. Tsuruishi here?"

"Yosh died last night."

"Oh dear," said Riyo, "Oh, dear." She was unable to say anything more.

She had thought it strange when she saw the candles burning on the sooty family altar, but it had never occurred to her that Yoshio might be dead.

The young men told her what had happened. Yoshio had gone out on a truck loaded with iron, and on the return from Omiya it had fallen cab-first off a bridge into a river, and he and the driver had been killed. Today people with the company and Yoshio's sister were cremating his body in Omiya, and they would return tomorrow morning. Riyo was stunned. She blankly watched the two men clear away Yoshio's things. There on the shelf she noticed the two bags of tea Yoshio had bought from her that first day. One bag was half empty and folded over on itself.

"Did you know Yosh, lady?"

"Yes, I knew him slightly."

"He was a good man. There was no reason for him to go to Omiya. Somebody just happened to ask him, and they left after noon. It's really crazy. He survives the war and comes back and then. . . ."

The other man, a heavyset youth, took the postcard of Yamada Isuzu from the wall and blew the dust off it. Riyo's mind was a blank. The small stove, the teakettle, the boots stood there just as they had before. The chalkboard caught her eye. There was a message in red chalk, written in a rude scrawl.

Riyo, waited until two.

Riyo took Tomekichi's hand, and swinging the heavy rucksack up over her shoulder, started around the high wooden fence. Hot tears suddenly began flowing down her cheeks as a piercing numbness seized her face from within.

"Did Uncle Yoshio die?"

"Uh-huh."

"Where did he die?"

"They say he fell into a river."

Riyo wept as she walked on. The tears poured forth, and she cried until her eyes ached.

Riyo and Tomekichi reached Asakusa around two o'clock. They came within sight of the bridge at Komagata, then walked along the river toward the Shirahige bridge. Riyo looked at the river as they walked, blue-black like the sea, and guessed that it was the famous Sumida River.

The morning they had separated, Riyo had told Yoshio that it would be a disaster if something went wrong and she got pregnant, and Yoshio had said he would assume any and all responsibility, that she needn't worry. He had told her he wanted to take care of her, that he would give her some 2,000 yen a month. He had licked the end of his pencil and written down her Inari-chō address in his little notebook. Before they parted, Yoshio had bought a baseball cap for Tomekichi with a team's name on it at a haberdashery in Tawaramachi. They had finally found a milk hall along the main street, a muddy bog after the rain, and the three of them had each ordered a bottle of milk.

Riyo thought of what had happened as she strolled along the river, the wind from its surface blowing against her. A flock of waterfowl rose up indistinctly in the distance at Shirahige. All sorts of cargo boats were plying the deep blue current. In her mind Yoshio's image was fleshed out and clearly defined, more so than her husband's.

"Mama, buy me a comic book!"

"I will later."

"We passed by a store full of comics a little while ago."

"Did we?"

"You didn't notice?"

Riyo turned around and went back the way she had come. She had no idea where she should walk. It seemed to her that she was unlikely to run across such a man a second time.

"Let's get something to eat, Mama."

Riyo was suddenly exasperated with Tomekichi, who had been pestering her for first one thing, then another. He looked cute in his white baseball cap with its team name in red. She wandered aimlessly. She gazed at the jerry-built shacks along the river and envied the people their homes. A house where bedding was being aired from a second-floor window caught her eye, and she opened the latticework door.

"I have tea from Shizuoka, tea with a good bouquet," she called out with a charming lilt in her voice. "Would you like some?"

There was no response, so she called out once more. A young woman's voice sounded harshly at the top of the front stairs.

"We don't need any!"

Next Riyo opened the glass door of the house adjoining it.

"I have some Shizuoka tea."

"Yeah, but we don't need any," answered a man's voice from a room off the entryway.

Riyo doggedly stood in the entry of house after house, but no one told her to set down her burden. Tomekichi trailed behind her complaining. Riyo liked standing in the doorway of each house, even if no one was buying anything, for it diverted her from her depression. It beats begging for money, she told herself. The heavy rucksack numbed her shoulders, so she put a hand towel under each strap where it pulled at her flesh.

The next day Riyo left Tomekichi at home and set off by herself for Yotsugi. She was free now in her solitude to think of Yoshio as much as she wished. She made her way around the construction site fence and found to her surprise a fire crackling inside the hut. Pulling up her rucksack, Riyo approached the glass door; she was thinking fondly of that first day. An old man in a *happi* coat was feeding wood into the small stove. Smoke from the smoldering fire billowed from the small window.

"What is it?" he asked. Coughing, he had turned away from the fire.

"I've been selling tea here."

"Oh, I don't need any 'cause I still have a lot of first-class tea."

Riyo took her hand away from the glass door and quickly left the shack. There was nothing to be gained by going inside. It wasn't that she didn't want to ask the old man where Yoshio's elder sister lived, go there, and, at the least, burn a stick of incense for him, yet she gave that up as well. Nothing would have come of it. Everything depressed Riyo now. She had come to feel that if by chance she were carrying Yoshio's child, she could not go on living, though how she had reached that conclusion was not clear to her. Her husband would at some point return from Siberia; even so she had decided that if things had gone wrong, she had no choice but to die.

And yet the sun shone with uncommon brightness all around her, and the green grasses on either embankment above the dry riverbed burned into her eyes like plants of fire. Riyo's conscience was, to her surprise, unimpaired. She felt not the slightest twinge of guilt for having known Yoshio. Riyo had come to Tokyo to try her hand at selling and had intended to go back to Shimizu if she couldn't sell any tea, but she liked Tokyo, business or no business, and would stay now, even if it meant dying in the street.

Riyo sat down on the green grass of the embankment. Near some chunks of concrete below her lay the body of a kitten that had been abandoned, its back to her. She immediately stood up again, swung the rucksack over her shoulder, and started walking toward the station. She abruptly turned into a narrow side street and called out at the lattice and glass front door of a rundown house repaired with assorted odd boards.

"Would you like some tea from Shizuoka, I wonder?"

"Well now, how much? Is it expensive?"

When Riyo opened the door several women turned to look at her. They were sewing facing into *tabi* socks, apparently piecework.

"Hold on just a second," said a petite woman, disappearing into the next room. "I'll go look for a can to put it in."

Women not unlike Riyo were busily sewing the soles of the *tabi*. Occasionally a needle would glint in the light.

Fireworks

MISHIMA YUKIO

Mishima Yukio's Hanabi *(Fireworks) is a compelling vignette of conservative politics and the underworld, an unsavory and commonplace meld that continues to titillate observers of power in Japan to this day. The 1953 story is set in a* ryōtei, *an exclusive Japanese-style restaurant — "geisha house," if you will — of the sort that used to be found throughout the Yanagibashi district of Tokyo. These appurtenances of the Establishment are almost all gone now, replaced by wholesalers and nondescript office buildings, and the banks of the once accessible Sumida River are encased in high and massive concrete antiflood walls, a sure barrier also to any would-be viewer of fireworks displays or any real communication with the storied river. Fashionable dining continues, but largely in Akasaka and the luxury hotels about town. We can, however, take some comfort from the fact that the annual fireworks survive, though further up the river, and that trains still make their way across the Sōbu line railway bridge.*

In Japan in the old days there was the custom known as *migawari-kubi*, giving one's life so one's master could live. Today in movies we have the stand-in. And there is truth, I can assure you, in the saying "Strangers, yet alike as peas in a pod."

Summer vacation would be starting soon, so I was looking for part-time work, something that would pay well. I talked the situation over with a friend, a fellow college student who was self-supporting and would do anything to keep the pot boiling. I wanted to go back to my home up north in Sendai for the latter half of summer vacation and needed to make a lot of money during the first half.

I spent an entire day job hunting, my friend at my side, going to several places he considered promising. As it turned out, either they had nothing for me or the jobs were not to my liking, so to console me, worn down by a day of failure, my friend took me to a watering hole he drank at now and again.

The tavern was a congenial, very inexpensive place near the sumo arena in the Ryōgoku district of Tokyo frequented by fledgling wrestlers and arena ushers. My friend was familiar with the place because he had been invited there for drinks by coworkers when he had a part-time student job at the summer sumo tournament as an usher, outfitted in the skirtlike *hakama* they wear.

When we got there we found that the sumo wrestlers were out in the provinces on tour, so there was no one particularly noteworthy amongst the clientele.

We immediately sat down at a table, and the woman who ran the place, plump and quick on her feet, brought us the cheap potato gin and appetizers my friend had ordered. He joked with her, affecting a worldly air, and—to make things worse—asked if she knew anyone who might have a good part-time job for his friend here. This embarrassed me, and I wordlessly nursed my potato gin, wishing he hadn't brought it up.

"You mean to say you're a student?" asked the proprietress, apparently somewhat taken aback by this information.

The two of us were wearing our white shirts and had put our student caps on a chair.

"We're classmates," said my friend, lifting my cap and putting it on top of the table. "I don't guess he looks like a student."

"It's not that. It's just that he usually dresses more stylishly. I had no idea he was a student. Now that I think about it, today's the first time you've been in together, isn't it?"

"Hey! This isn't the first time you've been here?"

"It *is* the first time! It's even the first time I've been to the Ryōgoku district."

"Well, I must say it's dreadful of you to pretend we've never met."

There seemed to be no way I could exonerate myself. The proprietress was tenacious in her insistence that I had been there a half-dozen times before, and my friend persisted in assailing what he called my "pointless lying."

As all this was going on, the cord curtain at the entrance parted and a man wearing a dark blue polo shirt and light pants entered.

"Evening!" he said affably to the proprietress, his wooden clogs noisily slapping the floor as he walked in.

We were astounded. Both in looks and age the man and I were identical, two peas in a pod. The woman who ran the tavern was especially startled and uttered a strangled cry.

"You could well be twins, the two of you!"

She was obviously delighted by this commonplace vagary and insisted we drink together as brothers and had drinks brought for us on the house. In spite of the fact that we had no particular desire to do so, my friend and I found ourselves introduced to my look-alike and drinking together.

Her introductions were not what you would call adroit.

"This is Mr. Naa. And you are Mr. Kawai, am I right? He's a student at Chūō University."

She did not seem to know the man's full name, and he did not volunteer it. He was, however, a jovial, amiable young man, so we had no special objections to sitting with him. I assumed that quite probably he was a blue-collar worker or salesman from the neighborhood, but that because we were introduced as college students he doubtless found it difficult to tell us what he did for a living.

"You certainly look alike, I must say."

At first this wonderment provided our only topic of conversation. As we drank the differences between the two of us slowly grew obvious: the way he drank, for example, dropping his head and bringing his lips to the rim of the cup; his habit of suddenly falling silent in the middle of an utterance, even though the way he spoke was straightforward; his inordinate desire to avoid anything controversial; the impression he gave when he smiled, eyes unsmiling. As these differences gradually became apparent I could clearly see another personality taking form before my eyes, one different from my own, and this I found reassuring. It had been somewhat unsettling to watch my own face before me. He was interested in our conversation about sumo wrestling. It was my friend, of course, who brought it up.

"You know a lot about sumo, don't you?" the fellow said to him.

"I had a part-time job as an arena usher," said my unreserved friend, "and they had me wearing a *hakama*."

By the time I realized what was coming next it was too late to stop him; he had jumped in feet first: "Do you know of a good part-time job for Kawai here?"

"A part-time job, you say?" He looked at me from over his saké cup.

His look was penetrating, the eyes unmoving. He was cheerful and affable, but it was his eyes, I think, that created the somber impression overall. When he looked at me I felt I was being studied like some sort of object.

"I've got an idea. How about the fireworks? Your friend worked in sumo, you, in fireworks. And kind of an interesting connection, wouldn't you say? Both being in Ryōgoku."

"What do you mean by 'the fireworks'?"

He explained that one of the posh geisha restaurants in the Yanagi-bashi area, borrowing a leaf from the sumo arena's book, was hiring students to work as ushers for the Ryōgoku district's annual river festival on July 18. The restaurant was called the Kikutei and was perhaps the premier establishment in Yanagibashi.

"How about it?" He continued in a monotone that managed to be neither enthusiastic nor indifferent. "It's just now occurred to me that while the pay is good, there's also a way you can get yourself a big tip. You know the minister of transport, Iwasaki Sadataka?"

"I've seen his picture in the paper." I recalled his very elongated face, the buckteeth, the white hair, the nonetheless strangely impressive face that so often found its way into political cartoons.

"The one with the long face."

"Yes, I know the one you mean."

"He's sure to go there to watch the fireworks display. When he does, give him a hard stare two or three times. You mustn't say anything. All you have to do is stare squarely into his eyes for just a little bit. That done, you'll get a big fat tip afterward. I'm telling you the truth. All you have to do is stare at him."

"That's a curious proposition."

"With that face of yours that's the spitting image of mine, eh."

I took another look at his face. An ill-made mirror could not have reflected so accurately this face that resembled mine to a T. I am not a handsome man. Having said that, however, I don't think you could call me ugly, either. If there is anything special about my looks, it is a certain severity. My eyes and eyebrows are hard against each other and the shape of my nose is definitely on the fashionable side, though my mouth is large and ungainly. I despise my mouth, which strikes me as canine. To say that my forehead is low and my face swarthy is to put it in the best possible light.

I was at a loss for a reply.

"Well, whether you apply for the job or not is up to you—your being hired is guaranteed—but if you do and you're given a healthy tip, I would appreciate it if you'd split it half-and-half with me. I'll be waiting here the night after the fireworks."

The proprietress and her help, now preoccupied with other customers, did not hear our conversation.

Though my friend was against the idea, I applied for the job, unable to restrain my curiosity. And as my look-alike had said, they took me on immediately. They told me to show up early on the morning of the river festival.

On the 18th, unfortunately, it rained off and on all morning. The weather had been mostly cloudy for several days.

When I got there in the morning I found that everyone was being given a pass. Crowd control barriers would be put up throughout the area at three, so we would be required to show these slips of paper whenever we went on errands and the like. Each pass had a number and the Kikutei's vermilion seal was stamped on the border.

1953 RYŌGOKU RIVER FESTIVAL
DATE: SATURDAY, JULY 18, 1953
IN THE EVENT OF RAIN PROGRAM WILL BE POSTPONED
TO FIRST GOOD DAY
1 P.M. TO 9:30 P.M.
ENTRANCE TO STANDS: NATIONAL AND MUNICIPAL
RAILWAYS ASAKUSA BRIDGE STATION
(PLEASE SHOW THIS PASS TO GUARDS)
SPONSORED BY
THE RYŌGOKU FIREWORKS ASSOCIATION

During the morning I busily went about my work in hemp-soled sandals and a *happi* coat with the characters "Kikutei" dyed into it. My misgivings about the weather notwithstanding, I carried tables into the banquet rooms, put together bleacherlike seats in the garden, and was sent running to the police with messages. In the afternoon, however, there was a break in the rain and we were notified that the fireworks display would go on as scheduled.

I had never before had a look at the demimonde. Certainly there is nothing that so excites the curiosity of a student from the provinces. The prodigious amount of money expended on this one night of fireworks, needless to say, was there to be used because patrons had earlier left it behind here and at the other restaurants. As for the purpose for which all this extravagance was undertaken, we students had not the faintest idea. The geisha had assiduously applied themselves to their gaudy dress and makeup and now milled about in the banquet rooms, paying us no heed whatsoever. An utterly different world was revolving before us and it was extremely difficult to feel the insignificant turning of our gears was in any way contributing to these revolutions.

Stools for us to sit on had been placed inside the Kikutei's gate and racks for footgear had been set up on both sides of the stone-paved entryway, now sprinkled with water. The regular rack could not accommodate all the footgear. In each of the banquet rooms from which the fireworks would be visible, wooden tables had been quickly hammered together and placed wherever there was space for them. These now sported white tablecloths, and neatly set out at each place awaiting the guests were a fancy tiered lunch box, a little gift, the fireworks program, a water glass, a saké cup, and a pair of chopsticks festively wrapped in red and white paper and lying on a chopstick holder. In the riverside garden there were rows of picnic tables especially made for the occasion and from each of these hung a strip of paper with the name of the party's firm grandly brushed in India ink. Dozens of colorful paper lanterns advertising a brand of beer hung in the trees from electric cords, swaying in the breeze that blew off the water. For those who wanted to view the spectacle from the river itself there were several moored boats to choose from.

Boats already moved about on the Sumida River, and a number fitted with fireworks racks sat in midstream. On shore, people with chairs and stools brought from home began to gather, and on every building rooftop, at each window, heads jostled with one another for space. There were policemen assigned to crowd control, tents erected here and there by the neighborhood associations, the incredible confusion of people coming and going, and above it all, the relentless booming of fireworks, invisible in the light of day, rending the lowering sky that once again began to let fall a spattering rain. Only the smell of those unseen fireworks could be detected in the gunpowder smoke that wafted toward us. Now and again smoke would spread itself over the river and obscure the rail bridge in haze. Then a whistle shriek would slice through the veil, followed by a train thundering across the bridge.

Sometime after three o'clock expensive automobiles slowly began to make their way through the narrow street to the restaurant. The greeting of patrons at the entrance was now unceasing. The proprietress kneeled smartly on the red carpet at the entrance, greeting her customers and giving instructions to the geisha and waitresses, all of whom were excited and ran frantically about, their chatter a shrill cacophony. From time to time conversations were drowned out by the roar of fireworks.

When this happened people would look skyward amidst the commotion—it gradually having begun to threaten a real downpour—and lament the state of the weather.

Those of us on our stools at the front gate had a tent over our heads. When a customer arrived, it was our job, in our matching *happi* coats, to stand up and bow. Since the one who ran up to the car and opened the door could get himself a nice tip, an old fellow, slight of build and feisty-looking, doubtless once the head of a construction gang, took the job for himself. The other ushers stood by waiting for something to do and were expected to chase away any undesirables who might try to enter. Only a handful of students had been hired. I eavesdropped on a conversation two were having.

"They say two cabinet ministers are coming today."

"Really?"

"The minister of transport and the minister of forestry and agriculture."

"What're their names?"

"The minister of transport is Iwasaki. The agriculture and forestry guy is Uchiyama. Dunno their first names."

"Hey! We can't see the damn fireworks from here!"

"Yeah, and it's gonna be dark soon, too."

We could be sure that the fireworks would be hardest to see from the front gate, which was on the other side of the restaurant, away from the river.

"Lemme see the fireworks program. Huh? What's this? 'Heavenly Autumn Rain on the Willow,' 'Draw-first Brocade and Crimson Dew.' Makes no sense to me, none."

I stole a look at the program, illuminated by the light of the paper lanterns. The names listed were absurdly gaudy and abstract.

The Dance of the Blossom-Vying Geisha
Silver Garden
Splendor of the Pride of Chiyoda
Pentachromic Necklace Fall
Multilayered Smoldering Blossom Swirl
Five Flowers of the Ascending Silver Dragon

A little after five the rain became a veritable cataract. People ran along the street holding handkerchiefs over their heads. The roar of the fireworks continued unabated. A parade of expensive automobiles rolled up to the restaurant's gate, the rain pelting their roofs deflected in a lush turf of spray.

The sun finally set and now and again I was able to catch glimpses from under the tent awning of pyrotechnic rings spreading out across the night sky.

At every burst the old fellow responsible for opening the car doors fretted and fidgeted, amusing us between guests with his show of impatience.

"Damn! I'd sure like ta watch! I'd like ta go up to a secon' floor room an' watch, even if it meant givin' back all my tips."

He was not joking, but apparently dead serious. And so he forsook the post that he had heretofore monopolized. He was the first to volunteer himself when there was a call for several ushers to go and help restore order out of the chaos of moving patrons in the boats and at the garden tables out of the rain and into the first-floor rooms. Shifted to the garden to work, he would at least be able to watch the fireworks.

Only a few of us were left under the tent at the front gate. Intelligence was brought to us by the minute, someone saying at one point that all the stationary fireworks were now being ignited ahead of schedule for fear they would get wet and be ruined. This meant that all of the stationary displays that were scattered throughout the program would be finished by early evening.

It was now past six. The arrival of patrons slackened somewhat.

A waitress I had seen before hurriedly spoke to us from the entrance: "Mr. Iwasaki hasn't come yet, has he. He's so late!" She abruptly disappeared inside without waiting for a reply.

It was a little after seven. A jet-black car pulled up at the front gate. It was a government limousine.

I stood up on impulse, an umbrella held aloft, went over to the car, and opened the rear door. A lone gentleman sat crouched over in the car, which was only weakly illuminated by the light at the gate. He was having trouble returning papers he had been looking at to an inside pocket. I thus had ample opportunity to scrutinize the face of Transport Minister Iwasaki, a face I was accustomed to seeing in political cartoons.

The oblong face, the buckteeth, the white hair were just as I had seen them in photographs. My initial impression of him, however, was that his skin was sallow, very enervated and unhealthy. I had always assumed a cabinet minister would somehow have a ruddier complexion.

It was taking him quite a while to put away the papers, so to keep the rain out of the car I closed the door halfway that I had just opened with a flourish. Suddenly aware of the movement, he casually looked up at me. This was at almost the same time he was rising from his seat to get out of the car.

The minister's eyes and mine met through the window glass for only a split second, yet I have never seen in a person's face a transformation so aptly described by the expression "lose one's color" as I saw at that moment. Dread suffused his face in an instant.

I could see with absolute clarity the instantaneous contraction of his facial muscles. So intense was his fright I was disquieted lest he lunge at me as he left the car.

However, when Iwasaki Sadataka wordlessly got under my umbrella, his face had become a picture of cold and distant tension. I escorted him to the entrance, where he was greeted by shouts of joy from the proprietress and geisha. Engulfed by the women, he receded down the gleaming cypress floor of the corridor without once turning back to look at me.

Dumbstruck, I returned to the tent.

"Well," asked one of the more forward student hires, "did he give you a tip?"

I suddenly realized I had received nothing whatsoever. But the feeling that next assailed me was no mere pecuniary discontent. As I recalled the indescribable look of sheer terror on the minister's face, it was now my turn to be assailed by an even greater dread.

About thirty minutes later a waitress came to tell me the proprietress wanted to see me. My heart was palpitating crazily. The role I had chosen to play now struck me as preposterous. This, however, turned out to be only paranoia on my part. She had summoned me to do some message carrying that required a bit of thinking, a task she had misgivings about entrusting to someone who was not a student. Her tone cheerful, she told me I was to run over to the neighborhood association's tent and explained the nature of my errand.

She had called me to the hallway outside a first-floor banquet room. In the room a crimson carpet was laid wall to wall. The color riveted my gaze as I listened to her talk. Over it moved endlessly the shadows of stunning geisha as they arose or sat down, now up, now down. I could see at a glance the tabletops were in grand disarray. Whenever fireworks exploded nearby and the room was filled with a quick succession of flashes, gasps of admiration from the geisha and their customers ran through the room like ripples over water.

I received my instructions and went back along the long corridor toward the entrance. There was a commotion as a group of people came down the stairs. I pressed my body against the wall to make way for them.

It was Transport Minister Iwasaki coming down the stairs surrounded by several geisha. He appeared to be a bit drunk already, though his face did not betray it. His ill-fitting black suit in the midst of the women's gaudy kimonos created a curious impression of isolation.

He took a good look at me this time. His fear did not manifest itself as blatantly as it had the first time, yet obviously he was struggling desperately against an awareness of dark dread. He looked at me with no change of expression, without batting an eye. When he had finished, he quickly looked away, lest the geisha notice his interest in a mere usher, and went on, passing right next to me. I sensed, however, that Iwasaki's frozen expression, quite contrary to its purpose, had nakedly exposed a terror growing still more intense.

I went out into the street on my errand. The rain had slackened to a drizzle, ironic weather for a display of pyrotechnics. Passersby walked past me complaining that it was not much of a show this year thanks to the rain.

When I reported back to the proprietress she told me to help with the cleanup in the garden, so I started clearing the rain-drenched outdoor tables. The beer company's lanterns hung limp and soggy in the rain, their colors running. It would have looked better had we torn down those very bedraggled lanterns.

I stared out at the surface of the Sumida, over which an endless procession of rockets still rose as I cleared away empty beer bottles, a little rainwater now collected in each. Depending on how the wind blew, gunpowder smoke now and again lay like a blanket over the Kikutei garden and the river. The engine of a canopied sight-seeing boat grew louder within the smoke, then a string of lanterns under its eaves emerged from the haze. Tiny white parachutes made of paper released in a rocket burst fell softly through the air to plaster themselves on the wet tables.

As we were carting away the piles of dirty dishes, I passed several foreign patrons, Westerners who had just gotten off one of the boats under cover of umbrellas held aloft for them against the rain. One, a woman, pulled up the collar of her light green raincoat with both hands and looked back with obvious regret several times at the boat she had been riding in.

The rain had tapered off to little more than mist, and this, paradoxically, made the opposite bank even more indistinct and reduced the soaring railway bridge to a flat silhouette.

Finally under the open sky, I was at last able to watch the fireworks as much as I pleased.

With a blast like a cannon's roar, a pillar of flame suddenly erupted on the surface of the river. The head of the column soared powerfully heavenward. As it reached its apex it exploded. Concentric circles of purple, scarlet, and green spread out, chasing after countless silver stars expanding into a circle. The inner rings disappeared first and as the outer ring collapsed an orange circlet blossomed low, dissolving into a rich cascade of light. Then everything vanished.

The rockets that followed rose aloft in a rapid volley. Several zigzagged their way upward, leaving countless fire blossoms in their wake. The flash of yet another exploding rocket would then cast into high relief the smoke lingering from the previous display.

I heard laughter and the hum of voices and looked up at the second floor. I could not see the source of the commotion, only the face of someone leaning against the railing and staring down. The face was obscured by darkness. Another rocket reverberated in the sky, its unnatural bluish light illuminating that white head of hair and the oblong face.

Iwasaki Sadataka was pale with terror, his expression isolated, tyrannized, his eyes following my every movement.

My eyes met his three times. Each time I was struck, undeniably, by the same indescribable dread he felt. Perhaps my own fear unerringly conveyed to me his profound and intolerable dread.

The minister of transport finally moved, disengaging his eyes from mine and concealing the white shock of hair behind the railing.

Some thirty minutes later when I was in the garden, a young geisha I had not seen before motioned to me from the edge of the verandah. She quickly handed me a bulky envelope.

"From Mr. Iwasaki," she said, turning to leave.

"Has he left already?"

"He just left," she said over her shoulder without the trace of a smile. The back of her white crepe kimono with its purple fireworks design disappeared into the crush of people in the corridor.

The following night, of course, I went to meet my look-alike at the tavern in Ryōgoku, for I had been given a very handsome gratuity that, even split fifty-fifty, left me richly rewarded.

He came, accepting his cut without so much as a thank you.

"Well," he said, pouring saké into my cup, "it went as I said it would, didn't it."

"I was really surprised."

"There was nothing to be surprised about. It was because you and I are as like as two peas in a pod. Which is to say, he mistook you for me."

"I wonder," I said, offering a different interpretation with forced joviality. "Perhaps it may just have been that he knew I *wasn't* you and gave me a tip out of a sense of relief."

My logic was something less than logical. Nonetheless, we drank late into the night, amusing ourselves with this harmless sort of disputation, then went our separate ways.

I had not lacked, of course, a venturous sense of curiosity to ferret out the terrifying. Those eyes, however, precluded any question.

Azuma Bridge

NAGAI KAFŪ

In contrast to Hayashi Fumiko's account of love and suffering in "The Old Part of Town," Nagai Kafū (1879–1959) has created in Azumabashi *(Azuma bridge) a postwar vignette of easygoing, matter-of-fact sexual commerce. Published in 1954, it is one of the many prostitute pieces Kafū wrote in his later years. Whether or not the general contentment of Michiko, the central character, comports with the reality of the time, it certainly runs counter to most tastes and expectations today, but Kafū naturally viewed the chaotic world around him through the eyes of a Japanese male of mid-twentieth-century Japan. One passage in the story is nothing less than a practical guide to the streetwalkers of Asakusa. Kafū baldly shifts into the immediacy of the present tense and has a character inform us where a man might find a prostitute and what it will cost him, much in the manner of an Edo-era* sharebon, *works of light fiction that also functioned as practical guides to the premodern world of "blossoms and willows." The streetwalkers of the late forties are long gone, but fortunately the river bus still departs regularly from its mooring next to Azuma Bridge and propels itself down a considerably cleaner Sumida River. Less fortunately, the bridge has recently been rebuilt and is now grander and wider to accommodate the private automobile, that superfluous curse and bane of modern Tokyo. An old inn on the Sumida-ward side of the river several doors down from Azuma Bridge that could well have been the inn mentioned in Kafū's "Azuma Bridge" disappeared less than a decade ago.*

From time to time Kafū lapses into a pseudoclassical, Saikaku-like diction where—to our Anglophonic horror—meandering sentences may brave the world bereft of various parts of speech, even their verbs, but it is also true that Kafū inevitably rewards us with the grit and smell and unfaded traditions of shitamachi. *This is no small contribution to modern Japanese letters. With the passing of Kafū and others of his generation, we find a relative paucity of writing firmly set in the metropolis. As Edward Seidensticker bluntly puts it, these days "Tokyo is not the subject for distinguished writing that it once was."*[1]

· I ·

The women of the evening who stood around every night at the approach to Azuma Bridge in Tokyo had gradually grown in number since the end of the rainy season and the onset of warmer weather, more summerlike with each passing day, so that now as many as ten would be waiting there to tug at the sleeves of passersby and importune dalliance.

One was a bright-eyed, moonfaced woman of medium build and height whom everybody called Michiko, or Mit-*chan*. She had first come there to ply her trade the previous summer and had not taken a single night off, though autumn and its piercing winds off the river were quickly followed by winter, when even gloved fingers nearly froze. Of all the women, she had been there the longest.

Inevitably a skirt of black and a white blouse trimmed with just a little lace at the collar. Her lipstick was on the heavy side, but her makeup

1. *Tokyo Rising: The City Since the Great Earthquake* (Cambridge, Mass.: Harvard University Press, 1991), ix.

was otherwise so light you could not be sure she was using face powder at all. She appeared, in fact, more refined than the respectable young women who came to the Asakusa district to see a movie, concealing her calling so well that one might take her, in the dim, feeble light at the bridge railing, for one of the women who worked in the nearby shops or for an ordinary office girl. She could pass for twenty-two or twenty-three, though in actuality she was doubtless a few years older than that.

Michiko leaned against the railing of the bridge. Her gaze, which had been directed at the neon signs coloring the roof and windows of the towering Matsuya building behind Sumida Park—now in utter darkness—moved from the pier directly below the bridge to the surface of the river. The water was illuminated by a neon sign advertising Asahi beer that shone in the sky on the other side of the river and by the flickering lights of the unending succession of trains that ran back and forth across the Tōbu Railway bridge. She could clearly make out not only the figures of young men and women rowing boats they had rented, but also melon rinds and discarded geta floating amongst the refuse carried along by the current.

On the rental boat dock a summer excursion boat, its mooring lines cast off, was about to depart; countless paper lanterns hung from its gunwales. A woman's high, shrill voice continued to call out to prospective customers, but with greater urgency now.

"Thank you for coming on board. Those who would like to ride the river bus, please hurry aboard! The river bus will make a round trip, stopping at Kototoi Bridge, Yanagibashi, Ryōgoku Bridge, and the Hamachō waterfront. The trip will take one hour. The cost is 50 yen per person."

Up on the bridge a crowd no less in number than you would find in the shopping arcade on the nearby temple grounds or along the Rokku promenade lined with movie houses watched the bustle of activity on the river.

The people leaning against the bridge railing jostled one against the other. Whenever the smallest space opened up at the railing, someone walking along would immediately squeeze into it, then look down at the flowing water and the lights reflected in it.

A man wearing white slacks and a dress shirt suddenly made a space for himself right next to Michiko. She pulled back slightly and in that instant casually looked at his face. Two or three years had gone by, but she recognized him, a customer who would occasionally stay overnight with her when she was going through some hard times, working in a whorehouse in Koiwa called the Palace.

"Well, if it isn't Kii! . . . It's me! Do you remember?"

Her tone was spontaneous and familiar. The man was startled and looked at her in surprise but said nothing.

"Number 13 at the Palace. Michiko."

"Oh. I remember."

"Let's have some fun." Mindful of the crowd of people around them, Michiko, pulling on his arm and shirtsleeve, led him from the railing toward a part of the roadway that was in semidarkness. She was now the complete coquette.

"C'mon, Kii, let's have some fun! It's been such a long time."

"I can't. Not tonight. I don't have any money."

"You can pay what you paid there. Come on. Please! Only the price of the room will be extra." Michiko was pulling him, step by step, toward the darkness at the other end of the bridge.

"Wait a minute! Have you got a hotel?"

"There's a nice, quiet place on the other side. They'll give us a room for 200 yen an hour."

"That right? I thought the reason you left that place was because you fell for someone and moved in with him. It never occurred to me you were out working like this."

"I have to do this because I'm still paying off my debts at the Palace and after I got my training there, I worked for half a year without any wages, just like I was supposed to. If my ma was still alive I'd have gone back home and made an honest living, but you know that both my mom and dad are dead, and I'm all alone now, that's why. I have to do this or I can't make it."

The man acknowledged Michiko's rambling soliloquy, nodding and grunting, but his expression showed he had heard it all before. As he listened he changed the heavy-looking flapped briefcase from his right hand to his left; she took his free hand and led him across the bridge.

Michiko turned right at the first side street.

"Here we are."

It was a two-story building sandwiched between two private homes, their front gates shut. The inn's lighted sign stood on the street in front of it. Michiko opened the latticed front door and took a step inside.

"Hello!" she called out, letting them know they were there.

A maid, a young girl, kneeled on the polished wooden floor at the entranceway and turned around two pairs of slippers for them to step into.

"Good evening," she said. "Please go upstairs. The room at the end of the hall is available."

They went up the stairs. On one side of the hallway there was a bathroom with a door made of *sugi* wood and a sink to wash one's face. On the opposite side were three rooms, three and six mats in size. They were all obviously being used by guests, who had abandoned their slippers outside the now-closed sliding doors.

Michiko went into the room at the end of the hall with her customer. The door had been left open and the bedding was laid out, with two pillows side by side. Along the windowed wall a small vanity, an old lantern-style lamp, an ashtray. On another wall hung a portrait, a picture suggestive of an old-style erotic print. Yellow summer chrysanthemums had been placed in a vase that stood beneath the picture.

Michiko had her clothes off before her customer did and opened the shoji-style window by the bed.

"It's nice and cool here, isn't it," she said. They could see in the river below the reflection of Komagata Bridge and the lights of the city on the opposite side.

"Let's make a night of it, shall we, love? Can you stay overnight?"

The man stared at this woman who was sitting naked on the windowsill smoking a cigarette.

"When you were working at the Palace they used to say you were an exhibitionist. That hits the nail on the head, I'd say."

"What's an exhibitionist?"

"Someone who shows off every inch of her body without giving it a second thought."

"Well, then, all strippers are, too. It feels good when it's hot. C'mon, you get undressed too," she said, pulling off his unbuttoned shirt from behind him.

· 2 ·

Michiko was the daughter of a carpenter who had eked out a precarious living in one of the poorer tenements of Tokyo's South Senju district. She had had an older brother, but he was felled by disease soon after he was sent off to the war, and her father burned to death during the fire-raids. This meant the end of their family line, so she then went with her mother to Matsudo, just north of Tokyo, where her grandparents were farming outside town, but they had trouble making ends meet there as well, so in order to put food on her mother's table she turned to prostitution in the Koiwa quarter, just then established, by enlisting the services of a broker and using to good advantage the fact that she had just turned eighteen.

This is an age at which a woman has no experience with men, but then we are talking about a trade that any woman can practice, if she puts her mind to it. Before three months had gone by she was a top moneymaker, and her remittances to her mother went out like absolute clockwork. Soon afterward, however, her mother took sick and died, after which Michiko earned more than she could spend, no matter how big the house manager's cut. At the end of her three-year term of service, she had a dresser and a tansu, and more than 10,000 yen in her postal savings account. She had no home to return to, however, so when a man named Tanaka promised to make her his legal wife by and by, she agreed. He was a telephone broker and one of those customers whose footfalls over a good half a year came eager and often to her door. She moved into his apartment first, then into a house he rented on the main street running through Tokyo's Minowa district, whereupon his younger sister, who had been married but had come back home, and his mother, forbidding and moody, came in from their home in the country to live with them. And so Michiko, who was good at neither needlework nor cookery, had her hands full attending to various and unaccustomed household chores. Her relationship with Tanaka's family, with whom she was temperamentally incompatible to begin with, went less smoothly with each passing day. Mutual provocations to red-faced anger and exchanges of sharp words at the drop of a hat came to be daily routine. Michiko found herself sulking and thinking back to her life in the trade at Koiwa. To make matters worse, business was not going at all well for Tanaka's telephone brokerage, so after a year they decided to separate, the man taking his mother and sister to the Kansai area. Michiko found an apartment in the same area they had been living in and began her life alone, but the savings in her postal account were almost gone and she had fewer clothes than she would have liked. Under the circumstances, Michiko—at the suggestion of the old caterer woman who often came to the apartment building on business—began seeking out customers in those Japanese-style inns and restaurants of dubious repute scattered throughout the backstreets of postwar Ueno and Asakusa. This is not to say, however, that she was able to work day and night. She was lucky if she had a customer or two every four or five days, so she decided to become an Asakusa Park streetwalker, the subject of endless discussion at the time.

She had no idea just where she should go, however, so one day she waited until it got dark, then walked around from one likely spot to another to get the feel of the park, acting as though she were returning home from a movie. It was then she realized that she had come to the Kannon Hall, the main building of the Sensōji temple, then being rebuilt. She had just thrown a 10-yen note into the collection box and clasped her hands together in prayer when she heard someone call out to her.

"Mit-*chan!*"

Startled, she turned around to see Chōko, a woman who had been as close as a sister to her when she was at the unlicensed brothel in Koiwa, and a woman who had walked the streets of Asakusa. Michiko explained her situation, invited her to a nearby noodle shop, and interrogated her at length about working the streets.

The places in the area where girls solicit customers, she told Michiko, are from the open ground behind the scaffold-covered Kannon Hall to the front of the Asakusa Shrine, from the Niten Gate area to the foot of Benten Mound where Kanetsuki Hall is. Here women begin soliciting in the daytime. Next is from the open land made when Hyōtan Pond was filled in to the area encircling the Hanayashiki amusement park. Here you might also see male prostitutes. On the opposite side of the temple grounds, that is, in the general area of Kaminari Gate: next to the Kamiya Bar at the bend in the road. Around the stop for streetcars bound for South Senju, across the boulevard. From the pitch-dark park entrance fronting the river to the approach to Azuma Bridge. Under the eaves of the sandal thong shops that close their doors early even though they stand along the district's main street where the streetcars run. On the dimly lit street encircling the Matsuya department store building. Not a night passes but there are four or five girls at each of these places. How they set their fees varies, but on average the women take in 300 to 500 yen per customer, not including the cost of the hotel, and an overnight stay costs more than 1,000 yen.[2]

Michiko, for reasons she could not quite put her finger on, felt that the approach to Azuma Bridge would be best and decided it would be the site for her debut. Business was good from the first night. She had customers in the early evenings, and any customer she snared around the time the last streetcar went by usually told her after they got to the inn that he wanted to stay until morning.

Men had always found something attractive and appealing about Michiko's personality since her days at the Koiwa brothel. After she had come to understand a bit the nature of her calling, there were few nights when she did not have an overnight customer, no matter how slow a night it was. Her ability to attract customers did not diminish after she began frequenting Azuma Bridge, and at the end of the month the purse she kept in her handbag was stuffed to bursting with 100 and 1,000 yen notes.

Michiko began once again to make savings deposits at the neighborhood post office.

---

2. The exchange rate at this time was 360 yen to a U.S. dollar.

· 3 ·

A little after ten one morning. Michiko left the riverfront inn in the Honjo district where every night she took her overnight customers, parting company with last night's on the main street. When she came back to her apartment, on a backstreet in Minowa, it seemed to her that the incense smoke from the temple cemetery next door beneath her window, its pervasive scent more pungent now than usual, was streaming directly into her room, borne through the trees by the wind. She looked down on the cemetery as she lay out her bedding for a nap and noticed that even the timeworn gravestones that usually lay buried under leaves had been neatly tidied up and provided with offerings of flowers and incense. From the main temple came the sound of sutra chanting and a bell being struck. It was then Michiko realized that July 13, the first day of *Bon*, the festival of the dead, had come round and surprised her once again. She caught the sound of a woman's voice, an unfamiliar voice, and once more stuck her head out the window. She saw beneath her a young woman, obviously married, her hair in the traditional Japanese coiffure and wearing a kimono, and an older woman, probably her mother. A temple worker carrying a wooden pail had just led them there. They stood before a still-new gravestone and set out a bundle of incense sticks.

Michiko suddenly thought of her mother, her ashes interred in a temple in Matsudo, and what had happened when she died. Because she had been working in the Koiwa red-light district then she was not her own boss, free to go at will, and considered herself lucky to get time off to go to the funeral. Now, several years later, Michiko did not know if the ashes were still there or not, and when this realization came upon her she suddenly felt she had to find out for sure. Leaving the bedding where she had spread it and her food uneaten, she shut the window and immediately went back out to the street.

Michiko took the train from Ueno, getting off at the Matsudo station. She could recall the name of the temple but had not the faintest recollection of where it was, so she hired a pedicab in front of the station. The temple was about where the road, which rises gradually as it goes along, begins to drop toward Kōnodai. It was a Nichiren sect temple, and the top of the main gate rose up from within a grove of pine. Here, too, people paying *Bon* visits to family graves were streaming in and out of the grounds. She walked straight toward the entrance to the priests' living quarters. Fortunately, a monk of some years who was probably the head priest happened to be standing there looking over the mail, apparently just delivered.

"Pardon me, uh . . . the grave of a woman by the name of Tamura," Michiko asked, hesitating somewhat, "uh . . . I wonder if it might be at this temple."

The expression on the monk's face offered no suggestion that he had the slightest idea there was such a grave, but he forced a smile nonetheless.

"When did she pass on? How many years ago was the funeral?"

Michiko reckoned to herself the years she had been a prostitute in Koiwa's sex district and the time she had lived with the telephone broker.

"The funeral was about five years ago," she told the monk. "It was still cold, around the first of the year. The arrangements were taken care of by the Tamuras, a farming family from Matsudo."

"I see. Let's take a look. Just a moment, please. Have a seat there, if you would."

The monk came out leafing through an old register made of rice paper and bound along its width.

"Aha, I see what's happened now. No one contacted us about a grave after the funeral, so that's where things stand. There is no grave yet. Are you a relative of the deceased?"

Michiko replied that she was the daughter of the woman for whom the service had been performed and that she was living in Tokyo.

"If there is no grave, I would like to have one, and a proper stone erected. Who should I have do the work?"

"Our temple knows a good stonecutter. If you have him do it, he will make one for you right away."

"I would like to engage his services, then, but I wonder just how much a stone would cost?"

"Let's see," said the monk, "even little gravestones like those over there—everything costs more since the war, doesn't it—even for those you can expect to pay 5,000 or 6,000 yen."

Michiko's body would bring her no less than 1,500 to 1,600 yen a night. The cost of a gravestone did not dismay her, not at all. It was nothing compared to buying a winter overcoat.

"I do not happen to have the funds with me now," she said, using the most formal diction she could muster, "but if that will be sufficient, I can pay you any time, so would you be good enough to take the trouble to discuss the matter with the stonecutter? I should certainly appreciate it."

The monk, apparently looking upon her as a good and unexpected customer, suddenly clapped his hands and summoned a young novice to fetch tea and cakes.

Michiko went on to talk about her father as well, that he was missing after an air raid and thus still without a grave, and she asked the monk to have a posthumous Buddhist name for him chiseled in the stone along with her mother's, giving him several 100-yen notes, wrapped in paper as decorum demands. The monk extolled Michiko's filial devotion as a rarity in today's world and saw her as far as the temple gate.

Michiko saw her bus go by as she was walking to the bus stop. She asked directions of someone waiting at the stop and returned home to her apartment, this time by way of the Keisei line from Kōnodai to Ueno.

The sun was just beginning to set at the end of one of the long days of midsummer. Normally she would go to the public bath, then—after she had dinner—get ready to go out and make some money, but this evening Michiko went nowhere. She stretched out on the bedding she had laid out just before she left and, thoroughly exhausted, fell asleep.

Evening, the next day. Michiko went a little earlier than usual to Azuma Bridge.

"Mit-*chan!* What happened to you last night?" asked a nightly regular, one of the girls she had become friends with. "It's a good thing you didn't show up."

"Someone was giving us a bad time?" she asked but did not wait for an answer. "I went to a temple out in the country to visit my ma's grave. I went to bed early last night."

"Early in the evening some toughs got into a fight on the bridge, and after that plainclothes cops started hanging around and hassling us. I heard three girls were finally picked up next to the Matsuya."

"Then it really was a good thing I didn't come, wasn't it. If I had, they probably would've got me too. It was just like what the monk at the temple said. He told me your luck gets better when you're a good daughter, and no misfortune can come to you. He was right as rain."

Taking a packet of Peace cigarettes from her handbag, Michiko gazed about her. Wherever she looked, she could see the crush of people out for this second night of *Bon* growing ever more brutal.

An Unclaimed Body

IKEDA MICHIKO

Ikeda Michiko, born in Kyoto in 1914, has been writing about the down-and-out of Tokyo for over half a century, both in her fiction and her essays. Her first work just after the war led critics to label her a chronicler of what they called the Carnal School, but her focus later shifted to the grittier, impoverished folk-ways of the city. In these pieces she clearly writes in the naturalist mode, a naturalism that only occasionally burdens the reader with the laundry-list hyperrealism of the Japanese I-novelist. Her concern is largely hardscrabbling women, particularly the women of San'ya, the most prominent of Tokyo's skid rows.

In Muenbotoke *(An unclaimed body), originally published in 1977, Ikeda traces the last years of Hideko, a hapless ex-prostitute who in her old age struggles to survive on the outer fringes of life in San'ya. And the narrator's self-reflection mirrors the author's own struggle to write and, at the same time, keep up the accommodating, if not cheerful, facade expected of a wife and helpmeet in Japan.*

Because of her work with a left-wing organization in the 1930s, Ikeda came into intimate contact with those at the bottom of the social ladder when she was arrested many times by the Tokkō, the ubiquitous thought police of authoritarian Japan. She writes that the jail experience instilled in her a lifelong sense of kinship with prostitutes, thieves, arsonists, and beggars, people she lived with twenty-four hours a day while in detention. She was able, she later wrote, to recognize in herself as well the weaknesses that hobbled these people.[1]

"An Unclaimed Body" is her first work to be translated into a foreign language.

An ambulance siren wailed past the window. This happened almost every night. Perhaps someone had collapsed on the street again or been injured in a fight. It was quiet inside the bunk hotel, however; I could hear only the footsteps of someone passing by in the hallway.

I rolled over on my stomach in bed and pulled the ashtray toward me. The only boundary marker between my bed and the next was a single horizontal bar 20 centimeters high. The old woman who had moved in the day before yesterday was in bed. Her salt-and-pepper head of hair was just inches from my nose. When I lit my cigarette she stuck her head out from under her quilt and drew her own ashtray toward her. I had never seen such a wrinkled face. That she should have wrinkles on her forehead and at the corners of her eyes was natural enough, but countless furrows ran from the corners of her eyes toward the edge of her lips. Her upper lip was creased with dozens of vertical lines and her jaw with rows of horizontal. The strangest thing were the wrinkles on her nose. One expects wrinkles between the eyes, but she had two running across her nose. To make matters worse, all the furrows cut so deep they looked like lengths of black string. The overall effect was of a mass of vertical, horizontal, and diagonal lines that had come together to form a human face.

---

1. Ikeda Michiko, *Muenbotoke* (An unclaimed body) (Tokyo: Sakuhinsha, 1979), 216.

I was not favorably disposed toward the wrinkled crone. She had come two days ago at night, a large *furoshiki* bundle in one hand and a shopping basket and umbrella in the other, taking the only unoccupied bed, the one next to me. She had stared at me and said mockingly: "Well, we have a new face, do we?"

I had made it a point not to get involved with people in the bunk hotels or to get drawn into arguments, so I didn't say anything, but I had already been staying there a good half year, and in the women's room I had been there the third longest time. I thought to myself, *You're the new face, you funny old girl.* I realized she was a regular who had been staying there off and on when one of the other women returned late that night.

"What's this?" she called out to the old woman, "You've come back again?"

The old woman dug around in her ashtray, finally finding a butt that was long enough.

"Got a match?" she asked me.

The cigarette she had in her mouth was a short butt good for one drag. I couldn't look on with indifference. I took out three cigarettes, together with some matches, and wordlessly set them down by her pillow beyond the metal bar that was our boundary line. The old woman quickly glanced at Miwa on the bed across from her. There were only three of us in the room then. Miwa was facing us, eating rice. In her lap were the pot she had cooked the rice in and soy-boiled kelp, still in the paper-thin wood shavings it had come in. That's all she was eating, no pickled vegetables or anything else. Having made sure that Miwa was simply staring off into space, the old woman gave me a mechanical smile, then, whispering her thanks so that Miwa couldn't hear, lit up and spoke in her normal voice.

"You're doin' okay, eh? Well, you're still young."

I was not at an age you could call young, only young compared to a wrinkled crone. I was first to finish my cigarette and pulled the quilt over my head.

Soon after the lights were turned off, I began to hear a light clunking. At intervals, like a clock ticking away the seconds: one, two, three, four. I had heard the sound the night before, too, and the night before that.

Since it was a soft sound that could well elude the ear, I don't know if I heard it before then. But a sound that catches the ear will keep you awake if you don't know what it is. I was certain it was coming from somewhere in the room. I suspect that I began to notice it the night the old woman moved in, and that it was coming from her bed. It wasn't the sound of water dripping, or of something hitting against something. It didn't sound like knuckles cracking, either. The sound would go on for twenty minutes or so, then suddenly stop.

A San'ya bunk hotel—a Simple Accommodation, in municipal official-ese—in this case, the Tokuya, had twelve six-tatami-mat rooms. The first room you came to on the second floor was the women's, the rest were for men, most of whom were day laborers. Initial construction had begun on the track-and-field stadium in preparation for the 1964 Tokyo Olympics, three years in the future, so there was plenty of work for the laborers.

Our six-mat room had in its center a wooden floor three feet wide, on both sides of which were bunk beds. There were me and the old woman to the left in the lower beds, and Miwa and Yuki to the right. The upper level were beds, too, so the room could hold eight, but there was never a time when all eight occupants were there at the same time, since the women got back to the room all hours of the day or night, depending on the sort of work they did. Women working in factories in the area or at construction sites would leave for work early in the morning and come back as it was getting dark. Women working in bars would go out in the afternoon or at dusk and return late at night. Prostitutes would leave at night and return the next morning.

The next morning when I woke up the wrinkled one and Miwa were gone. But now women were in all four upper bunks. Only Yuki across the wooden floor from me was still absent, as she had been yesterday. When I had first moved into the room, I slept in the bed Yuki was now using. When you sat up in it your head hit the "ceiling," which is to say, the bed above you, so I had to sit with my back bent. I had waited for an upper bed and moved when one opened up. The room had no ceiling;

it was open all the way to the roof, plenty of room even if you stood. Well and good, but I didn't appreciate just what climbing up and down the perfectly vertical ladder to my bed would mean. The ladder would be no problem if you used the bed just for sleeping, but a bunk hotel bed is where one's everyday tasks are done. I had to go up and down the ladder endlessly: to buy cigarettes, to drink some tea, to go to the bathroom. So when a lower bunk opened up, I moved into it.

I was hungry, so I got up. Wire was strung at the entrance to the beds; we hung our towels and laundry on it to dry and also used it as a clothes hanger. I took my skirt off the wire, put it on, and slipped on the sweater that I had rolled up and put at the head of the bed. The lavatory at the end of the hall that had been alive with the clamor of laborers at daybreak was now empty and the bunk hotel was as still as a tomb. I put on my coat—it doubled as a raincoat—got my shoes, which were wrapped in newspapers at the foot of the bed, and went downstairs to the front door.

Restaurants in San'ya open at dawn and close up after the laborers have had their breakfast. I was thinking how nice it would be if they were still open when I bumped into my elderly roommate on a corner on San'ya's main street.

"Oh!" I asked in surprise, "You're taking off work today?"

The old woman had gone off with the laborers every morning since she had moved into the hotel (though it was only her third day), so I had assumed she was doing odd jobs and the like at a construction site. When you saw her on the street her wrinkles were not that obvious. The hotel room had a single light bulb hanging down from the roof and its light hit her from the side and etched those deep, dark lines in her face. However, I could see now that the old woman was so short as to seem almost freakish. I hadn't realized she was so short.

"They played me for the fool, so I knocked over their mop bucket for 'em!"

She seemed quite angry. Her lips were trembling. She was wearing *mompe* trousers of *kasuri* weave, faded from countless washings, and a jacket. The sleeves of the jacket were rolled up to her elbows and its hem came down to her knees. I felt pity for the old woman; if she went around looking like that, everyone would doubtless treat her as a beggar.

"Who played you for a fool?" I asked, hoping to cheer her up.

"A new girl came in yesterday. She had me, an old person, doing the cleanin', an' she just sat at her desk shufflin' papers, pretendin' not to notice me. I told her right in front of the boss to help me. An' when I did, he said *I* had to do the cleanin'. Lecherous old fool! That got to me, so I dumped out the dirty water in the mop bucket."

"You dumped it on the president of the company?"

"No, on the girl. She was wearin' a white sweater, so I dumped it on her sweater."

She fell silent, then: "She can try an' wash it, but it won't come out."

She laughed at the humor of it, her shoulders hunched. But her laughter soon stopped and she seemed to be on the verge of tears. She had most certainly been fired.

"I'm going to get something to eat. Come with me. Eat something tasty and cheer yourself up. I'll treat."

I knew putting food on the table at that age was no easy matter.

All the restaurants on the main street had closed.

"I know a place that's still open," I said, and she fell in step beside me.

"I shouldn't let a woman treat me, y'know," she said as she walked. " 'Kindness is rife in this journey through life,' as the proverb goes. That refers to you, Missus."

My position had suddenly been elevated; I was now someone's wife.

"It's miserable gettin' old, I'll tell you," she said, looking up at me. "You don't know what it's like yet, Missus, but nobody pays any attention to you. I should've given things more thought when I was young. If I was twenty-seven or twenty-eight, you know . . ."

"How true."

There was a small meal-ticket restaurant that I frequented at the edge of the San'ya district near what had been the old Yoshiwara prostitution quarter. It was between meals so we were the only customers. The breakfast set was *miso* soup, pickled vegetables, and fermented soybeans. Strips of calligraphy paper were posted along the wall, and on these were written the à la carte dishes you could order.

"Have whatever you want," I said, looking over the paper strips.

"I really shouldn't, but I'd like to have vinegared octopus."

"Vinegared octopus? They don't have that, I'm afraid."

The eatery was a typical meal-ticket restaurant. Other restaurants in San'ya had customers who began drinking in the morning, so they had vinegared octopus and sashimi.

"Order whatever you want from what's on the wall," I told her, indicating the menu strips with my gaze. I ordered dried horse mackerel.

"I don't want a damn thing!" she suddenly shouted angrily.

I looked at her, startled. There was no reason for her to be angry simply because they didn't have any vinegared octopus. I wondered if she was abnormally short-tempered and snappish all the time. Such a personality would certainly have narrowed her horizons. Nonetheless, when they brought the trays of food to our table she was in good humor again and began to eat. She apparently hadn't had a proper breakfast.

It was then that the glass-paned front door opened and a woman entered. When I recognized her I gave her a nod. It was the woman in the bed over Miwa's. She had still been asleep when I left the Tokuya. She was called Ibaraki, but I didn't know if that was her surname or it simply meant that she was from Ibaraki prefecture. It was not uncommon for someone to be referred to by the name of their home area. If it were her surname, one of the characters was probably different from the *kanji* used in the prefecture name. In any case, I didn't know if it was actually her name or a pseudonym. She was over forty, had a slender face, and was dark-complected but was not an unattractive woman. She wore a brown overcoat and black shoes and carried a handbag. Of the eight in the room, only Ibaraki and me somehow or other managed to have overcoats. We were also the only ones with shoes.

"My! What good friends you are!" Ibaraki said, standing next to me and looking down at us. There was an edge to her voice.

"I'll have the breakfast set, too," she called to the back of the restaurant.

"You're not working today, Deko?" she asked the old woman.

Deko! A nickname not without humor, I thought.

"They played me for the fool, so I quit."

She had spoken with such anger moments before, but now, unaccountably, she was mumbling.

"You quit again, Deko?" The woman's tone was teasing. "You forget yourself when you blow up and you make a mess of things. I don't suppose you got the money due you, did you? Will you have to get Kanasugi to go get it? Kanasugi's a good-natured guy, and that's a fact. He can't bring himself to turn you down if you ask a favor of him."

"That's because," she went on, "he has religion. I have my doubts about religion as well, I'll tell you. People are using him all the time."

Ibaraki then turned to me.

"May I sit next to you?" she asked with affected politeness as she sat down. The dried horse mackerel, which only I had, looked terribly extravagant on my dish.

After I finished eating I lit a cigarette and offered the pack to the old woman. She made no move to take any.

"Why don't you take one," Ibaraki said, "since she's been good enough to offer them to you."

Only then did the old woman take a cigarette. Why should she be so concerned about someone seeing her take a single cigarette? Last night she had also quickly glanced over at Miwa to make sure she wasn't watching. I was concerned that it might cause trouble if Ibaraki saw me pay for two meals, yet if I didn't it would probably leave the old woman sitting there flat broke. I got up and went back to the kitchen and paid for the two of us.

It was a time when I had lost confidence in my ability to do my work as a writer and my literary ambition had disintegrated. I was living day by slothful day, an overripe piece of fruit waiting to drop from the tree. I was writing short stories for a regional newspaper—twelve manuscript pages every Thursday—under the title *A Look at Women*. It was a series in which each installment featured a woman of a different occupation and age. I had been given strict orders to make each episode as erotic as possible. I had no enthusiasm for the series and no desire to write it, but since this job was my only source of income I could hardly refuse. Readers would seem to be critical of fiction written with no enthusiasm; I wondered when my editor would pull the plug on the series. During the two or three days it took me to wrap up my twelve pages I would live at home. As soon as I finished I'd hurry back to the Tokuya.

My family was convinced I was an honest-to-god author. And they were unaware I was pushing myself to write something I had no desire to write, that I found intolerable. A parent does not notice that a child is hiding a failed exam paper, and a wife does not know that her husband's business is on the brink of bankruptcy. Perhaps this is how families are. Even so, it is no easy matter to silently bear a burden so that others can interpret things according to their own lights.

While I was home I would contrive a good-humored facade the instant I got up from my desk. And I was an agreeable conversationalist, chiming in even when I had no interest in what was being talked about. The consideration everyone gives a family, doubtless unconsciously, because one is a member of the family, was, for me, onerous. As I lost confidence in the work I was doing I found I could no longer endure this onerousness. In such a state the cheap hotel was a welcome change for me. I could look as sullen as I wished. I didn't have to talk to anyone. That is to say, I needn't give a thought to the feelings of others. On top of which, observing the daily lives of the laborers and the women who constantly came and went fascinated me. It was like journeying by oneself through an unknown land; I never wearied of it. At the same time, I had time on my hands during the day. Because the people who stayed in the bunk hotels all went off to work, leaving the entire district deserted.

"I'll see you later," I said to Ibaraki, who was still eating.

"You going back to San'ya?" she asked.

"I am going to Asakusa."

"I'm going there too."

"But I am walking," I said. I wanted to walk to kill time. I usually took the bus, given the distance.

"Hey, I'll walk if I've got someone to walk with. It'll save bus fare. Maybe you'd rather not have me go with you."

"No problem."

"Today the New World is opening after remodeling and two of my friends are already there. I'm on the second shift, so don't hafta hurry, but I was so hungry I couldn't sleep."

I hadn't a clue as to what sort of business the New World was. Ibaraki quickly finished her meal, then got up.

"You seem to smoke a lot, doncha," she noted. "I'll sell you smokes cheap. Get 'em every day. You'd probably like to have 'em cheaper, even if it's only a yen or two."

I suspected that the New World was a cabaret or some such, and that she was buying from someone the cigarette or two that customers were leaving behind in their packs. I had a reason for thinking that might be the case. A woman who had been staying at the Tokuya until just recently used to go to Tokyo Station every day and pick up the lunches people left on the trains. Passengers in groups—students on excursion, for example—were given lunches at noon whether they were hungry or not, so they threw away half-eaten lunches and those with only a bite out of them. She would gather these together, repack them, then sell them at a discount. So I guessed that's what was happening to the cigarettes.

"And it sure isn't fake tobacco," she confided. "They're cigarettes from the government monopoly."

I didn't respond.

The three of us left the restaurant and Ibaraki and I began walking toward Asakusa. Neither of us said a word as we went along. I looked back after a bit. The old woman was standing in front of the restaurant watching us go. As soon as she saw I was looking at her she turned away and started walking.

Our route to Asakusa took us through what had been the Yoshiwara quarter. I'd guess it was the third year since prostitution had been abolished, yet most of the buildings were still as they had been; all the front shutters had been shut. Paradoxically, the district, utterly silent at high noon, struck me as ominous simply because of its still splendid buildings.

"Things will be starting up again before you know it," Ibaraki said as we walked. "They're biding their time, waiting for the hubbub to die down. You can't expect men to lose their lust."

Then she changed the subject.

"You seem to be thick with Deko."

"Not really."

"They say she used to work in Yoshiwara," Ibaraki said, drawing her words out for effect. "She's a bad one. Better watch yourself. She sponges off everyone. 'Lemme have a cigarette. I'll pay you back. Lemme have some rice. Lemme have some tissue paper,' all borrowing and no returning. She thinks she's ahead of the game if she can score a single matchstick."

I recalled that the first thing the old woman had said to me was to ask for a match.

"She's just too brazen-faced and annoys everyone, so I gave her a damn good beating, after which she ran off with her tail between her legs. Now she comes running back and right away is sponging off someone."

"She didn't try to sponge off me. I treated her."

"It amounts to the same thing, doesn't it."

We had now passed through Yoshiwara.

"Which way you going?" Ibaraki asked.

I'd been thinking as I walked along how I might respond if she asked me where I was working or where I stayed when I was away at night so much. That's why I wanted to go off by myself, but I didn't know which way Ibaraki was going, so I couldn't tell her where I intended to go. I didn't know then that the unspoken custom of the people in the bunk hotels was not to ask the sort of questions that delved into a person's background or work.

"It looks like my coming with you is a drag," Ibaraki said.

"Not really."

I hadn't told her which way I was going; the two of us walked on shoulder to shoulder. We came to International Boulevard, one of the Asakusa thoroughfares.

"Look!" she said, pointing. "There it is."

I could see at the edge of the sidewalk a row of floral wreaths in celebration of the reopening. I guessed that was the remodeled establishment, but I still didn't know what sort of place it was. As we approached I could hear the torrential metallic click of pachinko balls.

"We wait in front for the place to open, then run in before everyone else, and look for a machine with loose pins so we can win extra balls. If the same person plays until all the balls are gone and the machine shuts down, the guys working in the parlor will spot her, so I relieve the first to go in. Day after tomorrow two pachinko parlors are opening across from each other in Setagaya. They'll each be letting people win balls to beat the other guy. It'll be a cakewalk."

The pachinko parlor was crowded.

"I don't suppose you'll play some pachinko?"

I declined her offer.

"You're unsociable, I'll tell you, a cold fish," she said over her shoulder as she disappeared into the pachinko parlor.

I saw the same *yakuza* movie two times, then fed the pigeons on the grounds of the Sensōji Temple in Asakusa. It was finally nightfall, so I returned to South Senju by subway. The cars were packed. Many of the passengers were laborers returning to San'ya. The main street running from South Senju to San'ya continued on the other side of the Namida Bridge—the Bridge of Tears—intersection to become San'ya's main street.

The Tokiwaya restaurant was crowded. There was a seat at the end of a table at the very back, so I squeezed in. The five others at the table were day laborers; they were all drinking saké. They had not come in as a group of buddies but had straggled in one at a time and just happened to be sitting next to each other. As I looked at the men sitting in front of me I thought of how the day's wages they had earned with their sweat a few hours before had been transformed into beer and pork cutlets and sashimi and cigarettes, and was now draining into their stomachs. The food a worm has taken in at one end of its cordlike body is excreted at the other end. Every day they repeat the same hand-to-mouth motion with the same monotony of the worm. I thought of this each time I ate with laborers.

Only Yuki, who had been gone one whole day, and the wrinkled crone were in bed when I returned to the flophouse. All the other women were out. The old woman got up as soon as she saw me. She was wearing a man's old shirt and a man's long underwear, also secondhand; the sleeves and cuffs, too long for her, had been simply and roughly cut off with scissors, leaving her head and arms and legs looking as though they were protruding from a big, floppy bag. Looking at this comical figure, it was all I could do to keep from bursting into laughter.

"Welcome home, ma'am," she said with intentional humor. She affected a smile, turning her face into a mass of wrinkles: "I've cleaned up your bed for you."

I saw that my futon had been folded and stacked in the corner. The way she had folded up the bedding was the way the flophouse clerks did it when a bed opened up and they squared things away for the next occupant. Normally one simply folded the bottom half of the bedding back on the top half.

"Will you be retiring now? Shall I make things ready?" the old woman asked, setting two quilts on the floor and spreading out the futon on the bed. She did not seem to be joking now. Her attitude had abruptly changed, and she was now prepared to fuss over me. Heedless of my confusion, she turned to me after she had laid out the futon and asked— in the politest of language—if the bedding was satisfactory.

"Never mind," I said, flustered. "I'll do it myself."

I tried to stop her, but she ducked under my arm and laid out the quilts and the pillow. She had washed the ashtray clean. I had no belongings, so one tatami mat gave me enough room, but the other women laid out their futons only the length of their bodies, folding under the excess at the wall, leaving twenty or thirty centimeters open at the head of the bedding to put their belongings in. That was why the old woman had asked about the futon. Only she lay out her bedding in the normal way. Her short legs only extended partway down the bed, so she had room for her baggage at her feet.

I was terribly embarrassed to have the old woman fussing over me, so I quickly crawled into bed, taking off just my overcoat. I suspected that she had an ulterior motive in fussing over me: had she eaten dinner? I had been told that the old woman had been in Yoshiwara in the old days. Perhaps she had treated her best customers just as she fussed over me now. She could hardly put on an act with such equanimity unless that were the case. Only Yuki was in bed now. Would the old woman fuss over me if the other women were there? She had been anxious not to let anyone see her receive even one cigarette from me, so she might not have given me the time of day if the others had been there. And yet, how pathetic it would be if the old woman had launched into this song and dance just to be treated to dinner. Nonetheless I simply pretended I was asleep.

Yuki was not asleep. I could hear her munching on *sembei*. Yuki was the only one who would seclude herself in bed to eat. In our cramped room you even knew when someone had chewing gum or rice cakes, not from the sound, of course, but from the smell. You could even smell bean jam and rice balls. Last night I could tell without looking that Miwa was eating her kelp—in its wood-shaving wrapper—with her rice.

The door to the room swung open and a man spoke: "The front office says you have something for me to do."

"Oh, Mr. Kanasugi, I have to ask another favor of you," the old woman said. "Wait in the hall. I'll change in a jiffy. 'Kindness is rife in this journey through life,'" she added, using the same proverb she had with me this morning. Miwa came through the door as she was going out.

When I went to the toilet, the old woman and Kanasugi stood facing each other in front of the restroom. Kanasugi had apparently just come back from a job site and still wore a sweat cloth wrapped around his head. I wondered if this was the kindhearted day laborer who was a believer.

"Is that really what happened? Is that all? It would be unfortunate if the story I hear from you and what I hear from them are at odds."

"I stumbled over the mop bucket and overturned it and it splashed her clothes and got 'em dirty. That's all. They don't respect San'ya people, I tell ya."

"The last time with the ice dealer—right?—they said they wouldn't give me your money without a note from you saying it was okay—you remember? A note would be proof you'd asked me to get the money. If you go buy paper and ask the front desk, they'll write it for you. All you have to write is your name. You got money to buy paper?"

This was all I heard from the toilet. As I returned to the room I could hear the old woman shouting: "You're bringin' up all this petty crap! Why aren't you honest enough to tell me you aren't goin' 'cause you don't want to go."

That night I realized all eight of us women were in the room together, which was quite unusual, but close to midnight Yuki got up and began putting on her makeup. She then changed into a gaudy check-patterned suit and left. It was a suit of heavy material and looked warm. She was young and attractive enough and didn't look like a San'ya woman. She probably had a date with a customer.

The lights were turned off soon after Yuki left. It was then that I once again heard that clunking sound. I was sure it was coming from the old woman's bed. Suddenly someone shouted.

"Quiet!"

It was the woman in the bed right above me. She apparently worked in a tavern somewhere and stayed out overnight from time to time. She had been here longer than anyone else.

"Deko, you're keeping me up! Get the front desk to change that into thousand-yen bills. Thousand-yen bills don't make a sound."

The old woman made no response and the noise was heard no more. Had it been the sound of her counting her money? Perhaps she had been counting under her quilt, so the sound was muffled and obscured. I still couldn't be sure what she was doing. Had she been dropping coins into a box and making what otherwise would have been a clinking sound without the quilt? She apparently always carried it with her, so I didn't think she could have many copper or nickel coins. Perhaps she had been counting and recounting them over and over again. I was relieved to realize that she did not have to go without dinner.

The next morning I lay in bed for a while after I awoke. I was planning that day to go to the art museum in Ueno. A woman friend, a painter, was exhibiting some of her pictures. I intended to stay another night in San'ya, then return home the following morning. I already had an idea for the story I would get started on the following day.

When I got up a little before nine and washed my face, the old woman came over to me; I guessed she had been waiting for me to get up.

"Good morning, Missus."

"Don't call me 'Missus,' " I said with some vehemence. "It's ridiculous. We're both San'ya types. There're no proper wives or well-bred young women here."

I changed the subject.

"You've a job lined up? There seem to be all sorts of jobs for helpers of one sort or another if you go to the employment office in Iidabashi."

The old woman was a stickler for cleanliness. She was the only one of us who tossed out all her bedding onto the wooden floor every day and wiped clean her single tatami with a damp cloth. Her hand towel and underwear hanging on the wire were always snow-white. Even if one couldn't sew a stitch or cook, there had to be low-level slots where all that was required was that you be good at cleaning.

"She can't go to the employment office," a voice behind me said. "There's no point in Deko doing that."

I turned around to see Ibaraki standing there brushing her teeth. I sensed that she had been keeping an eye on the relationship between the old woman and me.

"They have you fill out cards at the employment office, right? Someone there might fill it out for her, but then they'd ask her her name and how you write the characters. And she wouldn't be able to read the name of the place she's suppose to go, so she couldn't take a train or a bus. It'd have to be someplace she could walk to."

So that was it. The old woman could not read. That's why she blew up when Kanasugi told her to write her name. And why she got angry when I suggested, as I looked as the names of the dishes on the menu strips that lined the wall of the restaurant, that she pick out whatever she wanted. Both I and Kanasugi had been well meaning. Would it have been so difficult for her to come out and admit she couldn't read? She doubtless thought we would have made fun of her. The old woman was brushing her teeth, a look of feigned nonchalance on her face that said everything was just fine.

"What's the problem? She doesn't have to be able to read."

Ibaraki grunted and made a show of peering into my face: "You're taking Deko's side, a kindly expression on your face! You think you're Jesus or somebody?"

This time it was me who pretended not to hear. I looked across the room.

"Phone call!" the clerk said as I was slipping on my shoes at the entrance to the hotel. I looked back to see him with the receiver in his hand.

"It's for you."

My husband was the only one I had given the number of the Tokuya to.

"Ms. Tsukamoto called and wants to talk to you. When I told her you weren't in and asked if I should have you call her, she said she'd call again around noon."

I guessed that Tsukamoto Suzuko had come up to Tokyo from Nagoya.

"I'll be back home by noon."

Suzuko had helped me get my series of pieces in the provincial newspaper. Perhaps she was going to tell me they were stopping publication of them.

The eateries along San'ya's main street were still open. I realized at the entrance to the Tokiwaya that the old woman had been following me. The instant I noticed, she smiled.

"Nice weather, isn't it, Missus," she said, her manner affected. Her brazenness clung to me like sticky birdlime. If you displayed the slightest kindness to her, she would immediately take advantage of it, and there would be no end to her audacity. I felt I understood why Ibaraki looked at the old woman with a baleful eye and bullied her. But I certainly could not bring myself to rant and rave at her and send her packing. And the next day I would be leaving the bunk hotel for a while; I resigned myself to the situation and nodded to her. I had only myself to blame. I shouldn't have sympathized with the old woman and treated her to a meal. No, I had even blundered in impulsively speaking to her.

To my surprise, Yuki was at a table in the back of the restaurant. The gaudy check suit caught my eye as soon as I opened the door. She was with a man, apparently last night's customer. He was a well-built man, fortyish, perhaps someone in construction, maybe the boss at a job site. He wore a leather jacket and work pants, and his shoes were ordinary leather ones, not the hard-soled *tabi* that construction workers usually wear. It was late, so there were no other customers. A number of dishes were arrayed on their table, and three beer bottles. Yuki had seen us as we came in and gave a nod and a quick smile. This in spite of the fact that when people come face-to-face in the bunk hotel they give no sign they've seen each other.

We walked straight back toward the kitchen at the rear of the restaurant. A display case marked the boundary between the kitchen and the rest of the establishment, and contained a variety of food samples. Doors on both sides of the case provided easy access from either the kitchen side or the customers' side.

"They have vinegared octopus," the old woman said, watching my face for a reaction. I nodded permission.

"Vinegared octopus bright and early in the mornin'. It's paradise. 'Kindness is rife in this journey through life,'" she said once again. "This makes me so happy."

She carried the octopus and pickled vegetables, one in each hand, to a table. The waitress brought our rice and *miso* soup. The old woman was beaming, clearly pleased as punch. The wrinkles in her face, so unmistakable in the flophouse, were less obvious here. The unexpected thought suddenly came to me: she had probably been a pretty little thing when she was young. Her shortness would not have been as noticeable years ago as it is now, and I could see that her eyes and nose were normal enough.

"That damned Ibaraki," the old woman began as she picked up her chopsticks, "woman or not, she's got together with a guy an' is workin' con games, you know, a regular female *yakuza*. Her hand's quicker than her mouth, so when one of us gets hurt it's me who loses out, doncha know. She's too much for me."

She paused, but only briefly.

"Pachinko parlors hire bouncers, right? That damned Ibaraki's gonna get her butt kicked one of these days. She'll be beaten black and blue."

After we had eaten the old woman reached over without an invitation.

"Gimme a cigarette," she said and lit up.

"You know, I lost my mother when I was four. They tell me that at the funeral I was so happy to see people gathered together that I raised quite a merry ruckus. One of the older women, a relative, burst into tears when she saw this. 'Poor child,' she said. 'Course, I don't remember a thing. My father drank. He argued with my stepmother all the time. She had a child an' they had trouble making ends meet, I guess, so they sent me off to be a nursemaid when I was seven. An' the babies were hefty ones. The strap that held 'em on my back cut into my shoulders. That hurt, you can believe it. The father was a fertilizer wholesaler an' had five kids. They'd steam a mountain of sweet potatoes in a big bamboo basket, an' I could eat with their kids, as much as I wanted. The mother was a nice lady. I was much better off there, that's for sure. But babies grow fast, don't they. An' when they do, they don't need a nursemaid anymore, so off I went to other places, families where I couldn't get enough to eat. They'd be eatin' great stuff and I'd get the leftovers. If I'd cry they'd get mad an' call me pigheaded. My father drank an' got my money up front, so it was like I was sold off as a nursemaid. I was quite the dutiful daughter, I'll tell you. Sent him money while he was alive. I brought in quite a bit of money after I got to be a young woman, I'll tell you. A dutiful daughter, I was."

She didn't seem to resent her father.

"I was finally free when my father died and set up house with the manager of a movie theater in Asakusa. We were together three years. I lived the good life, with people respectfully callin' me 'Missus.' If my patron had lived I'd have spent my days as I damned please, the wife of a manager. He dropped dead one day of a heart attack an' it was hard times after that. My younger brother was doin' well, livin' in Kameido. A big tatami maker. He insisted I live with 'im, but his wife was a terrible woman an' I couldn't stay there."

I had no idea where the truth ended and the lies began.

Yuki and her friend got up and left, after which I and the old woman also left the restaurant. One of the restaurant workers followed us out front and took down the *noren* curtain that had been hanging over the entrance. The old woman once again recited the "kindness is rife" line, this time bringing her palms together at her chest and nodding. I was weary of all this. The thought of returning to San'ya after I had finished my work and being with her again was unbearable.

The Tsukamoto who wanted to talk to me wasn't Tsukamoto Suzuko. She was a magazine editor who was asking me to write fifty pages of short fiction. This request out of the blue was about to lift me out of my depression. As I had been lazing around in the bunk hotel, I had come to see all human beings, myself included, as little better than insects. I realized I had to stop seeing myself so. As soon as I realized this, I went round and round on this point: well, what does it matter if I *am* an insect? I suspected acceptance of this possibility was something that might well pull me up from the depths. I am a terribly ordinary person. Having others ignore me had soured me and made me spiteful. I relaxed when I understood this. For I knew the lack of attachment to life—I had twice tried to kill myself when I was in my teens—remained within me as part of my character.

I had forty days until the deadline. I decided to set to work after I wrote out several episodes of my serialization for the provincial paper. It was right at the end of the month, and I had already paid for next month's lodgings, but I didn't go back to the Tokuya, virtually living at my desk and writing at full speed five twelve-page short pieces for the newspaper. I finished my task, not even taking time off to go and see my friend's exhibition.

One day toward the end of the next month when I could afford to take a break, I felt like relaxing and going out for a night of drinking. There was a bar I had frequented in back of the Sensōji temple when I was staying in San'ya. It was a tiny place run singlehandedly by a good-natured woman, fiftyish, who had been a music hall performer. Her homemade dishes were delicious and the talk was interesting. I had blown one month's worth of rent at the hotel, but I intended to go back again the following month when I finished writing the fiction I had been commissioned to write, so as long as I was in Asakusa I decided to go pay the next month's rent. I had always made an effort not to get involved with others, but while I was away from the hotel writing I felt an overwhelming desire to take a long, hard look—unafraid now of entanglements and heedless of getting embroiled in disputes—at the women who floundered about in that cheap hotel. I saw in the wrinkled crone a personality I never could have conceived of before. Though I might be able to enumerate her failings—greed, servility, perverseness—I still did not understand the nature of what was at the heart of these failings. It seemed to me it did not necessarily follow that she was, at bottom, unalloyed wickedness.

I took the National Railway train and the subway, riding past Asakusa to South Senju. It would be a while before the laborers would be returning from work, so no one was at the Tokuya's front desk. I ascended the stairs carrying the shoes I had just taken off. The women's room was gloomier than I had remembered it and smelled musty, but this was curiously reassuring. I had become a doss house denizen without really being aware of the transformation. I felt neither shame nor sadness over this fact.

The bedclothes on my bed were neatly folded in the corner and my face towels and handkerchiefs no longer hung on the wire. I opened the box attached to the wall; my toothpaste, toothbrush, soap, and comb were gone without a trace. I had paid for the month. What had they done? The wrinkled crone's bed was also empty. And Yuki had moved on. Only Ibaraki was in bed. All the other beds were empty. It struck me as odd that everyone had moved out.

I called out to the resting figure.

"Excuse me."

A woman looked out from under her quilt. It was someone I'd never seen before. She sat up in bed.

"I'm so glad you're here," she said. "I'm all alone and surrounded by these laborers. I couldn't get a good night's sleep, I was so afraid."

She was a fair-skinned woman, fortyish.

"What happened to the others?"

"Others?"

"You don't know about the old woman who was here?"

"No. Somebody you knew, was it?"

"More or less."

"I was terrified and woke up again and again in the middle of the night. I took off work today to rest. I was so groggy from lack of sleep. I'm okay now that you're here. I'll be able to relax and sleep well tonight. The upper bunk is safer. C'mon over here."

She indicated the adjoining bed with a thrust of her chin. I had no interest in staying in a room that had no one in it. I decided then and there to leave the hotel. Yet where had everyone gone? With prices rising by the day, a woman now found it difficult to live on her own earnings, even if she did her own cooking. I wondered if they had all found work at places where they could also live. They were women who did not like living in like that, but maybe they could no longer afford the luxury of their distaste.

"You know," I began, looking up at the pale face of this middle-aged woman as I stood on the bare wooden flooring, "laborers drink, gamble, fight, and appear irresponsible, but they're better behaved than you'd think. They're all from the countryside. The second or third son in farming families becomes a laborer. They're not going to force their way in when a woman's sleeping, believe me."

Yuki had been young and not a bad-looking woman, but none of the laborers ever directed any obscene humor at her. And no one laid a hand on her in the hallway.

"That may be true enough, but I hear there're plenty of men who come here from prison."

"Well, maybe so, but—"

I fell silent. I did not know how I might explain the timidity peculiar to day laborers, and their basic goodness.

I noticed blue paper stuck between the futon and the wall. I had forgotten about this package, a secondhand magazine I had bought in Asakusa. When I unwrapped it the magazine was still there.

I couldn't bring myself to tell this middle-aged woman who was delighted by my arrival that I didn't intend to stay, so I left, pretending I was going to the bathroom. The clerk was on the stair landing, bending down over a cooking hibachi he was fanning. The hibachi, a teakettle atop it, sat in one corner of the landing, which was about six feet by nine; the kettle had boiled away through the night. There was also a cheap wooden desk and chair, and a tea strainer and mugs. The women had also cooked rice on this brazier. They would prepare the rice by turns, concerned all the while about inconveniencing the others. Bunk hotels had no cooking facilities for tenants. When I called to the clerk he stopped his fanning and turned to look at me.

"You've come back, have you?" he said with some surprise. "We didn't hear from you so we thought you'd been snared."

"Snared" apparently meant being held in the lockup or sent off to jail.

"Where'd everybody go?"

"Dunno where they went. They don't tell me and I don't ask."

"Did old Deko get work?"

The clerk grinned and held up his thumb, the sign for a man in Japan. "She found herself a good one and moved out. No woman is entirely useless."

I was dumbfounded.

"She's over seventy!"

"No, no! I'd guess she's fifty, give or take a year. She was a prostitute in the Tamanoi quarter. She made a bundle with her body when she was young, so she was quick to age. I've known her for a good while. She lived in a bunk hotel in South Senju with a projectionist guy who worked for the Shōchiku chain in Asakusa. She was already over the hill then. Maybe ten years ago—no, more than that."

I gathered this was the "movie theater manager" she had mentioned.

The woman who ran the place was at the front desk, so I got back my money for the two days left in the month.

"We're gonna stop renting to women as of next month," she told me. "It'll be all men from now on. Women are too much bother."

Was that why everyone had left? Women cook their meals even though there are no cooking facilities as such, and the hotel also has to set aside a special time for women to bathe. The Tokuya was the last place taking in women, and now San'ya would have none. I concluded that I would not be staying in San'ya again.

Midsummer more than four years later it turned out that I did stay in San'ya, where I had thought I would never stay again. I rented a private three-mat room in a Simple Accommodation called the Kotobukiya in South Senju, across the Namida Bridge intersection from San'ya. It was South Senju, but because there were so many bunk hotels there—the "simple accommodations"—everyone considered it part of the San'ya district of cheap hotels. I'm certain it was about this time that the name San'ya disappeared from the maps of the area because of the Domicile Designation Modification law. The Asakusa San'ya bus stop was changed to East Asakusa, 2-chōme, then to Kiyokawa, 2-chōme, which is what it is called today. But in everyday conversation people still call it San'ya and the day laborers refer to it as the Mountain, from the first character in the word San'ya.

I had chosen the Kotobukiya for my workroom because I had a project that needed to be done quickly. I put a desk in the middle of the three-mat room and spent all my time there. Most of the people staying at the Kotobukiya were there as families, so there was a community kitchen, but I took my meals at an eatery on the main street. The Tokiwaya hadn't changed, but all the employees were new.

A laborer called out to me one day as I left my lodgings for dinner.

"Miss! Miss!"

It was the time of day when laborers getting off work would go from bar to bar. I paid no attention; it's not acceptable for a man to call out to a woman like that. The man then quickened his pace to catch up with me.

"Miss, weren't you at the Tokuya?"

This stopped me in my tracks. I had thought that I might run into at least one of the women I knew from the Tokuya, but I had not met a single one.

"You were at the Tokuya?"

"Sure was. And I remember you. Hideko's sick."

"Hideko?"

"You were there about the time she was. The short one," he said, holding out a hand to show her height. "Deko. She was called Deko."

"Oh, I know who Deko is! You say she's sick?"

"You've got to help her!" the laborer said, his face now contorted and near tears.

"I can't give you a thing. I've run out of money myself."

If you gave someone money, 100 yen even, they would never leave you alone.

"I look like the sort who sponges off people, do I?" he asked, abruptly drawing himself up to his full height and looking down into my face. "Listen, I've been working in subway construction for a long time. Money's no problem. I've been taking care of Hideko."

I suddenly remembered.

"You're Mr. Kanasugi?"

The laborer nodded.

"Sorry for what I said. When you're poor you tend to be wary."

"I'd like to pick your brains about Hideko," he said, "that's all."

Had the clerk at the Tokuya been talking about Kanasugi when he said Deko had "found herself a good one"? Or had she left the Tokuya to be with another man, then got together with Kanasugi later? In any case, Kanasugi was a man in his forties, still in his prime. A laborer who was starved for affection might well be beguiled by the old woman, who had once been a prostitute and was not shy about playing up to men. No, doubtless Kanasugi, who was a religious man, was looking after the pathetic old woman's welfare simply out of kindness. I wanted to hear what Kanasugi had to say, but there was no place in San'ya where we could sit down and talk. Every establishment served liquor. Even places that sold rice cakes had beer. Kanasugi appeared to be a good-natured fellow, but I didn't know if he was surly in his cups or not, so I could hardly invite him for a drink. I thought about it for a minute.

"I'd like to hear what you have to say. Let's go to the South Senju Station. We can sit in chairs on the platform and have a leisurely chat."

"I've enough money for drinks," he said, pulling out a large purse from the waistband visible where his shirt was hanging open.

"Look," he said, opening and showing me what was inside, "You have a drink now and again, don't you?"

"Let's walk and talk," I said, starting to walk. "It's cooler walking. You asked to pick my brains, but I don't think you'll find much wisdom there. What's wrong with Deko?"

"You know, Hideko has no friends. You were with her at the Tokuya, so I'd like you to talk to her. She's bedridden with rheumatism, and when I took her to the welfare center and had them examine her, they found she has a bad heart. I wanted to get her into the hospital and did the paperwork to get medical assistance, but she doesn't want to go in. She says if you're hospitalized for free, they'll take your blood. She's convinced of it. When I tell her she has to, she goes into a rage like a madwoman and says I want to kick her out because I think she's a burden."

We walked along the street as it led us past one cheap inn after another, turning right, then left. Day laborers were squatting down in front of every inn, taking advantage of the cool evening air. Most were still in their working clothes, but some were wearing thin summer kimonos or had changed into lightweight *jimbei*, long, sleeveless jerkins. A man and woman walking together was not a common sight on these streets, so everyone stared at us.

"After I leave you, I'll go home and cook up some rice and feed Hideko. Got to give her a bath, too. It wears me out. I get up every morning while it's still dark, prepare the rice, make lunch as well. It's getting to me. I'd like you to convince her to go into the hospital."

I nodded. Twice I had visited people who had received financial aid and been hospitalized. Both had been at municipal hospitals in Tokyo. I knew that the hospitals had provided them the same food everyone else got and gave them the same medical care. I decided I would explain this to the old woman.

"I didn't say anything about it to Hideko," Kanasugi continued, "but I went to her younger brother to ask if he would look after her. He rejected the idea flat out, I'll tell you. Said he'd taken her off the family register, so he'd no connection with her anymore. If we're going to talk about family registers, what do you call Hideko and me? We're nothing. We've no relationship whatsoever!"

"So her brother's really in Tokyo, is he?"

She had told me her younger brother had a big tatami operation, but I had put that down as so much hot air.

"He and his wife are renting an apartment. It's a big room, six mats. With a room that size they could let her sleep in a corner, no problem. You'd think they could put in an extra portion when they cook their rice, that it'd be nothing with a wife in the house."

"He makes tatami mats?"

"Dunno. They've got a TV, so it doesn't look like they're hurting for money. They really have it in for Hideko. He said he couldn't stay out in the countryside because of her, because he had a sister who's a murderer, so the whole family ended up in Tokyo."

"A murderer?" I asked in astonishment.

"It happened a real long time ago, apparently when she worked as a nursemaid. He said she set fire to the home of the family where she was in service. The fire moved fast, burning to death the wife and baby. I don't know if it's true or not. There's no damn way I could ask her if she set fire to a house and killed people. And don't let her know you heard it from me."

I nodded. I certainly couldn't ask her such a question either.

"But Hideko is a kindhearted person, for all that, I'll tell you. She's fond of cats, you know, and was always giving sweets to the cat at the saké shop, and delighted when they let her hold it. I wanted to make it possible for her to live where she could have her own cat, but I couldn't."

He had one more thing to say: "She's not the sort of woman who'd kill someone."

In any case, I decided I would go see how she was. Whether she had set fire to a house or hadn't, I had to feel sorry for the old woman; she had been unable to go even to primary school and now she could not get around. Kanasugi had said she would eat anything, so I picked up thirty pieces of *inari-zushi,* rice balls wrapped in fried bean curd; he would not have to prepare dinner that night.

The Satsumaya, a Simple Accommodation, was a street beyond the sushi shop. It looked as though they had no lodgers with children; the concrete floor at the entrance was neat as a pin, without the clutter of kicked-off footwear.

"Hideko's friend's come to see how she is," Kanasugi explained to the desk clerk as he took out two pairs of slippers, one pair blue, the other red, from the footgear box to the right of the entrance. The red pair was still new and both had Kanasugi's name written on them in India ink.

"Who bought these slippers?"

"I did."

"You went shopping for them?"

"No, Hideko did."

I could guess how the old woman must have felt buying red slippers at her age, and I had the feeling I understood the nature of their relationship.

There were stairs going up to the second floor at the left of the entrance and a hallway about six feet wide running to the back of the building. The layout of the place was exactly the same as the Kotobukiya, except that the staircase was on the left side, not the right. Rooms lined both sides of the corridor. The very last door on the right had been left open. A woman's voice welcomed Kanasugi.

"I'm glad you're back. I missed you, all by myself here."

I can't say I had remembered what the old woman's voice sounded

like, but when I heard it I knew it was her. As I was about to follow
Kanasugi into the room I saw the old woman's face for the first time. I
stopped stock-still in the hall, stunned. She was swollen up like a bal-
loon; her wrinkles were gone. It was as though she would audibly pop
if you stuck a pin into her. Her face so puffed up she was no longer
recognizable, the old woman had been leaning against a pile of quilts,
her feet thrown out into the doorway and her gaze on the hallway as she
waited for Kanasugi. He stepped over her legs and went in.

"You wanna pee?"

He squatted down over her and lifted her up in his arms. As he did
so the air moved and a fetid smell wafted up to me. I suspected her
bottom was festering with her own filth in the heat. It seemed to me she
would soon be dead. Kanasugi had said earlier she had rheumatism, but
it was more than that. She appeared to be suffering from all sorts of
maladies. The old woman, resting her chin on his shoulder, looked at
me as I stood in the hall with an expression of tenderness in her eyes
that I never would have thought her capable of. She apparently did not
recognize me, however. Kanasugi, Hideko in his arms, went down the
hall and turned right. The washroom was at the end of the hallway, so
the toilet was probably to the right.

He didn't come back for a good long while. There was apparently a
bath to the left of the washroom; a man wearing only boxer shorts, a
wash towel in his hand, emerged from the bath and passed by, giving
me a quizzical stare as I stood in the corridor. Then the man who had
the room across from Kanasugi's returned from outside. Judging from
his appearance—white jacket, dress shirt and necktie—he was an employee at a trading house, a man with style. He also looked at me with
curiosity.

Kanasugi finally came back a good thirty minutes later.

"Not being able to pee is a real problem," he said to no one in particular as he came in. "Doesn't look like the medicine's helping any."

I had bought the *inari-zushi* because Kanasugi had said she would eat
anything, but as I entered the room I realized you couldn't very well
give it to someone this sick. The room was two and a half mats in size,
not three. The builders had been able to get it to a half by cutting a mat

lengthwise. Kanasugi, still carrying the old woman, pushed the piled-up quilts toward the entrance with his foot and set her down, this time with her back to the door.

"You passed water this morning, right? Once a day is enough, I reckon," he said, then indicated me with a thrust of his chin: "A friend has come to see how you are. And with a present for you. It's your friend from when you were at the Tokuya."

Kanasugi apparently didn't know my name. I suspected Deko didn't know it either. I didn't know her last name. She made no effort to look in my direction, so I went around and stood in front of her.

"Deko, it's me."

"Your friend's given you something to eat, so tell her thank you," Kanasugi said, getting up. "I'll go boil water for tea."

There was a tea cabinet in a corner. He opened the door. Inside were all sorts of things: pots, kitchen knives, a teakettle, rice bowls. A bottle of soy sauce and Mikkan vinegar stood atop the cabinet. I wondered if she still wanted to eat vinegared octopus, as sick as she was. If so, it seemed to me that Kanasugi would have gently fed it to her. The old woman fixed me with a steady gaze.

"Her eyes've got weaker," Kanasugi said as he started out of the room, kettle in hand.

Suddenly the old woman shouted.

"Damn you to hell!"

Her tone was vehement, not that of an invalid. Kanasugi, shocked, stopped in his tracks. I was also surprised. I looked at the old woman, then Kanasugi.

"I'll throw you out on your ass, you miserable whore! Making a pass at someone else's man! I'll kill you!"

I was aghast. It was me she was damning to hell. She looked as though she was about to leap at me. I was out of the room in an instant.

On summer nights people in San'ya are out and about. Being shouted at and called a whore had put me in a sour mood. I was not about to return to the Kotobukiya and simply sit there with no one to talk to. I went to a coffee shop on the second floor of a small building at the Namida Bridge intersection. I had been there before. A corner booth was empty, so I sat down, my face to the wall in front of me, and ordered a water high. As I sat there picking at my peanuts and mechanically drinking highballs I really didn't want, I began, willy-nilly, to feel the effects of the alcohol. I'm always able to develop a boundless magnanimity when I'm feeling my liquor. For the gritty old woman, uneducated and with death close at hand, Kanasugi was her one and only lifeline. Doubtless she herself knew that Kanasugi had his hands full with her. Thus while her illness might well be a trial for her, she would not utter a word of complaint, and when he came home at night she would tell him—in as charming a tone as she could muster—just how lonely she had been. And did this not require that she pull out all the stops? It was to be expected that she would see disaster looming if another woman intruded, and that she would explode in a jealous tirade. Since she herself had been a prostitute, she judged others by her own standards, reviling me as a "miserable whore." It took me five highballs and two hours to arrive at this conclusion.

There was a laborer sitting at the entrance to the Kotobukiya. He stood up when he saw me. To my surprise, it was Kanasugi.

"Here you are, miss," he said holding out a paper-wrapped package. I knew right away it was the rice balls. I took it without saying anything.

"I got you to come as a favor to me," he said, bowing deeply. "I'm really sorry. That's how crazy she is. Please don't hold it against her."

I had nothing to say. I still felt like shouting, but I had no anger for Kanasugi. He appeared to want to tell me something. I remained silent, however, so he left without broaching whatever it was. The dejected droop of his shoulders struck me as terribly pathetic.

I placed the rejected *inari-zushi*—three apiece—in the hands of children who had not yet gone to bed and were playing in the hallway.

After I went to bed that night it suddenly and inexplicably came to me that Kanasugi would abandon the old woman and disappear.

I'm sure it was in summer two years later. I had gone to San'ya for the first time in a good while, to a meeting at a Christian mission. I was making one of my infrequent appearances at an editorial meeting of a mimeographed magazine being published in San'ya and had gotten to know people from the mission, the result of my involvement in a relief organization for day laborers arrested in the San'ya riots.[2] There were fewer than ten people at the meeting, held in a room in one of the bunk hotels, but since we became so comfortably settled in, I failed to notice that my wristwatch had stopped, and by the time I realized it, the buses and the subway had stopped running.

"Now what am I going to do?" I said, looking about at my companions. "Should I stay here in San'ya? I wonder if there's an empty room somewhere?"

"There're empty rooms all over," someone assured me. Construction work was down because of the recession. Day laborers who could no longer make any money in San'ya had drifted off to laborer barracks at various job sites outside Tokyo. They said even the ambulances had stopped coming by.

I took a room on the second floor of the Matsuya, which faces Tamahime Park. The room looked out on the road. Next to the park was Hōrai Middle School.

The hotel hallway should have resounded with the footsteps of day laborers with the coming of the dawn, yet there was not a sound. I wondered if my watch was off again. When I opened the window I saw a canopy tent with gaudy red, white, and blue stripes, the sort of thing one associates with a beach umbrella at the seashore. The tent was on a street near the park. It grabbed my attention because the color scheme was not the kind one often encountered in San'ya. Day laborers were hurrying along the street beneath my window. Apparently none had stayed at the Matsuya.

No one was in the washroom and the curtain was still drawn over the window at the front office. I undid the latch on the front door, opened it, and let myself out. I could see what the canopy tent was all about as soon as I got out into the street. They were selling griddle cakes at the side of the road. In the park the so-called morning market, a flea market, was underway as usual. I went into the park from the Hōrai Middle

2. There were a number of riots in San'ya during the 1960s, most of which were directed against the police in response to what the laborers saw as unfair treatment of them.

School side. I was astounded at how the look of things had changed. When I had been staying at the Tokuya, the morning market had been the usual seedy flea market that had nothing you would want to buy: well-used washbasins, tea mugs, almost half of which had chipped rims, mud-caked *tabi* of the sort laborers wear; and when you spread out a charming light serge kimono, you'd find it full of moth holes. I had heard stories about how they were selling stolen goods, imported wrist-watches, precious gems, and the like, but I had never seen any myself. Nonetheless, the women at the Tokuya had been steadfast in their rum-maging, though buying only things to wear. Ibaraki was said to be an expert haggler, so they had all invited her to come shopping with them.

And how was it now? Vendors still spread their straw mats out on the ground to display their merchandise, but now everything for sale was new. There were all the clothes a laborer needed: work pants, rubber-soled *tabi*, undershirts, boxer shorts, belts. Every seller had at least an assortment of overnight bags large and small, surely a necessity when leaving San'ya for job sites in the countryside. One of the vendors was selling timepieces, fountain pens, toothbrushes, soap, and so on. I squat-ted down and picked up one of the women's wristwatches. The name of the manufacturer on the dial was so small I couldn't make it out. As I was thinking the unthinkable—surely this isn't a stolen Omega; if so, it's a good deal—I wound the stem of the watch, which was not running. It came off in my hand. I pushed the stem back into the watch and put it back down, my face a picture of innocence. As I moved away my heart was in my mouth lest I be called back.

I left the flea market on the side the gaudily colored canopy tent was on. Under it an elderly couple was hard at work. Day laborers stood about eating breakfast, or what would pass for it. The awning blocked out the morning sun, leaving all their faces in shade.

"It's good stuff! Shrimp! Squid! We've got everything!"

The old woman, shouting at the top of her lungs, put a griddle cake into a small scrap of newspaper she had folded in half, walked over to me, intent, willy-nilly, on putting it into my hand. I looked indifferently at the old woman's face as I resigned myself to accepting the food. I was flabbergasted. It was Hideko, the wrinkled crone. I had been certain the old woman was dead. The swelling of her face was gone without a trace, nor was she as thin as she had been when she was at the Tokuya, and this now made her look surprisingly healthy. She was wearing a brown, short-sleeved dress, which fit her well enough and was not at all baggy. She appeared not to have taken particular note of me; perhaps her eyes were failing or she had forgotten who I was.

The old woman continued to bellow out her wares—"Shrimp! Squid!"—putting a griddle cake into the hand of a passing laborer as she had done with me. A man who appeared to be her husband wordlessly cooked the cakes. He was probably younger than she was but was himself over fifty. He was a good match for her, a small, lean, dark man. The old woman kept up her strident shouting, giving it her all and then some. I had the impression that she even enjoyed the hawking. The tent was brand new, so they had probably started up their enterprise only recently, yet the squid in the griddlecakes was tough and salty. It was all I could do to eat the unpalatable squid. Because they were day laborers, I realized, they would not complain at having the tasteless cakes pushed off on them by high-pressure selling tactics. Human beings, nonetheless, are not mere insects, and in order to go on living they try to be resourceful and put their wisdom to work.

One day some time after that I decided to drop by San'ya on my way back from Asakusa, where I had business. I had heard that an elderly man I had developed a nodding acquaintance with at the mission was sick, and I wanted to see how he was.

I met the woman who ran the Tokuya standing, shopping basket in hand, in front of a fruit and vegetable shop in the Iroha Arcade, San'ya's shopping center. More than six years had gone by since I had stayed at her hotel.

"Well, hello," I said, "it's been a while, hasn't it."

She turned around and looked at me, but I could tell from her expression she didn't recognize me.

"I stayed in the women's room at your hotel."

It seemed to come back to her at last.

"You've been in San'ya all this time?" she asked in obvious

amazement, taking in from head to toe my smart outfit, not the sort of clothes you see on the tenants of bunk hotels.

"What happened to the women I shared that room with?"

"I haven't run into any of them, you know, and of course I would expect to if they were still in San'ya."

Then she remembered something.

"Oh yeah. Someone killed Deko."

I caught my breath. I had assumed the old woman was still selling her griddle cakes.

"Happened quite a while back. A month ago, I guess. Got into an argument with a laborer and he hit her. Must have caught her in the wrong place. They say she died in the ambulance. It was even in the papers, I hear. A short piece, though."

She made a gap of two centimeters with her thumb and forefinger.

"We didn't notice it either. The police came to ask about her. Someone told them she'd been at the Tokuya. When they showed us her picture we knew right away it was Deko. But we didn't know anything about her background. They said an argument started over a vendor getting stiffed by a customer, so we figured Deko had tried to get away without paying for something, right? She could well've done something like that. She caused us headaches, you know, leaving without paying her bill. But then the police told us Deko had been selling fried octopus cakes, and it was a laborer who tried to walk away without paying. You knew her, right? A little old woman, dark complexion, skinny."

"No, I didn't," I lied without a moment's hesitation. As I did so, I remembered that I'd heard Deko had a younger brother in Kameido. I did not want to talk about Deko with the woman from the Tokuya. It may well have been that Deko was killed the day I saw her.

I recalled Deko, whose body had lain unclaimed by kin, in the various guises she has taken throughout her life. I thought of how sad it was to have this happen to her after she had thrown herself so energetically into selling her griddle cakes. Then it suddenly struck me: when she had been a young prostitute in Tamanoi hadn't she tugged at the sleeves of the men who happened by with just the same determination?

From Behind the Study Door

NATSUME SŌSEKI

It is perhaps enough to say of Natsume Sōseki's stature in Japan that his portrait is on the 1,000-yen note. Sōseki (1867–1916) is a transcendent figure in modern Japanese history and literature who has enjoyed a continuing and robust popular interest both in his work and his life. He was born into a not-impoverished Edo family the year before the city was renamed Tokyo and became Japan's capital. Like other modern literati, he had an archetypal unhappy childhood and apparently became an unhappy adult who struggled throughout his life with depression and the ulcer complaint that would eventually kill him. Notwithstanding his embrace by the cultural establishment, he was an uncommon Japanese, an unpredictable eccentric who, for example, left a prestigious position in the capital to teach at an obscure middle school in the provinces. His education was a mix of traditional Confucianism and English literature, the climax of which was a tortured sojourn in London, where he apparently spent most of his time shut up in his room reading. While his serious works, novels such as Kokoro, *take up the question of individualism and the individual's relationship with others, the following reminiscences, four selections from his* Gurasu-to no uchi *(literally, Within the glass door), are a nostalgic recall by Sōseki of places from his childhood in the Shinjuku area of Tokyo. This was, of course, a time when Japan was just beginning the process of moving from an underdeveloped feudal society to a modern industrialized state. Readers familiar with his work will notice places and situations that have served as models for his fiction.*

The essays translated here were written in ill health the year before his death.

My old home, the one I was born in, was in a district of Tokyo known as Lower Baba, several blocks further out from where I'm living now. It was a district of the city, yet when I was a child it seemed to me a depressing place, one that had certainly seen better days, and that I could only think of as an absolutely insignificant highway post settlement. The name came from the fact that Lower Baba was below Takatanobaba, thus though you might find it on an old map of Edo, it would assuredly be in a remote corner, where you would still be at a loss to know whether it was within or outside the red lines that marked the boundaries of the city proper.

Nonetheless, several houses in that small district were built in the impressive godown style. One of them was the herbal pharmacy of Ōmiya Denbei, visible on the right as you went up the road. And when you went along the road to where it goes downslope, there was a saké shop called the Kokuraya, which had a wide frontage. This, of course, was not in the godown style, but it was a place with a history: when Horibe Yasubei, one of the forty-seven Loyal Samurai, avenged his lord at Takatanobaba, he first stopped at the saké shop and had a drink. I remember that tale from when I was a child, but I never actually saw the saké cup kept there that Yasubei was said to have put to his lips. I did, however, listen countless times to the *nagauta* ballads sung by O-Kita, daughter of the owner of the grog shop. I was a child, so I hadn't the slightest idea whether she was competent or incompetent, but when I stepped out onto the flagstones to go out into the street or wherever, I could hear O-Kita's voice quite clearly. On spring afternoons, for example, I often lingered a bit, leaning absentmindedly against the whitewashed wall of our godown, not exactly listening—or not listening—to O-Kita rehearsing her songs, my rapt soul enveloped in a serene glow. It was because of this that I in the end found myself knowing such *nagauta* lyrics as "Sycamore is the raiment for my journey."

There was also an oak woodworking shop and a smithy. A little toward Hachiman Hill Road there was also a covered vegetable market ringing a spacious dirt floor. Our family called the master there Sentarō the Wholesaler. I was told that Sentarō was a very distant relative on my father's side, but judging from their interaction, they were utterly estranged. It seemed to me their relationship consisted of nothing more than calling out comments on the weather when they ran into each other on the street. I remember hearing that Sentarō's only daughter had gotten involved with the storyteller Teisui,[1] a liaison so serious that the two threatened to kill themselves if they couldn't be together, but I can find in my brain no hint of how it all turned out. What I, as a child, found more intriguing was the sight of Sentarō sitting on a platform, brush-and-ink case and account book in hand, looking out over the mass of upturned faces and asking in his animated voice: "Hey! How much for these fine vegetables?" I watched the stirring spectacle of twenty or thirty hands raised as one beneath him, all directed at Sentarō as voices shouted out, strident as insults, the price argot of the market, using numbers quite different from *ichi, ni, san,* and all the while baskets of ginger, eggplant, and squash were being spirited away in thick-knuckled hands.

There was, of course, a bean-curd merchant, which you would almost always come across, no matter how remote the village. A *noren* of cord, thoroughly permeated with the oily odor of a tofu shop, hung in the doorway, and the wastewater that coursed past the front of the shop was so clear you could imagine yourself in Kyoto. The front gate of the Seikanji[2] Temple, around the corner from the tofu shop and halfway down the block, stood on a slight rise. The area behind its red-painted gate

---

1. Possibly Shinryūsai Teisui, who died in 1917.
2. A Pure Land temple in Kikui-chō.

was completely covered with a dense stand of bamboo, so that from the street you could not see inside, yet even now my senses recall the peal of the bell from within at morning and evening service. The clangor of the Seikanji bell, especially from the often fogbound autumn and through winter, when the icy winds blow, inevitably dampened the spirit of the small child I was then, as though something forlorn and chill was being thrust into my being.

I retain only a vague recollection that there was a variety hall next to the tofu shop. Perhaps my memory has been clouded; you would not expect to find a variety hall on the edge of town. Inevitably, every time I recall the place and look back at this long gone past, my eyes wide in wonder, I find myself struck by how singular this was.

The manager of this variety house was the head of the local fire brigade. He would often walk about in front of his hall shod in old Edo-style zori and the like, sometimes wearing a red-lined *happi* coat over a workman's apron of blue woven cloth, finely striped. His daughter O-Fuji also lived there, and I still remember quite clearly that she was a woman whose beauty was a topic for comment in our household. Later they adopted a young man to be her husband, a splendid-looking gentleman with an imposing moustache. This was a bit of a surprise for me. Even O-Fuji thought highly of this man, this new son that everyone was so proud of, but I later learned that he was merely a clerk or the like in a ward office somewhere.

They had apparently quit the variety hall and gotten out of the business by the time they brought the man into the family, but before that, when a dingy signboard still hung forlornly from the eaves at the front of the building, I often got spending money from my mother and set off for the hall to hear a *kōshaku,* a historical recitation. I'm pretty sure the name of the storyteller was Nanrin.[3] The strange thing was that apparently no storyteller but Nanrin ever appeared at the variety hall. I don't know where he lived, but wherever it was, his coming was certainly no easy feat, looking back on it now when we have decent roads and street

3. Tanabe Nanrin, one of a number of oral storytellers named Tanabe.

after orderly street of houses. On top of which, the house head count was always some fifteen or twenty, so I can only think of it as pure fantasy, no matter how much I give free rein to my imagination. I'm baffled now and don't know whether I learned the bizarre lines

"Hello there, Oiran," someone said, and the instant Yatsuhashi turned and asked "What is it?" there was the glint of a slashing blade.

from Nanrin then or picked them up later from a *rakugo* raconteur imitating such recitations.

If at the time I wanted to go to a neighborhood worthy of the name, the first thing I had to do was pass through a deserted field of tea plants or a bamboo thicket, or along a long path through rice paddies. Any real shopping usually meant going as far as Kagurazaka,[4] so it should not have been all that hard for me, used as I was to the necessity of it, and yet when I came to the straight-arrow road of five or six blocks, having gone up the hill at Yarai and made my way past the Sakai family's fire lookout, I would come to Temple Town where everything was in eternal dimness even at midday, as though the whole of the sky was overcast.

Numberless huge old trees with trunks some two to three arm spans in circumference stood along the embankment there, and since the breaks now and again between the trees were blocked by deep stands of bamboo, on any given day there was not a single moment that allowed a glimpse of sunlight. It goes without saying that were I to step into my fair-weather geta and go down to *shitamachi*, the plebeian area of Tokyo, I would certainly find myself in trouble. That the thawed ground there was more terrible than either rain or snow is branded in my memory.

There appeared to be the fear of fire even in an out-of-the-way place like Lower Baba, and so it was not surprising to find a high ladder standing where the road curved. And atop this ladder was suspended, not unexpectedly, an old fire bell. I well remember those days as though they were yesterday. The small eatery, too, immediately beneath the fire bell presents itself spontaneously before my mind's eye. I cannot forget the

4. At the eastern edge of what is now Shinjuku Ward, Kagurazaka in Sōseki's youth was largely known for its brothels. Today it is home to a wide variety of restaurants.

mix of smoke and the aroma of piping-hot boiled vegetable dishes waft-
ing through the cord *noren* hanging in the doorway and drifting out into
the road, to meld with the twilight haze. A haiku I composed when my
friend, the poet Masaoka Shiki, was still living was, in fact, to memori-
alize the bell.

> Standing in a row
> Together with the old fire bell—
> Tall trees of winter

Generally, the memories I have of home are these sort of rustic recollections, a lodgment of suggestions of the plaintive, the vaguely lonely. So
I was surprised just the other day by my still-surviving elder brother's
description of my sisters' visits to the theater in those days. On reflection
I can only feel that our having lived so ostentatiously long ago is truly
like a dream to me.

The theaters of the day were all in Saruwaka-chō.[5] He told me they
always wanted to get to Kannon Hall, the main temple in Asakusa, by
early morning. At a time when there were no rickshas or trolleys such a
trip was apparently no minor enterprise. My sisters would get up in the
middle of the night and make their preparations. There could be distur-
bances along the way, he said, so as a precaution a manservant always
accompanied them.

Leaving Tsukudo, they would go from Kakinoki Backstreet to Ageba[6]
and board a canopy boat they had arranged for beforehand from a boat
rental shop there. I can imagine how filled their hearts were with anticipation as they were rowed along the Kanda River, going ever so slowly
from the front of the gun works in Koishikawa to Yanagi Bridge, passing
Ochanomizu on the way. Their progress, of course, could not come to
an end there, which is why those days long ago when people were unconcerned about the constraints of time are all the more a source for us
of pleasant retrospection.

5. An area north of the temple complex, to which Kabuki theaters had been banished
in the mid-eighteenth century.
6. All three places are in the northeastern corner of what is now Shinjuku Ward.

My brother told me that once their boat made it out into the Sumida, it would head upriver, passing under Azuma Bridge, and arriving near the Yūmeirō[7] in Imado. My sisters would debark there, walk as far as the teahouses that fronted the theaters, then, finally having been brought to their theater, take the seats that had been set aside for them. These seats were always *takadoma*, raised box seats in front of the galleries at either side. Such a location nicely lent itself to exposing their attire, faces, and coiffure to the gaze of the run-of-the-mill theatergoer, so those who fancied ostentation contended with one another for those seats.

Between acts an actor's assistant would come over and invite them to visit his dressing room. Whereupon my sisters would follow the man, who would be dressed in a patterned crepe kimono under a man's *hakama* skirt, and go to the dressing room of one of their favorite actors, perhaps Tanosuke or Tosshō,[8] and have the actor draw something on their fans. This was doubtless a display of their vanity, a display that could only be bought with money.

On the way home they would be rowed back in the same boat to the landing at Ageba, returning the way they had come. A manservant would go to meet them with a lantern, again for safety's sake. They would arrive at the house around twelve o'clock, to put it in the time-keeping terms we use now. Which is to say, they were able to see a play only by leaving in the middle of one night and returning in the middle of the next.

When I heard this tale of theatergoing extravagance, I was inclined to doubt that this sort of thing had really happened in our family. I felt as though I were hearing a story of the old days of a wealthy townsman's family somewhere in *shitamachi.*

Of course, our family was not of the samurai class either. My father was a townsman, the head of our district, and had to take part in gaudy social give-and-take. The father that I knew was a bald-headed old man, but when he was young he had studied the *jōruri* epic-ballad in the Kyoto

7. A fashionable restaurant on the Asakusa side of the river.
8. The Kabuki actors Sawamura Tanosuke III (1845–78) and Sawamura Tosshō III (1838–86).

style and, they say, sent a woman he was a special patron of new crepe bedding for house display, as was the custom.

There were rice paddies in Aoyama then, and I was told that the rice brought in from them alone was adequate to feed our family. My third eldest brother, for example, who in fact is still with us, tells me one could hear the ceaseless sound of rice being hulled. In my recollection, everyone in the district was much impressed by our entryway, a frequent topic of conversation. At the time I did not appreciate the significance of this, but when I think back on it now, it occurs to me that was probably because we were the only house in the district which had such an intimidating entryway with a small porch attached. I still remember the barb pole, sleeve hook, and throat fork[9]—all implements for subduing wrong-doers—that greeted you as you came up on the porch, which, together with a well-worn horse lantern, all hung there in a row.

There is a district near where I now live called Kikui-chō. I was born there—when it was called Lower Baba—so I know it better than most people. And yet when I left home, wandered the world, then returned home, I found that Kikui-chō had grown quite a bit, extending itself eastward in no time as far as Negoro.[10]

The name of the district, which has been such an important part of my life, has not the slightest nostalgic resonance for me, the sort that would summon up my past. Perhaps this is because I was raised daily hearing its name. As I sit alone in my study, however, chin resting on my hand, and let my mind follow its own course like a boat drifting on the current, my thoughts from time to time run straight into the four *kanji* that make up the name of Kikui-chō and linger there.

In the old days when Tokyo was called Edo, this district seems not to have existed. Perhaps when Edo was renamed Tokyo or perhaps much later—I don't know what the reign era was for sure—but in any case I know for a fact that my father coined the name.

9. These long-handled implements were employed by officialdom in the Edo era to subdue miscreants. The first two hooked the wide, floppy sleeves of the garments of the day; the working end of the body fork consisted of two sharp metal prongs separated by roughly the width of an adult throat.

10. Now part of Benten-chō in Shinjuku Ward.

Our family crest is a chrysanthemum inside the character for well,[11] so he used the words for chrysanthemum and well, which together are pronounced *kikui*. I don't know whether I heard this from my father himself or someone else told me, but be that as it may, it remains with me to this day. My father, after the position of village head was abolished, held the post of ward head for a while, so perhaps he may have been free to do so. He was very proud of this, but looking back on his vanity at this remove, any disgust I have quickly dissipates; it only makes me smile.

Above and beyond this, my father gave his family name Natsume to the long sloping road in front of our house that one had to go up whenever he left the house and went south. Unfortunately, this did not become as well known as Kikui-chō and today it simply remains a road on the hill. However, the other day someone came to visit and told us that if you check the place names around here on a map, you would find a Natsume Hill Road climbing the hill, so it just might be that the name my father gave the road is serving some useful purpose even now.[12]

How many years has it been since I left Tokyo, then returned again to the Waseda area? Before I moved into my present residence—I don't remember whether I was purposefully looking for a house or on the way home from a picnic—I was surprised to find myself for the first time in a long while beside the house I had once lived in. I could see from the front gate the old roof tiles on the second floor, which set me to wondering how it was it was still surviving, but I then went on my way without stopping.

I passed by the front gate again after I had moved to Waseda. Looking in on it from the front, I had the feeling that nothing had changed, but then I noticed a sign on the front gate that I had not anticipated: Rooms To Let. I wanted to see the rice paddies of old Waseda, but the area was now developed. I wanted to look again on the bamboo groves and the tea fields of Negoro, but I could discover no trace of them anywhere. I could not even tell if my suppositions—I guessed they were probably around there somewhere—were on the mark or off.

11. The sinograph for well resembles a tic-tac-toe grid.
12. The name, in fact, survives.

I stood there dumbfounded. *Why was it that only my old house exists here like a ruin from the past?* In my heart I wished that it had collapsed early on.

Time has its power. Last year on a walk toward Takata I found myself passing through the area and saw that my old home had been torn down and that a new rooming house was being built in its place. And a pawn-broker stood nearby now. A spare fence enclosed the front of the pawn-broker's and shrubbery had been planted behind it. Three pine trees had been pruned so severely they looked almost deformed, which made me feel I had seen them before. Years ago I had composed the haiku

> Mismatched shadows of
> Three pines, their heights uneven
> Of a moonlit night.

As I made my way home, I wondered if these were not those three.

Firefly Tavern

SAEGUSA KAZUKO

The unreality Saegusa Kazuko (1929–) offers us in her short piece Hotaru sakaba *(Firefly tavern) is subtlety itself, a mode we are not unaccustomed to in the Japanese cultural tradition. Again, as in other successful tales of the extraordinary and inexplicable, the narrative is rooted in the humdrum, in this case ordinary folk indulging in the venerable convention of* hashigo-zake, *"ladder drinking," as it is referred to in Japan, that is, pub crawling. Saegusa's characters, in fact, are only going from one particular bar to another, the latter in the western reaches of Tokyo, but the principle of hopeful adventure, the standard motivation in such excursions, is in place, as are the reader's expectations that something unusual is afoot. That the Möbius strip may be a bleak metaphor for the treadmill of life does not weaken these expectations.*

The Jindaiji Temple, much mentioned but never gained, is in Chōfu and is the second oldest temple in metropolitan Tokyo, junior only to Asakusa's Sensōji.

It was founded in the eighth century and is home to a bronze statue of unknown provenance that is believed to be even older than the Jindaiji.

First published in 1980, "Firefly" moves quickly, alternating its ample, but crisp, dialogue with brief description that is near staccato in patches, offering an interesting contrast with the extended style of many earlier writers, Mishima being only the most obvious.

Saegusa, who majored in philosophy in college and wrote her graduation thesis on Nietzsche, is seen by some as a difficult writer who seasons her variety of magic realism with elements from the classical tradition, both Japanese and Western. She has done considerable research in Greece and is currently studying the ideal of matriarchy in the ancient culture. She has won a number of literary awards and is also respected as a literary critic.

I don't know how you write the name Mizuyachi in sinographs. On the professor's bottle we keep in our bar his name is simply written in large *katakana* script, so I'd guess no one in the bar knows what the characters are.

The professor apparently teaches anatomy or something like that. I first realized he was a college professor when his students wandered in, saying we were the third stop for their class's night out. But I don't know whether he's a full-time lecturer or an assistant professor. From his age I can only guess he's not a full professor.

The professor tells us he's thirty-five, but sometimes he looks a year or two over forty. It just might be that he is actually forty. The crown of his flattish head steams when he's feeling the effects of alcohol. His broad, shiny forehead is covered with beads of sweat. His small bulging eyes—what you could call goggle eyes—begin to twinkle. Suddenly he is loquacious.

"Which is to say, this, uh . . ."

The professor twisted a chopsticks wrapper at its middle, then brought the two ends together.

"Which is to say, it's a question of the antiuniverse versus the positive universe. Antimatter versus matter. You see, the axis of coordinates X, Y, and Z . . . the natural law's—"

"You're talking about image, aren't you?"

"Exactly. The Möbius strip can do this in two dimensions."

"Uh-huh."

The one grunting agreement is the nameless youth. He's twenty-seven or twenty-eight. He's a regular customer at the bar. When I asked him what his name was, he curtly answered: "Me? I've got no name."

He invariably writes an equilateral triangle on his bottle, each leg about an inch long. And so he is the Triangle Guy. Next to Triangle is a young man who utters not a word, only smiles quietly to himself. The two of them always come together. They're apparently friends.

"So, *Sensei*," I said, putting in my own uncomprehending two cents' worth, "you mean you zipped along this road that's like a Möbius strip?"

Professor Mizuyachi wiped his brow with his handkerchief and nodded vigorously.

"Right."

"Let's go and take a look!" Triangle shouted. The four of us jumped up as one. It was two in the morning. Professor Mizuyachi hailed a taxi as soon as we got outside. He had me and Triangle and the Smiler sit in the back seat and he sat next to the cabbie.

"Well," he said, "head toward Mitaka. Of course, I don't know whether they'll be open or not."

"Right. It's two o'clock."

"If they're not open," I said, "we can just come back."

Triangle agreed with me: "That's true."

"Anyway," Professor Mizuyachi said, "it's right in the middle of a field. The area's pitch-black and when you hightail it along the road in the middle of the pitch-black fields you can see fuzzy yellow lights in front of you."

"Aren't they fireflies?"

"That's right. Fireflies."

The Smiler, who had been silent all this while, suddenly spoke up.

"Driver, are there fireflies around here?"

For some reason this startled the rest of us and we regarded the Smiler's face.

"Well, I haven't come across any. You might find some at the Jindaiji temple though."

Professor Mizuyachi: "There're fireflies at the Jindaiji?"

"I just have that feeling somehow, but I haven't seen any."

The Smiler interjected a mumbled "Fireflies need water."

"What's with you tonight?" asked Triangle. "You're talking."

Professor Mizuyachi opened the window and let in the cold air. "We've finally got away from the city! Smell that fresh greenery!"

"It really *is* pitch-black!" I said.

"Please take Shinkawa Boulevard," said the professor.

The taxi stopped for a stoplight at an intersection where there was not a single car, then started to move again. The darkness was rent. The asphalt road before the taxi, illuminated by the headlights, drifted pale before us. Everyone abruptly fell silent. The taxi continued on for some time with its silent passengers.

Then another signal. The road had a lot of signals for a street with so little traffic. As our taxi approached, the light, ready and waiting, turned red.

That's when it happened. The knocking on the driver's window. Incredulous eyes turned instantly to the sound and saw a bespectacled face peering in from the darkness.

"This is the road to Tsutsujigaoka, is it?"

The man outside the window appeared to be another taxi driver.

"Actually I'm not that familiar with this area," the driver answered, almost grudgingly. "Go left at the next signal or the one after it." He put the car slowly into motion. A little while before when he was telling us about the Jindaiji temple and the fireflies he seemed quite familiar with the area; was that just an act?

After the car started moving Professor Mizuyachi began muttering to himself. No one responded, however.

"Right. That's right. Anyway, you should go left. That should be the way to go, given our location."

What sort of fare was riding in the other cab? A drunk? A woman whose labor pains had started? That's usually the case in the middle of the night.

We were silent as the taxi went on. We passed two or three signals. The distance between the streetlights grew farther apart. Perhaps it was a residential area or we might even be driving past one side of a park.

Even so, there was an incredibly long wall. And again a signal at a break in the wall.

Quite suddenly the driver stifled a cry. Oversized eyeglasses had thrust themselves into the window on the driver's side.

"Say, you said left here, did you?"

It was the man from a little while ago.

"Yeah, that's right," the driver answered, his voice husky. He did not, however, complain about the other man surprising him. We had gotten the taxi in front of the Ogikubo station. We had then ridden it for close to twenty minutes. We could guess the general direction we were headed, but only Professor Mizuyachi knew where we would finally be taken. Since everyone had fallen silent, the driver also stopped talking. Perhaps he was feeling uneasy for some reason.

How much time elapsed after that? Five minutes. No, you can't calculate it quite like that. I thought we'd be there any minute now for sure, but I could see nothing resembling lights. This road . . . just what was it?

Then the professor craned his neck.

"Ah! Turn left at the corner."

The driver said nothing.

Then we could see them in front of us. Dim yellow lights.

"Thank goodness they're open."

The instant we got out the driver flipped the door switch, shutting the car door. His relieved expression was precisely that of a man disposing of something disagreeable. Absolute darkness surrounded us as the taxi's taillights sped away.

"Look! Look! Huge fireflies!" the Smiler said, his shoulders shaking with suppressed laughter.

Hiragana script spelled out the word MÖBIUS in yellow lights.

"Professor Mizuyachi," Triangle said, "you gave it that name, didn't you? You told the woman who runs it to give it that name. I'll bet anything you did. There's more to you than meets the eye."

Professor Mizuyachi emitted a guttural laugh. The expression on his face was somehow different now.

"Good evening," he said, pushing open the door. His voice was wheedling, quite unlike what it was when we were in the bar in Ogi-kubo.

"My goodness! An entire regiment today!"

The mistress of the tavern had used an old expression from the war, though she was not that old, about the age of the professor. She made no special attempt to make herself look younger. She had a small, compact face that held no suggestion of makeup. She resembled a particular stage actress, but the woman's name wouldn't come to mind.

"I really appreciate your coming all this way."

The woman affably handed each of us a steaming towel to wipe our hands and face.

"A solitary house," Triangle said, "in the middle of a field."

"Exactly. And come morning it will evaporate, lock, stock, and barrel. On the straw will be scattered two or three leaves, nothing more."

The mistress of the bar played along with the conceit. No, it wasn't a matter of playing along. That may have been the truth.

The place was bigger than I had expected. There were two booths that seated four people each, and a bar with space for seven. Three customers were at the bar. The three, their backs to us and their faces obscured, wore, starting from the man on the left, a black polo shirt, a snow-white dress shirt, and a red T-shirt. Each man had a close-cropped crew cut.

A poster advertising a pro boxing match was tacked to the wall at the side of the booths.

"*Mama's* guy used to be a boxer," Professor Mizuyachi explained, employing the English word Japanese use for a woman who runs a bar.

"Flyweight?"

"No, junior flyweight."

"He's here now?"

"No."

A middle-aged man emerged from the rest room.

"Him?"

"No." Professor Mizuyachi called loudly to the man: "Hey, Yasu! Yasu, come on over."

Yasu introduced himself as soon as he sat down.

"I'm a fisherman. I specialize in deep-sea commercial fishing. I'm more like a crewman than a fisherman. I've been on a five-day shore leave, but I go back to work tomorrow."

"He apparently manages the whole operation here," the professor explained, then introduced the three of us: "These are my friends."

"Intellectuals, eh," Yasu said sourly. "All Professor Mizuyachi's friends are intellectuals."

"Yasu," I joked, "you're Mama's boyfriend?"

Yasu's cheeks twitched abruptly in surprise.

"Don't talk nonsense. Mama has a fine man," he said. His eyes were suddenly red-rimmed.

"Well, Yasu," said the professor, "you and I are a couple of bachelors." The two men clinked their highball glasses together in a toast and drank.

"Say, *Sensei*," said Mama, calling to him from behind the bar, "we have some Chinese dumplings. Would you like some?"

Professor Mizuyachi answered with childlike energy: "Yes indeedy, I would."

It finally came to me: the woman looked like the actress Naraoka Tomoko, but somehow I couldn't bring myself to say as much.

The professor and Yasu began to talk about the refrigeration of fish. Triangle latched onto Mama and questioned her about the gym the boxers pictured in the poster were affiliated with. The Smiler sat next to Triangle and interjected not a word.

Yasu was suddenly making a point in a loud voice: "These days, because it's salt-broiled sea bream . . . I'm in commercial deep-sea fishing, but I really hate it."

Professor Mizuyachi said nothing.

"I'm a product of the Inland Sea. Used to be a fisherman working out of an honest-to-god fishing village. I'm no damn boxer!"

I listened uneasily to Yasu talk. The fact that a fisherman would come here to a place so far from the ocean deepened my confusion all the more.

Mama was standing behind the bar. Triangle took advantage of this to ejaculate: "Ah! This is getting to me!"

I don't know what Professor Mizuyachi made of this, but he forgot all about Yasu and fixed his gaze on Triangle. The Smiler merely shuddered.

I said nothing. At four I was going to suggest we leave. It was fifteen minutes to.

"We didn't see any fireflies," I ventured.

"There might be some," Triangle said, "if we go to Jindaiji temple."

"The Jindaiji, eh? I wonder if it's light out by now."

Yasu shook his head: "The Jindaiji? Listen, it'll take you forty minutes to get there walking. And you won't find many taxis passing by this time of night."

"Then all the more reason to walk there," Triangle countered, "since we have to wait for the first train anyway."

"People!"

The professor sprang to his feet.

"People! You really think you can get the first train or whatever? This road is a Möbius strip!"

"Professor Mizuyachi," said Mama amiably as she saw us to the door, "you're really in your cups tonight, aren't you."

Outside it was daybreak. There were, not surprisingly, cabbage fields on both sides of the road. The yellow lights of the Möbius glimmered obscurely amongst the cabbage fields. Its yellow lights in the flush of dawn seemed more like fireflies than they had in the middle of the night.

"That," said the professor, looking back and thrusting his chin toward the yellow lights of the Möbius, "will disappear without a trace in a little while." He abruptly began hurrying away, walking in the middle of the road.

"You're really going to the Jindaiji?"

"Of course. Weren't we going to look for morning fireflies?"

I and Triangle and the Smiler, none of whom had the slightest idea where he was, followed unsteadily after Professor Mizuyachi in, of course, the middle of the road. My skin grew hot as we walked along. It's the feeling I have when drunkenness takes sudden leave of me. It would be quite a while before the sun rose. There was not a soul on the main street, nor a dog in sight. Only the traffic signals repeated again and again their pointless flashing. They were wondrously vivid in the air, which was light now, but not yet touched by the rays of the sun.

"What would happen if we had something liquid here?" Triangle muttered as he approached a vending machine at the side of the road. "If gravity is merely curved space—"

"Hurry up, jackass!" the Smiler said. Each person deposited their 100-yen coin, then drank their coke. Suddenly we heard a dull, drawn-out sound. We looked back and saw that the Smiler had picked a dandelion and was blowing a tune on its stem. The dandelion, of course, was bereft of its flower; only its small, firm head from which its fluffy seeds had likewise long since flown away remained at the tip of the overgrown stem. The Smiler had picked a dandelion which had grown toward the road through an opening in the chain-link fence of a parking lot.

I immediately did the same, as did Triangle. Then Professor Mizuyachi. Four adults walked along intently playing a simple tune on the stems. But this amusement, too, soon came to an end. What remained: the absurdly wide road to the Jindaiji temple. A grove of trees came into view. We had been walking for almost an hour. Perhaps that was the temple.

"What's the time?" Professor Mizuyachi asked. He had his own watch. I wondered why he asked.

"Five to five," Triangle answered.

Professor Mizuyachi came to a halt.

"Hmm. If we turn here we'll be at Jindaiji," he said, pointing at a white bus-stop sign on which were written the words "Jindaiji Elementary School."

"But if we go to the temple now we'll find the morning fireflies have gone off," the professor said, looking at our faces. "So, we've come this far, but we needn't go to the temple." His words were like a muttered incantation.

I was dumbfounded, but since neither Triangle nor the Smiler said anything, I likewise made no protest.

The professor grunted and nodded with apparent satisfaction.

"Then would you mind coming this way?" He grinned and gracefully stepped off onto a side road. He briskly strode down the side road, a long and narrow open space that you could scarcely call a road. Beyond the space was a field of ten or twelve acres where someone was growing tomatoes and eggplants. A two-story apartment house had been built in a part of the field that had been cleared. No doubt the landlord of the apartment building was the owner of the farmland.

"Here we are."

Professor Mizuyachi climbed the stairs. He opened the door, the key clicking in the lock.

"This is my apartment. Please come in. I try not to return to my apartment before 5 A.M."

Then he emitted a high-pitched cackle.

"Ah, of course, you live by yourself," said Triangle, standing squarely in the middle of the room he had just been admitted to and scrutinizing it carefully. An odd smell hung in the air. Professor Mizuyachi opened all the veranda windows, but that was not about to dispel the odor. It was, indeed, the smell of a school lab on a hot afternoon.

The professor's closet doors were all open. Half of the closets had futons and suits in them, but the other half were filled with stacks of books. And books projected themselves from bookshelves and closets and stood in high stacks on the tatami. There seemed, in fact, to be more books on the tatami than anywhere else. The apartment had two rooms, one of which was taken over entirely by books.

"I finally made up my mind the other day to do the laundry. It was actually the first time in three months."

Half the room, from lintel to lintel, was strung with line, and clothes hung from these. They were clothes of all sorts: underwear, suits, dress shirts, windbreakers. It was not clear which of these had not been washed for three months. It was a strange sight: all of the clothing was on hangers, and these swayed over the piles of books. I felt a vague nausea as I stood there amongst books left open to colored illustrations of human internal organs and the sleeves of an undershirt suspended above them.

"Would you like some tea?"

There were apparently only two teacups in the apartment, so when the professor got to me he poured my tea into a consommé tureen with handles on each side. When I finished my tea, however, we had run out of things to talk about and were ill at ease.

"Shall we go?" Professor Mizuyachi asked with obvious discomfiture.

"I hate this place. I try my best to stay away. When I finally wander back at dawn it comes to me how happy I'd be if this apartment disappeared."

"Let's go," Triangle said, his hand on the Smiler's shoulder as they descended the stairs. Then he muttered yet again: "This is getting to me!"

The Smiler said nothing. But suddenly he stopped smiling and knitted his brows, seemingly on the verge of tears.

"Let's go back to Ogikubo," the professor said. "We'll be back on track once we get back to Ogikubo."

We started walking, Professor Mizuyachi in the lead.

I silently quickened my pace. For the first time that night the question of what in the world we were doing suggested itself to me. In any case, it took us some five minutes before we were finally able to get a taxi.

"Ogikubo."

Hearing the name of our destination, I suddenly felt my exhaustion.

"Professor Mizuyachi," Triangle asked, "there're no classes today?"

Of everything we had said the entire night, these were the first straightforward words uttered. Not surprisingly, everyone picked up on this and smiled wryly.

"Today's Sunday," the professor answered, "so I have no refuge." He shook his head in disgust.

The Smiler, who had been looking out the window, uttered a strangled cry and raised himself partway off the seat.

The professor, eyes fixed straight ahead, spoke in a voice that had not a hint of emotion: "That's right, the Möbius has vanished."

I looked back, slowly twisting my body around in the taxi. Though none of the men, not Professor Mizuyachi, Triangle, nor the Smiler, looked back, I turned and stared all the more intently.

No one said anything.

For whatever reason, the Möbius was not there. I had expected to see the cozy bar with the bay windows and the yellow sign, the lights turned off, as it should look in the morning. My eyes widened in surprise in spite of myself.

"You looked, did you?" the professor asked without turning around. "It's the women who have courage, after all."

I glossed this over with a laugh. I said nothing about the Möbius not being where it was supposed to be. What the woman who ran the bar had said was true after all: "And come morning it will evaporate, lock, stock, and barrel. On the straw will be scattered two or three leaves, nothing more."

After that no one in the car had a thing to say. We arrived in front of Ogikubo station at ten to eight. Professor Mizuyachi was suddenly flustered.

"A newspaper. I've got to get a newspaper."

He hurried off toward a kiosk.

"Hey! What'll we do?" Triangle asked the Smiler. "You wanna go to a sauna maybe, then go back to the room and sleep?"

The Smiler had no response. Professor Mizuyachi returned with four newspapers. I don't know what he had in mind, but he gave one to each of us and deftly set the last one atop his head.

"Well, I'll be off now."

Then he went down the station stairs, his newspaper shade obscuring his face. I rolled up the newspaper he had given me and started walking.

"Goodnight!" Triangle shouted right at my back. On my way home I threw away the paper, unread.

Sparrows

IROKAWA TAKEHIRO

Irokawa Takehiro's (1929–89) Suzume (Sparrows), published in 1985, goes beyond the magic realism of Hino Keizō's "Jacob's Tokyo Ladder" into surrealism, but one sufficiently tempered with autobiography to provide reassuring access for even the most literal-minded of us. Tokyo-born Irokawa's reminiscences of his youth in the city lay a foundation of realism on which incredulous readers can hunker down as the more fanciful patches whirl about them. And in fact, the author of "Sparrows" was briefly institutionalized in 1968 after a mental breakdown characterized by visual and auditory hallucinations. That this fantasy revolves around one of the most prosaic and dependable institutions in the world, the Japanese rail system, naturally makes Irokawa's bizarre tale all the more outlandishly effective.

Irokawa's youth was infinitely bleaker than what we might imagine from this short story. Like many of his generation, too young for military service but old enough to contribute to the faltering war effort, he was dragooned — amidst the intensive bombing of the cities — into work in factories. Unlike most of his contemporaries, however, he was rebellious and considered a troublemaker. When a mimeographed magazine he had secretly published came to light in the pipe factory he was working in, he was cut off from school, effectively ending his formal education. At war's end Irokawa embarked on a chaotic odyssey over the burned-out ruins of Tokyo, selling on the black market, peddling on the street, even making ends meet by gambling. He eventually found more traditional employment but drifted from one dead-end job to another. In 1961 he made a remarkable debut in the literary world by winning a short-story competition for new writers.

Irokawa was subsequently the recipient of major literary prizes and, like a number of other Japanese novelists, wrote both "serious" fiction — the pathogenic "Sparrows" is one of the better known of these — and more popular, lighter stories, works with whimsical titles such as Sixteen Previous Convictions *and* Chronicle of a Mah-Jongg Drifter *(written under the name Asada Tetsuya).*

When I was a young lad, which is to say, some fifty years ago, there were a lot of kids who, when asked what they wanted to be when they grew up, would answer "a motorman." I also remember giving such a reply. Doubtless this is akin to kids these days being interested in space aliens and robots.

Both electric and steam trains were running long before that, but they meant nothing to me. When you're young you take notice of the world outside and things around you as they come, one by one. In the process of doing this you come across things that are far beyond a child's everyday sensibilities, and I think the train was an instance of this for me. It's impossible to feel kinship with a steel object hurtling over rails, and, conversely, one might also be attracted to it. Adults would laugh when they heard the response "a motorman," but since I was merely stifling malice toward trains and giving a "sound" reply out of deference to the adult, the word motorman immediately came to mind. It was what adults wanted to hear. I certainly didn't think I could become a motorman. Quite the contrary, they seemed to me to be cold, distant creatures, like space aliens (at the time, my image of a motorman was of a somewhat bucktoothed cinder-faced man wearing thick-rimmed glasses, lines scoring both sides of the nose).

As for automobiles and buses, they were somehow gentle and sweet, and their movements were comprehensible, though that may have been because there were so few of them. Airplanes had yet to become ordinary. Once I was struck dumb when an airship appeared in the patch of blue sky visible from our garden, hemmed in by adjoining houses, but that only happened once.

The reason I couldn't skillfully cope with trains and the like, aside from the fact of the violent nature of these objects, may also have been because the world of the trains seemed, in its entirety, somehow to have something akin to a computerized structure. Each train appears simply to run about wildly and pointlessly, yet you don't know who is causing that, or why; it's hard to accept that someone is controlling it somewhere, and that the whole system is thereby running about in perfect harmony.

Other kids, not just me, lost themselves in train play, attempting to grasp in their little hands those things that controlled and were controlled. The insane roar and the menace that will crush underfoot whatever gets in its way are missing from the miniature world of train replicas. Yet the mass of the entire mechanical structure can be inflated to any degree by the power of imagination.

I, too, gave myself up to train play, imagining the black border around the tatami in my parents' home as tracks. I developed no interest in the electric toys being sold in department stores, for they were only objects. My trains were building blocks and picture postcards. It was necessary that I operate many trains on as complicated a layout as possible. Before long I was able to become not a mere motorman, but a mysterious demiurge who was off somewhere controlling everything. I left my infancy behind, but I did not outgrow this amusement. At the same time, its complexity increased. I had to set out an alarm clock and make the whole thing run according to schedule, and to the second. My tracks gradually expanded, extending over three rooms. Once I started, that was it; there was no allowance for stopping midway. And once I had determined the intricate layout, I then became a prisoner of the proposition that I had to

228   IROKAWA TAKEHIRO

act on this complexity, and rather than being amused by this, I was bored by the make-work and pointlessly enfolded in exhaustion and did not feel I was in control. It was as though I myself had sunk into that world and was the one being controlled. In truth, I may have perfected my play, controlling and being controlled, yet another condition—addiction—remained. I was unable to stop even when I became a middle-school student. This affliction infected my younger brother, six years my junior. He made the sound of a train by going "Maaa!" Not hackneyed blends like "woo-woo!" or "rattle! clank!" but "maaa! maaa! maa!" I don't know of anyone else who expressed it that way. And yet certainly such a timbre could be part of the sound of a train, mixed in with all the other resonances, and it showed everyone the confidence he had vis-à-vis the sound of trains.

And when we played train from morning to night, Father would give us a look of pure disgust. But I expect the only one in the household not engaged in games on the level of train playing was Mother. In Father's case, it did not take the form of playing train, yet he amused himself—just as we did—from morning 'til night cutting cards and laying them back down before him.

"Dinnertime, dear."

"Uh-huh."

"Please come. Your soup will get cold."

"I'll be right there."

"I'm calling you, dear!"

My younger brother is saying "Maaa!" I am moving the trains along with utmost caution, muttering softly to myself: "Zun, zun, tan, tan." My father is wordlessly cutting the cards. He's explained nothing to us about his game, but the fact is I and my brother know he is playing the same sort of game. The evidence for this is that my father writes, card by card, the outcome of a shuffle on the back of wrapping paper. After these slips of paper have accumulated, he looks at them with a hint of reluctance, then blows his nose on them. On the surface, it might appear to be fortune-telling or something. Perhaps it was for countless, unspecified people; for example, he may have been divining the fates of unknown people all over the world.

It may have been partly that, living on a pension, he had nothing else to do, but more than that, more than anything, having begun playing the game, he could not possibly leave it unfinished. Neither my brother nor I got up until our father did. Then he would shout at us.

"You won't eat when your mother calls you?!"

When I was small I thought that this was what life was. That is, something in which you are busy with trifles, bored, fatigued, and exhausted, even though you are involved in neither production nor consumption.

It is my sense that I was thus able to get thoroughly intimate with what comes under the heading of trains. Or perhaps you might say I was able to comprehend them.

I don't recall exactly when it was, but at some point it began to dawn on me that a Ministry Railway line (now the Japan National Railways)[1] ran four or five houses north of our house. It appeared in back of someone's house four or five houses to the north, leaped across a narrow road, ploughed into a nurses' agency on the other side, and went underground, then ran alongside our house. It was neither the Yamanote line nor the Chūō line, but a line that went from Iidabashi through Waseda to Ikebukuro. It was abandoned during the war, and I remember that the stations along its route were relieved of their roofs and left open to the rain. I recall the line, but not a vestige remains to suggest it once existed. Yet I have the feeling that I grew up hearing from time to time its rumbling sound close at hand.

You would lift up the tatami in a room, duck under the house, and jump down onto the tracks cut into the earth next to the toilet. Then if you walked at the side of the tracks along an arrow-straight path, you would arrive at Iidabashi. When a train came tearing along you would press your back against the tunnel wall and let it go by.

"Button all your buttons!" an older boy warned me. "If they're unbuttoned, the wind could catch the edge of your jacket and you'll be hooked by one of the cars."

When you came up to ground level near Iidabashi station you were instantly confronted with a railway overpass, and there the path

1. Privatized in 1987 and known today simply as JR.

narrowed and trains passing each other ran closer together. I was told not to stand there. In any event, it gave me a real thrill, and I frequently decided that I would never, ever go through the tunnel again. How is it that such memories have no connection whatsoever to reality?

When I was well on my way to becoming an adult the war became more intense, and the days when even I, a middle-school student in Tokyo, felt more dead than alive followed one after the other. I had gotten used to hunger and being pursued by flames and to bodies of the dead. At the same time, however, these experiences seemed to permeate my flesh and bones, and looking back on it now, I can even think of that time as having been the high point of my life.

So it is strange that what frightens me now is neither hunger, nor fire, nor bodies of the dead. It appears that great experience has not had as great an impact on me as I had expected. Why is this? Was it perhaps inevitable that I should turn out optimistic because I happened to survive when others died?

For us at the time, Shinagawa and Tabata, places where rows of tracks burgeon out and run as far as the eye can see—with their urban and interurban trains, and freight and private lines as well—were symbolic for us then of the violent nature of the train. I'm a coward, so I don't like such places. Yet under certain circumstances I did go there. And further, when it comes to basic circumstances, all tracks are the same.

Both at Shinagawa and Tabata long overpasses straddle the rows of tracks. Although it would be simple to cross over using the overpass, in my dreams I always scamper across the tracks below, one track at a time.

There are inbound and outbound trains. You must continually look to the left and right. Though you have let an inbound train go by and have an eye out for any sign of an outbound train, having once started across, you're always on a track somewhere, and while you're watching for only one inbound or outbound train and waiting for absolutely safe passage across, it can sometimes happen that the track you're on at that moment becomes a place of danger. That said, it can also happen that after you let a train go by the next train comes right on its heels on the same track, which should have been safe for a while.

National Railways trains are a bit wanting in power, but given their high frequency, they seem able to noiselessly sneak up on you, besides which, there are places where they drop into a dip, so they can close in on you before you know it.

Even so, I make no effort to return to safety. Like the circus performer challenging Ultraman C day in and day out, or perhaps like a matador, I attach myself to the train tracks. Motormen are watching me wordlessly from within the passing trains that I skillfully evade. And I quickly return their glances in kind, the glances of an alien race. Will I be run over or will I evade them? Will they run me down or pass without hitting me? I cannot avoid these decisive confrontations. And does all this mirror my experience with B-29 bombers?

There are many tracks still running next to each other. To my eye, it's almost impossible to tell the tracks apart, all jumbled together and clinging one to the other. But I can scarcely stay still. There's no sign of a car on the tracks before me, yet in the distance I can see a brutish freight train, looking more like a steamroller, hurtling toward me. Then an express train with special cars stretches itself toward me like a silver snake.

My estimation of my ability to dodge trains became even more suspect ever since the day a black ground-shaking mass trailing wisps of white steam abruptly changed its direction to the diagonal and switched to the track I was standing on. That is, up to that time all I had to do was pay attention to what was to my left and right and be aware of the existence of a train, but now I had to take into consideration changes made by the enemy. Yet whether he made changes or not was up to my adversary, and I wouldn't have the answer until I had drawn him to me.

The motormen were as expressionless as always, their eyes in their sooty faces looking straight ahead. Yet their ill will toward me was obvious, proof of which was that all trains that came switched tracks to target me.

If you slid down the face of the bluff at Ochanomizu and jumped down onto the tracks, at your back was the bluff and at the other side far below the Kanda River; there was no shoulder on either side. On top of which, countless rails ran parallel, as at Shinagawa and Tabata. For some reason traffic was in the doldrums; no trains were going by. Relieved, I made my way across the tracks, stepping unhurried over each. A utility train with a long, slender face approached on the track at the far side, a single car, its brakes hissing. Only the motorman's cab and the rear where the conductor was were enclosed. There was no roof or sides in the middle; helmeted laborers squatted there.

The utility train stopped halfway without even an ominous quiver. Then a five-car freight pulled by a small electric locomotive came along the track closest to the bluff, where regularly scheduled trains normally didn't run. Its approach was plodding. I could see it coming, but it seemed it would never pass by.

I could hear in the distance a train blowing its warning whistle, the sound hanging in the air. As though on signal, far down the track two trains, side by side and heading in my direction, eased into view. A number of trains flew like arrows from the opposite direction. Confused, I bounded back and forth, first to the left, then to the right. An inter-urban train that should never run there was passing on the far side of them. The engineer, his face familiar, stared straight ahead. Another train followed immediately on the heels of the one that had passed before me. There was no longer time to distinguish one train from another. Trains came from my left and right, as though a dam had burst. Nowhere was there an empty track. I realized now I was engulfed in the rush hour. The demon of time in an overly intricate schedule that demanded all tracks run to their limit once a day was on every track; anything in its way then would be cut down.

That experience had an impact on me, after which I made it a point never to take the railroads lightly. And yet there were instances when I would suddenly lose sight of this.

By then the utility train had come to a stop some distance away. Flustered, I flew to the face of the bluff and, hugging it, tried to make my way up inch by inch.

Sleep is a strange thing; since you're stock-still, you might think yourself safe, but you are not. On the contrary, it would seem you let down your guard and are defenseless. Which is to say, I always run out onto the tracks, forgetting that danger is part and parcel of it. With seasoned footwork, I let two or three trains go by. The ill-omened utility train with its section gang cargo has now stopped on the other side. As I look around, a toylike electric locomotive slowly lumbers along on the furthest track over. It comes along sluggishly at the side of the bluff.

I am startled, but it is already too late. All at once the tracks are jammed, a flurry of motion. I run blindly, like a wild pig pursued in the hunt, but I am cornered.

One day I encountered the demon of time at a crossing near the Nakano car barns. The ill-omened utility train, following its usual routine, ran past as I watched. Suddenly chaos was upon me: trains of malicious aspect came one after the other.

Hurray! I'm spared today!

The freight train approaching on the track closest to me suddenly made a right-angle turn at the crossing, smashed the barrier with a crunch, and headed toward me.

I no longer doubted their malice: their placing cross-ties on top on the tracks, changing signal lights, throwing switches the wrong way to see what would happen. The huge ebony devil slowly turned over before me. I had begun to master the technique of standing between two sets of trains and dodging them where they come closest to each other. Then, in the wake of this flood of trains, I can see a large black rhinoceros approach pulling a freight, its head lowered. The rhino advances zigzag, his gait savage.

At long last I am no longer engulfed in the demon time. When I realize it is that time, I find a signal and seek refuge behind it. Unfortunately for the train, it is blocked by the signal's iron pole and can only graze me as it rushes past.

One day a train with the face of a dragon stopped next to the signal. It then sent a jolting shudder along its length and suddenly lowered its pate at me. Sensing danger, I shinnied up the signal pole, but my enemy likewise wrapped itself around the pole, chasing me to the very top.

When I was in elementary school my father surprised me one day by coming over to me and telling me he was going to take me "someplace nice" that day. My younger brother was playing out front and Mother was doing the laundry.

I was delighted and got ready to go. *What's he mean, "someplace nice?"* Father said no more than that.

"We're walking," he said when we got outside. He extended his right hand and stuck his middle and forefinger down to me.

"Grab hold of this," he said.

I took hold of his two fingers and began walking, matching his stride as best I could. Before long, however, my hand fell away from his.

"Don't dawdle!" he scolded.

As I walked along I wondered if we were going to a movie theater. We crossed the rise at Sadohara, then from Outer Moat Boulevard passed along Hitokuchi Hill Road, coming to Kōjimachi, then went from Miyake Hill Road to Sakurada Gate. We then entered Hibiya Park, coming in through the back. Father sat down on a park bench.

"Ahhh!" he said with the expression of a man gazing at the wind, "I can't let something like this wear me out."

I was still wondering which movie we were to going to see.

"You know, when I was a kid everyone walked. Me, for example, I used to go from Ushigome to Shiba and back every day. And there was a kid who walked in from Saitama prefecture. In the old days people really wanted to study."

"How long did it take?"

"Good question. In any case, that kid was tardy every day and would come in when we were studying, steal in to a seat farthest to the back, peek at the page the kids around had opened their books to, and quietly open his own book to the same page."

"Didn't he get tired?"

"I felt sorry for him, I'll tell you. If he wasn't careful he'd have to get ready to return home as soon as he got to school. Because in those days it was pitch-dark at night, you know."

Father hated me to do any sightseeing as we went along. I wasn't supposed to look in shop windows or at people in stores. "Stop daydreaming," he'd say. For him walking meant moving your feet, your back straight and your eyes fixed intently on the empty air before you. When he was caught up in this, my hand would slip away from his two fingers.

And he did not consider it proper to step on the lines between the sidewalk paving stones. His stride would take him about to the midpoint of the third stone. Once he came to end of the sidewalk he would carefully look down to make the necessary adjustments as he set his foot down on the new sidewalk. The reason I began to notice such a trifle was that I always kept my eyes on the ground as I walked.

And when my younger brother turned a corner he would go out into the middle of the intersection and make a 90-degree turn there. When he was little he would mumble softly to himself "maaa" as he turned or make the sound of a brake releasing its air: "ssssh!" After he grew up he did it silently; I'll bet anything that even now he does it in his heart of hearts.

And when the two of us went to the public bath and took turns soaking in the tub, we'd get in pretending we were arriving on such-and-such track.

My brother told me that even when he went on his honeymoon he was, not surprisingly, thinking about trains. He was so busy taking pictures that he had his new wife take care of the luggage. The fact is, he was photographing the trains in the background; he said it would have been unseemly not to have his bride standing in front of them. Apparently my brother never once had the desire to work for a railroad, yet he inevitably carries a notebook and notes in it the car ID numbers of the various trains he rides. But he does more. He also puts down the car numbers of every single train that passes on another track and any others that catch his eye.

Whenever he boards a train he inevitably takes out his notebook, yet he never shows his wife what's in it.

"No looking!"

"You won't let *me* look at it, but you show it to others."

In his college notebooks my brother has recorded the car numbers for every possible model, and the tally marks themselves show how many times he rode them.

But if you were to ask him, he'd say I also seem to be doing the same sort of thing, but with different types of car. Our father was extremely displeased, not so much that his sons were empty-headed, but that they let something like that take up residence in their minds.

"Stop your daydreaming!" he would say. But we were no longer playing train. Even my father could not kick about the picture postcards in our heads. Thus he would say things like "You two are moths!" and "You're both insects!" I think a parent who has to talk like that is a sad person.

When the war situation worsened, my father, who had no job of any kind, was corralled for the post of head of the young men's association or the neighborhood association or whatnot. My father's personality abruptly changed; he diligently went out and bought a lot of loose-leaf binders and made a record of all the households in the district. He wrote down everything about a family using one sheet of paper for each household. When a particular household became a subject of discussion, he would open to their page and could see all the data at a glance.

"Look, it says so right here," he would say, but that's all he did.

"Boy," my brother said, "it really looks like we like to write down stuff, and so much you could never get it all down if you wrote 'til the cows came home."

"Well, you know, our interests don't seem to lean toward anything useful, do they. It's not that we sit around doing nothing. Our heads are full of pebbles or something, and we can't think of too much else. Pebbles are just pebbles and are good for nothing."

The two of us would sometimes take up that topic for discussion, smiling wryly at each other, but that was all we did. My brother has lived almost fifty years, becoming the epitome of the utterly ordinary white-collar worker, but as he approaches his life's goal, you can detect signs of distress.

"I'll tell you, when I retire I'm going to do what I want to do."

"And what'd you want to do?"

There was no response. He doesn't like others to realize that trains have not loosened their grip on him, and he makes something of a display of his other interests. Horse racing, for example. Yet, for all that, these things don't really hold him. He interacts with the world with those meager crevicelike portions between the pebbles in his head. Life for him: trains. Which is to say, this is what he honestly feels, and in any event, trains actually exist, so it becomes all the more complicated, and neither he nor I can competently argue our case.

It had been a newly built planetarium in the Yūraku-chō district that my father had taken me to that day. The world of stars was cast sharp and crisp up onto the vaulted ceiling, and a commentator who was apparently an astronomer explained it most graphically. I was deeply impressed that something that had practically nothing to do with our day-to-day lives had been transformed into such an elegant display.

A train station in the country. A single locomotive stood silently a short distance out of the station.

The station had no roof or supporting posts, and around it was only grassland. The sun was starting to set, so those waiting about here and there cast long shadows on the platform. I lingered at one end of the platform, my eyes in pursuit of a zone of safety. Once it starts to move, it will doubtless come charging, with me in its sights. Where should I be to prepare myself for its onslaught?

Perhaps it will run up on the platform. The side for inbound passengers is not safe; it's directly in its path. If I stand lackadaisically on the outbound side, that's an inducement for the locomotive to cut across and come at me at an angle. I can't go down onto the tracks. How about inside the waiting room? He would demolish in an instant the small waiting room, which is there only to protect people from a buffeting wind.

I crouched low behind the waiting room, out of his line of sight.

The time ripe, the locomotive shook itself several times, then immediately gave a short blast of its whistle. Sure enough, he was up on the platform in an instant, sweeping people off onto the tracks at the end of the platform. He came to the waiting room, where I was hiding, then spun around. Of course, I had moved to the side facing the outbound half of the platform, a blind spot for him. He came rumbling toward me. We continued to play tag for a while outside the waiting room. Then he suddenly let loose a blast of white steam, as one unable to hold his breath any longer, and began to run in circles of eight on the platform. Dodging back and forth, to the left, to the right, I at last discovered stairs leading to the station building and ran down them as fast as my legs would carry me. Tracks had also been laid down the stairs.

Thus I had to conclude that when a locomotive, black as pitch, appeared there would be tracks for it, wherever that might be. Thinking that he would not be able to go *there* surely—before he had yet to appear—I would flee to where the tickets were sold in the basement or into operations on the seventh floor, but when I got there I would discover tracks and, thoroughly rattled, run off. And he would inevitably make straight for where I was, as though he had dispensed with even the process of searching me out.

One day I found myself in the unfortunate position of having to work as a gandy dancer. I was supposed to stand on the near side of a large, arcing curve and tell the rest of the section gang doing pick work, men all senior to me, when a train was drawing near. Trains approached noiselessly, so it sometimes happened that I would fall to daydreaming. Once a train sped past my startled eyes and, in a panic, I shouted to the men and waved my flag. These older workers, sitting on the tracks, happened to look up and see the oncoming train. The train, however, did not reduce speed.

My fellow workers were willing to forgive me my blunder. They did not, however, forget to toy with me. They made a late-night meal in the laborers' shack. Laughing, they prepared chicken innards and told me to eat them. These older men, wearing round-frame glasses, all had large, sun-darkened faces.

I enjoyed myself only when I had left my work behind. Wearing my hat, I would return home walking along the edge of the tracks. The tracks closest to me on this side of Iidabashi station angle off up a rise and—looking down their nose at the tracks below—lead me to a siding. I would always hesitate there: had I been unable to get through before when I went up the rise or had it been when I transferred to the lower track?

In either case, I would end up at the same place. It was a single set of tracks and you could not change direction beyond that point. Before I knew it water had collected at my feet and carp were swimming in it. There was a row of official-looking buildings on both sides, where older women, part-time workers, toiled here and there. No station came into view no matter how far I went. Yet since I knew what I would find were

I to take the side road leading to the government buildings, I had no choice but to keep walking straight. As I walked along the side road I realized the women were dissecting corpses on an assembly line. What I had been trying to convince myself were carp were the internal organs of people run over by trains. I walked straight ahead, earnestly pretending that this was something I was quite used to.

"You know what Dad's doing now?" my younger brother said quietly some time after our father had died, as though he was letting me in on a secret. "He's somewhere around Ise."

"How do you know that?" I asked.

"There's a pencil on his writing desk. On it are the words City of Ise, embossed in gold."

"Is he at someone's house?"

"Uh-huh. He's sitting at the desk drawing pictures and writing words on lots of pieces of paper. He's surrounded by rice paddies and sparrows are everywhere."

"And did he tell you something?"

" 'I'm taking a census of sparrows,' he said when I asked him. Each sparrow has its picture drawn on a sheet of paper and every day he writes down what each bird is doing. He writes furiously, the tip of his tongue protruding in his earnestness. He seems to be somewhat better off in his afterlife than we'll be in ours."

"Uh-huh," I answered, "somewhat."

Morning Comes Twice a Day

INABA MAYUMI

Inaba Mayumi, born in central Japan in 1950, belongs to a cohort of fiction writers who have been laboring in the Japanese literary vineyards for some years and are now reaching their prime as storytellers. Inaba began her writing career at the age of sixteen by winning a poetry competition sponsored by the influential magazine Bungei shunjū. *She soon began writing fiction and in 1973 won an award given annually to promising new women writers for her short story* Aoi kage no itami o *(The pain of blue shadows), a look at a young woman succumbing to ennui. Her fiction, which addresses the isolation of women who choose to live solitary lives in the city and who seek "the other" within themselves, continues to win recognition. Most recently, she was awarded the Hirabayashi Taiko literary prize for her short story* Koe no shōfu *(The voice prostitute), in which an introverted library clerk finds herself the inadvertent recipient of calls from men dialing for phone sex.*

Asa ga nido kuru (*Morning comes twice a day*), *published in 1996 in the literary magazine* Kaien, *gives us a contemporary Japanese perspective on the isolating urban experience. It is Inaba's first work to be translated into English. Mimi, the cosseted cat of this autobiographical tale, placidly lived out her old age in a condominium on the southeastern edge of the city.*

——————

I had bought maps first thing. A booklet of maps of metropolitan Tokyo arranged by ward. I didn't know where I should go, so I unhurriedly leafed through the maps page by page. It was after I came up to Tokyo that I scoured the maps corner to corner. Where I was living, in Musashino, was still inside the city limits, but on the outskirts. Since I was renting, I knew I would have to look for another place if they had told me they wanted me to leave.

As I sat in the hallway of the old traditional-style cottage, the names of districts I had never heard of, the amenities, hospitals, the libraries in each ward, the names of the art museums assailed my eyes. The labyrinthine roads ran on from top to bottom, meshes in a net.

The first page, Chiyoda ward. When it was time to move I was reminded again as I opened up the booklet that Chiyoda in Chiyoda ward is the lot number for the Imperial Palace. Chiyoda, Chiyoda ward, surrounded by pale turquoise and green ink, was like a womb smack in the center of the body of Tokyo. It sat there in cheerful isolation, surrounded by the water in the Imperial moat.

Truth be told, I probably should have focused on the Musashino area, which I was used to living in, but when it came time to move, I found myself attracted to sections of the city I'd never even laid eyes on and traced my finger over the subway lines again and again, and when I read out the names of the JR stations—Asagaya, Nakano, Mejiro, Shibuya—I would remember the contours of districts I had heretofore only passed on the train. Anywhere would be fine. There was no area I really wanted to go to; all I need do was find a room to live with my cat.

It was already the latter half of March when the old couple who owned the cottage had come and told me their son was coming back to Tokyo and asked if I could be out by the end of May. The rent I had been paying was 80 percent of the going rate, and they had taken only the equivalent of one month's rent for the deposit and for the unrefundable key money. The understanding had been, however, that their son, who had been transferred to his trading company's Hokkaido branch, would be returning in about two years, at which time I was to move out. He didn't return in two years, so in the end the place was my and my cat's home for five.

Notwithstanding the fact that I could not expect to stay there indefinitely, I had grown attached to the house and quite at home there, and when I was faced with the prospect of leaving I hadn't the foggiest notion where I ought to make my new home. For my cat, who glided easily in and out of the openings in the corrugated vinyl fence around the storage shack behind my bath, I wanted to find something similar, a cranny-riddled house, but such a place in greater Tokyo could be found only in its rural outskirts.

Thus I first assiduously tramped from one rental realtor to another in the Kunitachi and Kokubunji areas, near where I was living, hoping to find an apartment with a yard, but even when there was one, keeping a cat was not allowed. A new condominium was out of the question. As soon as I mentioned my cat, no matter the realtor, I would hear a sympathetic tone of voice.

"That wouldn't work here."

"Oh, they don't allow pets here either."

"How about leaving your cat with someone?" one of the realtors suggested. "Have someone take it for you."

I couldn't imagine living without my cat.

I would explain things to my cat every night.

"We're going to a new house. Let's find one like this one. You'd like a house with a garden, wouldn't you. Even if there's no yard, you'd want a park you can go to, right? I'm going to find you a place like that. You can bet on it."

When I finally started looking—determined I would live with my cat, come what may—I couldn't bring myself to believe there were no houses where you could keep a cat.

I soon learned there were no longer any old, weather-beaten houses—

farm houses and such—left in the heart of Tokyo, and that in the case of apartment units and condominiums, there were extremely few where you could keep pets. It wasn't that I found no rental condos for people with pets, but the rents were way beyond my ability to pay. As for condominiums where animals were given consideration, most were in the exclusive residential districts in the center of town, available only for the select few, with unrealistic prices and appointments.

My booklet of Tokyo ward maps in my bag, I would make the rounds of the realtors, last week Shibuya ward, this week Nakano ward, on other days Setagaya ward, becoming more depressed by the day and by evening on the brink of tears at the futility of it. While I was looking at the listings in a realtor's office I would be attracted to the layout of a place, the ample sunlight, the reasonable rent, and immediately want to take it, but once I broached the matter of my cat, I was back at square one. The deadline that the couple had given me drew nearer with each day; at night I would hold my cat to me and feel myself a homeless waif. What would happen if in the end I couldn't find a place to live? More than once I looked up with bitterness at large single-family houses, the warm breeze of a spring night now on my face.

When you look around you see masses of houses everywhere. The view from the train as you commute: houses, houses, houses. It seemed completely absurd that in a Tokyo covered with houses eave to eave there was nowhere to be found a room where I and my cat could live, and every time I saw laundry flapping away in a yard or a verandah buried under plants or a front gate where a dog was tied up, I was possessed by a dark rage.

By the middle of April I was taking purely random walks about town every day off I had. I accustomed myself to sitting in the Real Estate Center, a place that had information on most of the rental housing in the city, and looking through dozens of listings. The picture, nonetheless, did not brighten. I made the rounds of all the realtors near the stations along the Chūō train line, passing out to one and all dozens of business cards, yet not one realtor contacted me to say he had found something that met my needs. There were any number of rooms for women with children, but not one room anywhere for a woman with a cat. Because they were aware of this, the realtors were perhaps disinclined to beat the bushes with any enthusiasm. The thought of my business cards lying quietly forgotten off in the corner on real estate office counters and in trash cans put me in a dismal frame of mind.

A man in a two-by-four real estate office in Shibuya that I just happened into one day listened to my story.

"Rather than a rental unit," he said, "why don't you consider the purchase of a condominium?"

I stared at him dumbfounded. I had never even thought about buying a condo, and I didn't have that sort of money about. He took out his desk calculator.

"Given the rent where you're living now of 55,000 yen and calculating with that figure, with a down payment of 2 million yen and a loan of 8 million or so, your payments would not be much more than your rent now. Why don't you give it some thought?"

He tapped his calculator lightly as he talked. Then he quickly took from the file cabinet by him a sheaf of leaflets slightly larger than a 1,000-yen note on condominium units that were to be resold and showed them to me.

"Uh," I began, "if I buy a condo can I keep a cat?"

"There are all sorts of condominiums. Some expressly forbid pets in the contract, but many are vague about it. If the animal doesn't go outside or doesn't cause problems for the neighbors, people would be willing to be flexible. I would think that nobody would care what's in your unit."

The man smiled gently and pulled out a number of contracts that said nothing about prohibiting pets in the management bylaws. My heart began to thump in my chest. I had never considered buying a place, yet now such thoughts roiled up in my mind: if I did buy a condo I could live with my cat, and what's wrong with buying one for the sake of my cat? The strange thing was that the phrase *no pets* that so annoyed me in the rental listings was practically nowhere to be found in condominium pamphlets. The owner of a condominium, no matter how small the unit, seemed to enjoy an extraterritoriality that others could not violate.

"Would you like to see a few?" the man asked. "It would cost you nothing just to look."

"I'd like to look. I'd like to look," I said, my response almost parrot-like. "Any condo would be fine as long as I can keep a pet."

One candidate, a condominium in Shibuya, was in a bustling commercial area near the train station. Someone was still living in it, and the kitchen was covered with grease. The woman who lived there, who had cut short her workday so that she could show us the unit, told us she was a hairstylist.

"I'd like to sell it soon," she said, cigarette dangling from her lips. "I'm tired of the place. Besides, I suspect it'll be quicker and simpler to sell than remodel."

It was a dreadful place that certainly had to be remodeled before anyone could live in it. The interior of the single-room, thirty-five-square-meter condo was awash with mirrors, either to make it look bigger or because she needed them for her work. The mirrors were dingy, clouded over with grease and tobacco tar, making the room look smaller, in fact. The carpeting was dark and undulating, here and there sporting grease stains and cigarette burns. The whole unit appeared ready to burst into flames at any minute. It was filthy and utterly without charm. How much would it cost in remodeling to extirpate the charmlessness? On top of which, the price for the unit far exceeded my budget. I sighed, realizing at once that this was not the place where I and my cat would live.

The next condominium I saw was in Koganei, not too far from Kokubunji. It was in an area that still had farm lots, a dozen or so minutes by bus from the train station. There was plenty of open space where the cat could play. The rooms were covered with a faint film of dust, suggesting it had been empty for a good many months. Bright and balmy sunlight shone into the main room. I almost leaped for joy.

"Ah, this is great! My cat can lie in the sun."

But on the way back when I looked at the bus schedule at the bus stop, I saw that service was greatly reduced at night and the space after 11 P.M. was blank.

I commuted to the publishing company I worked at in the heart of the city, so I could hardly live somewhere were the buses didn't run after eleven at night. It would be different if I had a car, but I didn't even have a driver's license. The only option would be to take a taxi every night.

For someone with no money to spare it was much too far to be practical. The next condo I looked at was along the Chūō line, a one-room unit in Mitaka. The exterior and interior walls were pure white; perhaps it had just been built. There was a dryer in the bath and a gas stove had been installed in the kitchen. Which is undoubtedly why it would have taken me far over my budget. With the very best possible loan, it would have exceeded the amount I was able to pay by more than 5 million yen.

If there was a phone call from the realtor, I would go see any condo I could inspect, not only on days off, but also at night. I often killed time in neighborhood coffee shops because the condo resident was late getting home, and there were units I rejected simply after looking at the floor plan. Those I was able to see were, at best, condos of 10 *tsubo*, or 360 square feet. Just looking at the floor plans of a unit of that small size, further divided into a three-mat room, a four-and-a-half-mat room and a six-mat room was enough to bring on claustrophobia. If I could find it, I wanted a single, wide open, unpartitioned room. A room where the inside and outside were of a piece. I had not the least desire for an at-tractive condo or anything elaborate. It would be enough if my cat could mosey about at her leisure.

The end of April was fast approaching. I ran to the Real Estate Center downtown, for I had to settle on a condo, come what may. My back was to the wall. If I were to find nothing, I would have to leave my cat with someone in the country or, failing that and unable to find a hotel or whatever where I could stay with her, we would be out on the street. As I flipped furiously through the listings, a floor plan suddenly caught my eye. The unit was a bit over my budget, but were I to borrow the down payment shortfall from my mother, the balance was such that I should be able to cover it with a loan. It was located in Shinagawa, an area where I'd never been. I don't know exactly what it was about it that struck a responsive cord, but I chose that condominium from the fat stack of listings and asked it be shown to me.

The unit was in an eleven-story building which had a large garden and a parking area at ground level. It was the tallest structure in the vicinity. The condo I wanted to see was on the fifth floor. It was a bright and cheerful corner unit with windows facing both east and north. A nine-by-twelve-foot dining room-kitchen and a traditional tatami-floored room of four mats. The two rooms were divided by four sliding doors, and when these were removed you had one large room. An ample wind blew from the east window to the window opened to the north, lazily puffing out the white curtains of both windows. The housewife who showed us her condo apparently had a fondness for cleaning. Though the building had been standing for thirteen years, the walls showed little wear, and the kitchen was clean and in need of no renovation. The floor, vinyl sheeting, was glossy and spotless.

The time when I would have to move was almost upon me; I concluded this was the place for me. I was also completely exhausted and lacking the reserves to continue the search for a better place.

I was buying thirty-three square meters, exactly ten *tsubo*. I hadn't been able to find my cranny-riddled house or my own garden, but with this purchase the pressure was now off, and I'd gotten a place for my cat and me.

I dreamed a lot about falling acacia blossoms. In the dreams the blossoms fell from trees endlessly. I would awaken, my mind white as snow. I could still smell the flowers under my nose. The sweet, heavy membrane of aroma lingered briefly even after I awoke and tended to hang in the air through the morning.

Having borrowed money, then emptied your savings account of its last yen, how is it you are then apt to dwell on the place and house you found so pleasant? In Musashino in the spring white acacia blossoms fell silently. When there was a breeze you would catch snatches of their aroma. Those days visited me in my room suspended in space in Shinagawa in the form of dreams.

When I would awake in the middle of the night, almost overcome by the heavy, sweet, yet somehow pungent smell, I and my cat were not in Musashino, but high in the air where there was no earth to be seen. In this one room where there was a large window facing east and another facing north, there was not a single green thing growing, and the balcony lay parched under a rubber mat. Though there might be the new greenery of May outside my windows, it did not have the fragrances of May that we had savored at our house in Musashino. Even the green that burgeoned within my sight, though it might be rich in color, was far below me, so far I could not possibly touch it with an outstretched hand.

You could open the condo windows, but it was near where Yamanote Boulevard runs, so I was assailed by unending noise and by soot and smoke: exhaust gas from cars that wafted up and black grime that collected on the floor, no matter how much I wiped it away. Yet I was happy. Even though I hadn't a yen to my name, I nonetheless had a place where the cat and I could be together, and I had a job. As for the money I had borrowed to make the down payment and the loan I'd just worked out, I could doubtless pay them off in my lifetime if I stayed in good health. Optimism washed over me like ocean waves and I couldn't help smiling when I was in my condominium.

White blossoms fluttered down upon the smile. I was optimistic, yet a vague unease about the future lingered, and the petals went on falling, the substantiation of my unease. Some nights I heard the cat, looking down at me from the branch of a huge tree she had climbed, say "I hate this place! I hate it! I can't get outside!" Other nights, when her meowing woke me, I found her prowling the room from one side to the other, looking for a way out.

Each time she did this I would take her in my arms and tell her there was no place she need go now. This was our new home. Whenever I murmured to her that our old, big house was gone now and that this room in the sky was our home, tears would well up in my eyes. Should I have, in fact, left the cat in the stand of trees in Musashino she had so taken to? Should I have bid her farewell at the path she had traversed day and night? I didn't know the answer. Morbidly responsive to her stealthy movements, her meowing in the middle of the night as she searched for a way out, I knew only one thing to do to mollify her: buy cat toys by the carload. I resorted to something akin to the cajolery of a mother humoring her baby. The cat would play with its new toy for a while but soon tire of it, at which point I would give it a colorful ball or a stuffed mouse.

There was only one plaything that seemed to catch the cat's fancy. A stuffed jaguar made so that a child could carry it on its back like a backpack. I'd got it as a premium of some sort. The jaguar, yellow with black spots, was made of soft cloth and sponge, and had a pocket on its belly you could close with a zipper. A small pocket that could hold no more than a handkerchief and tissue paper. My cat misapprehended this animal bag, very much something for a child, as a newfound companion. I would be awakened in the middle of the night by a playful-sounding meowing, to suddenly discover the cat dragging the jaguar across the floor. She would even bite its ear and give its tail a thorough licking. My cat, separated from the stray cats that hung out around the house in Musashino, had chosen the stuffed jaguar as her solitary companion in the condominium.

If living in our new condo outraged the cat, for me it was a delight. My commuting time shrank and even when I worked late I was usually able to make the train. Even when I'd missed the last train I could get back home from work in ten or so minutes by taxi.

And relations with my neighbors never went beyond a hello when we happened to run into each other. I passed my days in ignorance of the people who lived in the other units or what sort of people they were, and this did not inconvenience me in the least. On the contrary, the sense of isolation invited relief; on my days off I could loll about on the floor from morning to night with the cat, the windows wide open, reading books and listening to music. The din that rose from the expressway directly beneath me was absorbed by the timbre of violins and flutes, and my condo shone gaudily with scintillations thrown off by strings and brass. I had listened only to jazz in Musashino, but when I moved to Shinagawa, it no longer moved me, and I started listening to classical music. Perhaps this was because of all the variety of natural changes in Musashino; the shadows of the trees and the intensity of the wind nicely suited the rhythms of jazz. Or it may have been that, having come to live amidst the sounds of the city, I found jazz directly beneath my window and could not bring myself to listen to even more of it.

In the first six months since moving I placed leafy plants in planters in my room (encased, as it was, in thick walls of concrete), repainted the walls of the bath from white to pale green, took out the fluorescent lights and replaced them with incandescent lamps, and provided the cat with new food and water dishes. I hung no curtains, however. I wanted to leave the sky visible from the windows as of a piece with the room. With the windows open the boundary between the room and the world outside was less clear-cut and gave me the buoyant sense day and night of floating in the sky. And the sight of a bird flying past my window was not something I would have seen from my low-lying house in Musashino.

I stayed up until dawn to watch the sun rise out of the waters off Shinagawa. I delighted in throwing the balcony door wide open and watching the banks of pale sea-blue clouds as their color gradually took on a reddish cast. The building manager told me you could see the ocean if you got on the roof, but I could hardly wake him to get the key to the door to the roof, so I would stand on my fifth-floor balcony and catch the predawn breeze.

The cat never went out on the balcony but did like the window, and when the dawn light shone into the room she would jump down with a thump from her accustomed place on the sofa and lie down in front of the door to the balcony. She waited for morning, her face to the east. At the house in Musashino she would quietly go out at first light, just like clockwork. I don't know whether it was for a stroll in the woods or a physiological phenomenon that summoned her, but summer or winter this routine was unchanging; by the time I awoke the cat would be nowhere to be seen. This practice may have survived the move to the fifth-floor condo. When it got light outside, the cat would gradually work her way toward the light and stare at the sky. There was no place to go, however, so when the room filled with light she returned—with seeming dissatisfaction—to her place on the sofa.

A short while later I realized the cat would always stretch out by the window in the afternoon when the weather was good. When I was working at my desk in the afternoon on my day off the cat would thump down from the sofa and sit down by the window, her face fixed on the east, as she did in the morning, which puzzled me: why is she doing that at that time of day? I then realized that it was gradually getting lighter in the east and the room was filling with a bright, orange-colored light.

There is a street directly below my window, and across the street a fire station, and beyond that a white bank building and office buildings

built along the First Keihin Expressway. The sun setting in the west
reflected off the massive white walls and glass windows directly into my
condominium. Laundry, book pages, lamp shades, these were all dyed
a garish red. It was like finding yourself in the pulp of a ripe plum. The
rays of brilliant light, thanks to the white walls, were drawn together in
a point and carried into my room as dazzling reflected light. The cat,
unaware that the light was from the setting sun, moved to the window
as she did when it was morning.

Ah, morning comes twice a day to this room. The instant I realized this, I
smiled, filled with a sense of happiness. The cat's face, whiskers, her sun-
translucent ears, were tinted red, and doubtless my own body orange.
The light, which seemed richer than in the morning and bearing a touch
of weariness, warmly colored the cat's body and made her look pleasantly plump.

The cat gradually accustomed herself to the room to which morning
came twice a day. During the long daylight hours or at nighttime, shut
up in the 10-*tsubo* unit, she amused herself by walking about with the
jaguar in her mouth and licked it as you caress a baby. Yet it pained me
to see her look vacantly up at the sky, as she tended to do. I came to feel
I could do no less than create a means of egress for her. She had been
afraid of the balcony from day one and wouldn't set foot on it, so the
only recourse was my front door. And this would be in the middle of
the night when everyone was asleep.

The elevators for my floor were near my front door, and next to these
was a steel emergency stairway that ran from the ground to the roof.
Late one night when I left my door open to see what the cat would do,
she quietly went out to the stairway. At first she walked skittishly, her
breathing uneven as she sniffed about. Then she cautiously went out onto
the stairs, looking up, then peering down. Below her was Hell, and
above, the fifth floor landing from which the stairway rose up without
end. Not knowing which way to go, she returned to the condo, a bewildered expression on her face.

It was about a year after we moved into the condominium that I took
her in my arms and slowly made my way down the emergency stairway.
Having lived there for a year, I knew what time the residents put their

cars in the parking garage, and calculating the time when car engines
fell silent as 2 A.M., would go down then. My timorous cat clung to my
chest, her eyes ovals of fear. Nonetheless, when I set her down on the
asphalt-covered ground, she elected the darkness alongside a parked car
and began to move off in measured steps.

The first day she came back right away. During the next week she
would crawl under a car and wait stock-still for a while, getting used to
her surroundings. The route the cat took in Shinagawa was beneath cars
in the parking area. While the cat was taking her stroll I would sit on
the stairs and read a book under the pale white fluorescent light or peer
into the darkness with her. I could not tell just how the cat was moving
about under the cars, which were in racks one upon the other; the cat
would peer out from the least-expected places, returning to me via a
mazelike zigzag course. She made no attempt to go across the road to
the vacant lot on the other side, surely uneasy about finding herself unable to get back. She would stare hard at the lot, her ears cocked, then
turn around and look up at me.

We continued our walks in the dead of night; sometimes I would carry
the cat up the emergency stairs, sometimes I would let her walk up herself. The cat, now accustomed to the smell of the exhaust fumes that filled
the parking garage, inevitably wanted to play on the stairs whenever
my door was open.

A chronic lack of sleep settled drosslike over my eyes. Yet I was relieved that I had found a way out for my cat. It was an arid and cheerless
route, but I wanted to show her there was a ground she could go to. I
also wanted to show her—though she might not understand—that the
earth of Shinagawa was connected to Musashino. I stood on the emergency stairs, the cat in my arms, my pointing finger shifting around in
space like a direction indicator.

"That way, long time ago. Now, here."

It was in the spring six years after we moved to Shinagawa that the cat
disappeared. As usual, she went out the door, which I had left open, and
should have been playing on the landing. Because I happened to be
snowed under with work, I stayed at my desk and waited for the cat to

come back from her solitary stroll. I knew that she would scurry home if there was any sign of people. Unconcerned, I marveled at how quiet it was that night. The cat did not come back. It was a good hour after the cat left that I began to wonder how long she was going to play on the landing. Maybe she had found a bug that caught her fancy. When I poked my head out the door, my heart stopped. My cat, who should have been quietly sitting on the stairs peering below or playfully poking her paws through the railing, was nowhere to be seen. She would play in the darkness under the cars in the garage if I carried her down there, but she had never gone down there by herself. My cat could never turn into a runaway, no matter how familiar she became with the route to the garage.

Dubious that she had gone downstairs, I nevertheless went down to the parking garage, now silent as the tomb. I crouched down in the darkness amidst the odor of chilled asphalt and peered under the cars one by one looking for my cat. I even went over to the vacant land across the street. She was a cat who would come running from wherever she was if I called her name; now there was absolutely no sign or sight of her.

I wondered if she had fallen from the landing and was caught partway down. Overcome by a grim unease, I ran up the stairs to the fifth floor, leaned out over the railing, and looked down. There was no indication the cat was hung up anywhere and I could hear no meowing. Then maybe she went upstairs to a higher floor. I checked every floor up to the roof and in the end verified that, as I feared, she was not to be found. Was it possible that she had wandered over to the expressway and been run over by a car? The thought turned my legs to jelly, but the next moment I was running as fast as I could to the highway.

I don't know how many times that night I climbed the stairs, went down to the ground floor, knelt on the ground and looked under cars, prowled the vacant lot, or ran to the expressway. Half mad, I would decide she must have returned home while I was gone and would go back to my room, searching in the far corners of the closet, then fruitlessly open and close, and open again, the door under the kitchen sink. Torn with remorse and self-directed anger, my whole body was immobilized and my brain numb to its core: *Why had I been so absorbed in my work for over an hour? Why didn't I carry her downstairs and have her play in the parking garage as I usually did?*

When the youngster who delivered the newspaper came up the stairs, I was slumped in exhaustion in front of my door, which was still open, my face smeared with tears and snivel, sobbing convulsively. The young man, seeing this woman sitting in the hallway in front of her door, her hair disheveled and her face a mess, was doubtless startled and uttered a strangled cry as he froze in his tracks.

"My cat, it's disappeared. I've been looking for it all night, but it's really gone. She's brown and white and black, but with no special pattern. I can't find her anywhere."

I wanted to explain the situation to someone, regardless of their possible disinterest, but my voice was breaking. The young man, standing absolutely still, gingerly handed me the newspaper and uttered an indistinct monosyllable that was not really an answer. He undoubtedly felt sorry for a woman who was so disturbed she was unconcerned what people might think of her.

"I'm going to the upper floors now," he finally said, "so I'll let you know if I see it. But it wasn't on any of the lower floors. Your cat, you say. Ah, cats, cats."

The youth bounded up the stairs with the expression of one who has looked upon something truly terrifying.

It was right after this that the building manager stopped in front of my door. He was an early bird. He came around six o'clock to clean the stairs for each floor and the area in front of the elevators. His eyes opened wide as the paperboy's had and he stood frozen to the spot. I was still sitting in the entryway, staring with unfocused eyes at the landing.

"What's wrong, miss?" he asked, his tone incredulous. He had a broom in one hand and a dustpan in the other.

"My cat, it's gone," I told him. "I can't find it anywhere. I've been waiting for her to come back since last night, but she hasn't returned."

I was unable to stop myself from bursting into tears again. My nose was stuffed up and my voice nasal.

"Cats, they say a cat's attached to its home, right? I'm sure it'll come back. In any case, you're not safe like that. Have you been out there all night with the door open?"

The tone of the last sentence was one of amazement.

"Anyway, you'd better get some sleep. You haven't slept, have you? I'll be making my rounds now, so I'll look for the cat. I'll give you a holler if I find her. There's no point in you sitting here, is there."

Nonetheless, I was drained of energy and could not immediately get to my feet. My emotions were so wrapped up in my cat I certainly had no thought of moving or going to bed. First of all, if I shut the door the cat would have had no way to get back in. If I were going to move, I wanted to go out one more time, this time in the bright light of day to look under the cars and go over to the vacant lot and the expressway. But it could be that she had climbed up to the locked roof along the railing. *That's it! She might be on the roof!* My mind was in turmoil again and I was set to dash up to the top of the building. I was quite beside myself. The image of my cat stranded on the vast, windswept roof, wandering forlornly from one side to the other, filled, with my tears, every crevice in my brain. But before I could run off the manager came back with news.

"Just to be sure," he reported, "I took a look around the roof. She's not there."

I could only conclude now that the cat had intentionally gone missing. Disgusted with life in a condo, had she taken it in her head to go back to Musashino? Were that the case, where might she be now? Did she know in which direction to go? From Ōsaki to Gotanda, then Meguro. I visualized the terrain in the booklet of maps of Tokyo wards that I had once gazed at with such fascination. From there she would go north to the road to Itsukaichi. Filling my feverish mind with the map, I traced the route the cat would have to take. Could she actually be walking in the right direction, the direction to Musashino I had shown her from the stair landing? *That way, long time ago. Now, here.*

My mind was replete with the smell of Musashino's acacias that had been lost to my memory for some time, and when this smell came back to me, I again burst into tears. The time I had shared with the cat poured down upon my body like a roaring cataract. Waves of sorrow that seemed to flow from the very core of my being assailed me endlessly. I remembered the weight of her body in my hands as, entrusting herself to me, she went limp when I picked her up, the warmth of her sandpaper tongue, her diffident gait as she rubbed up against my leg. All these were not isolated incidents; they bound my entire body like a thick membrane.

It was almost noon, the sun high in the sky. Still sitting, distraught, in front of my door, I heard my phone ringing. It was the manager. He was shouting into the receiver.

"We've found her! We've found the cat! She apparently went into a unit on an upper floor by mistake. A woman upstairs says she slept the night with the cat in her arms. She just called me. She said she's on her way down!"

I heard the sound of someone coming down the stairs as he was talking. I sprang to my feet. A young woman was on the landing, the cat in her arms.

"Ah, the cat's not a stray, after all, is it," she laughed, petting the animal's head. My strength had deserted me the instant I saw my cat's face, and I could only mutter a few words. The truth is I wanted to wail at the tops of my lungs, but my throat was constricted as tight as a drum.

The woman told me that she had left her front door ajar late at night when she was doing some work, and the cat had slipped in, meowing three times as she did so. The woman watched in surprise as the cat sashayed in, right at home, and sat herself down on the kitchen floor. So she gave her something to eat and slept with her in her arms until morning.

I was getting angrier by the second. I had been calling and calling. I had looked high and low, and yet all that time my cat was in a condo on an upper floor, eating and sleeping as soundly as you please. But when I took my cat back from the woman, I immediately realized she had not been living the easy life upstairs. I could feel her body trembling. Doubtless she had realized she was in the wrong unit, but there was no way for her to get back home. When I called her by her name, "Mimi," she responded with a clipped meow, then uttered a drawn-out meow as her strength left her. What then followed was a long, long passing of water. The pungent, hot fluid soaked my clothes from my stomach to my feet.

The more energized drops of urine fell to become glistening, random dots on the landing.

I wonder if the aging cat notices. That fifteen years have gone by in the room with the stuffed jaguar, that the tatami in the four-and-a-half-mat Japanese-style room and the dusky eat-in kitchen vinyl floor have been changed to a warm-colored cork floor, that the heated carpet that was always laid down in winter has been taken up because it had absorbed the sun and cat hairs and faded and begun to smell. The stuffed jaguar, bitten and licked and dragged around the floor, is now torn and tattered. I've covered it with bits of colored cloth that matched the torn areas and then put other scraps on top of that, creating a mottled patchwork of light and dark. The sponge that had been all puffed up has lost its elasticity. Nonetheless, the delight the cat takes in the jaguar is undiminished. Even now she uses it for a pillow when she sleeps. When I'm not around she amuses herself in her solitary hours by chewing on its weary ears.

My cat hasn't used the emergency stairway since she went into the wrong condominium. She pokes her head out of the door and takes two or three hesitant steps beyond it but immediately comes back, a look of seeming uncertainty on her face. The condominium building I live in has the same layout on each floor, the doors are the same type, painted the same color. If she could no longer differentiate odors, all she had to go on was indistinguishable, identical doors. She has remembered this in her bones.

I suspect she had already been starting to age by then. When the cat disappeared I wondered if she had gone back to Musashino, but the place where she would have gone had long since disappeared. The cat, when she strayed into a stranger's home upstairs, most certainly knew that that sign of old age, of being unable to find one's way back home, was very close at hand.

The condo is filled with bright and cheerful light. The light of Shinagawa that has shone in my window immutably every day since we moved into the condo.

I became good friends with the woman above me who had looked after my cat here in the condominium building where I had not a single acquaintance earlier. She was single, a painter. She lived with her mother. She would come by and wistfully ask about the cat who had wandered into her condo.

"You're not coming back?" she would always ask the cat, stroking its head. "Come visit me again."

The invitation notwithstanding, the cat pretended not to know her and even seemed to have forgotten they had once slept together.

It was in the winter of the year before last that the young woman died in an accident. I heard she was taken to the hospital, but she had been killed instantly. In her room upstairs there was a picture of her when she was young. She was smiling sleepily, holding a white cat, and the cat also looked sleepy. She had told me it was a picture taken to commemorate finding the cat; the white cat she was holding had been dead for years, however.

I pick up my old cat twice, once in the morning and once at night, and feel its abdomen. I've discovered that when I find its distended bladder and push it gently with my finger, the urine, which she has difficulty expelling, comes out nicely. I used to run in a panic to the animal clinic every time there was a problem, but now I rarely take her to the vet. For a cat who can no longer go to the bathroom, the best thing to do is to gently push your hand into her abdomen when the bladder is full, and when she can't expel a stool, the hand is more effective than medicine.

If I press the wall of her intestines, moving my fingers gradually toward the back, as if I were squeezing a tube of toothpaste, she will excrete what she couldn't expel on her own. After I discovered this technique, it was quite obvious that her body, which had been swollen with excrement, deflated naturally and became lighter, and I could imagine her insides glowing with vitality.

A placid bag of flesh that eats and drinks, sleeps and wakes, then eats and sleeps again. When afternoon comes round, the cat has her second "morning" in a room filled with orange light and stretches out by the window. Supporting the cat as it crawls, I, too, am awash in the dazzling light of the second "morning."

Morning comes, noon comes, then it's "morning" again, then night.

The world's one and only almanac where morning comes twice a day, and one known only to me and my cat. In a room where from time to time, as in a dream, white blossoms still fall like snowflakes.

And there have been nights when the voice of the woman upstairs sounds in my ear like the wind.

"Come visit me again."

Glossary

Edo	the former name of Tokyo before it became the capital in 1868
furoshiki	a large cloth used to wrap and hand-carry belongings
Gigaku	an ancient dance using masks, some of which are humorous or grotesque
hakama	loose-fitting trousers usually worn on formal occasions or in certain traditional sports such as archery and kendō fencing
haori	a traditional jacket worn by both men and women with kimono or *hakama*
kasuri	cloth with a splashed white pattern on indigo
miso soup	soup made with fermented soybean paste, fish stock, and tofu
mompe	baggy, pantaloon-type trousers for women especially common during the Second World War and the immediate postwar period
nagauta	a narrative ballad accompanied by samisen and often flutes and drum, as in the Kabuki theater

noren	a short, split curtain (or strands of cord) hung above the main entrance of a shop to identify it and indicate it is open for business
rakugo	traditional comic monologue popular since the seventeenth century
ryōtei	a traditional upscale Japanese restaurant, often the site of commercial or political deal-making
sembei	rice crackers, often soy-dipped and wrapped in seaweed
sensei	a teacher, though the term is also used as a deferential title for politicians and others of a certain prominence
shibui	the quality in the vocabulary of Japanese aesthetics of understated, somber beauty
shitamachi	(pronounced *sh'tah-mah-chee*) traditionally the plebeian, working-class part of town
yakuza	the Japanese mafia
Yamanote	literally, "the foothills"; considered the better part of town, as opposed to the flatlands of *shitamachi*
Yoshiwara	the former licensed prostitution quarter; outlawed brothels have now been replaced by "soaplands"
yukata	an unlined summer kimono worn by both men and women

Suggested Reading

WORKS IN ENGLISH

Ashihara, Yoshinobu. *The Hidden Order: Tokyo through the Twentieth Century.*
  Translated and adapted by Lynne E. Riggs. Tokyo: Kodansha International,
  1989.
Bestor, Theodore C. *Neighborhood Tokyo.* Stanford: Stanford University Press,
  1989.
Ericson, Joan E. *Be a Woman: Hayashi Fumiko and Modern Japanese Women's
  Literature.* Honolulu: University of Hawai'i Press, 1997.
Fowler, Edward. *San'ya Blues: Laboring Life in Contemporary Tokyo.* Ithaca:
  Cornell University Press, 1996.
Goossen, Theodore W., ed. *The Oxford Book of Japanese Short Stories.* Oxford:
  Oxford University Press, 1997.
Greenfield, Karl Taro. *Speed Tribes: Days and Nights with Japan's Next Generation.*
  New York: HarperCollins, 1994.
Jinnai, Hidenobu. *Tokyo: A Spatial Anthology.* Translated by Kimiko Nishimura.
  Berkeley: University of California Press, 1995.

Mukōda Kuniko. *The Name of the Flower: Stories by Kuniko Mukōda*. Translated by Tomone Matsumoto. Berkeley: Stone Bridge Press, 1994.
Mulhern, Chieko, ed. *Japanese Women Writers: A Bio-critical Sourcebook*. Westport, Conn.: Greenwood Press, 1994.
Natsume Sōseki. *And Then: Natsume Sōseki's Novel Sorekara*. Translated from the Japanese, with an afterword and selected bibliography by Norma Field. Ann Arbor: Center for Japanese Studies, University of Michigan, 1997.
Ōoka, Shōhei. *The Shade of Blossoms*. Translated with an introduction by Dennis Washburn. Michigan Monograph Series in Japanese Studies, no. 22. Ann Arbor: Center for Japanese Studies, University of Michigan, 1998.
Popham, Peter. *Tokyo: The City at the End of the World*. Tokyo: Kodansha International, 1985.
Richie, Donald. *Tokyo Nights: A Novel*. Rutland, Vt.: Charles E. Tuttle, 1994.
———. *Tokyo: A View of the City*. London: Reaktion Books, 1999.
Seidensticker, Edward. *Kafū the Scribbler: The Life and Writings of Nagai Kafū, 1879–1959*. Stanford: Stanford University Press, 1965.
———. *Low City, High City: Tokyo from Edo to the Earthquake*. New York: Alfred A. Knopf, 1983.
———. *Tokyo Rising: The City Since the Great Earthquake*. Cambridge, Mass.: Harvard University Press, 1991.
Waley, Paul. *Tokyo Now and Then: An Explorer's Guide*. New York: Weatherhill, 1984.

WORKS IN JAPANESE

Hisada Megumi. *Han'ei Tokyo uradōri* (The backstreets of prospering Tokyo). Tokyo: Bungei shunjū, 1997.
Jinno Hitoshi et al. *Tōkyō tanken* (Exploring Tokyo). Tokyo: Hachiyōsha, 1988.
Maeda Ai. *Maeda Ai chosakushū, daigokan: toshi kūkan no naka no bungaku* (The writings of Maeda Ai, book 5: Literature in urban space). Tokyo: Chikuma shobō, 1989.
Tōkyōjin (Tokyoites). 1997–2001.
Tsuchida Mitsufumi. *Bungaku Tōkyō annai* (A guide to Tokyo literature). Tokyo: Ryokuchisha, 1956.
———. *Tōkyō bungaku chimei jiten* (A dictionary of Tokyo literary place-names). Tokyo: Tōkyōdō, 1978.
Unno Hiroshi. *Modan toshi Tōkyō: Nihon no sen-kyūhyaku-nijū nendai* (The modern city of Tokyo: Japan in the twenties). Tokyo: Chūō kōronsha, 1983.

Acknowledgments of Permissions

The estates of the following have granted permission for publication of their works: Hayashi Fumiko, Irokawa Takehiro, Kawabata Yasunari, Mishima Yukio, Mukōda Kuniko, Nagai Kafū, Sata Ineko. The original Japanese copyrights are as follows. *Asakusa kurenai-dan* (excerpt) by Kawabata Yasunari © 1930, Kawabata Hite. *Watashi no tōkyō chizu* (excerpt) by Sata Ineko © 1946, Kubokawa Kenzō. *Dauntaun* by Hayashi Fumiko © 1949, Hayashi Fukue. *Hanabi* by Mishima Yukio © 1953, Hiraoka Iichirō. *Ame no naka no funsui* by Mishima Yukio © 1963, Hiraoka Iichirō. *Azumabashi* by Nagai Kafū, © 1954, Nagai Hisamitsu. *Saikai* by Mukōda Kuniko © 1980, Mukōda Sei. *Suzume* by Irokawa Takehiro © 1985, Irokawa Takako; original publisher: Shinchōsha.

Grateful acknowledgement is made to *The East* 24, no. 3, where "Fountains in the Rain" was first published, and to Kodansha International, which holds the translation rights for the original story, *Ame no naka no funsui*.

The editor also gratefully acknowledges the cooperation of the Japan Foreign Rights Centre, the Japan UNI Agency, the Nihon Bungei Chosakuken Hogo Dōmei, and the Sakai Agency.

Compositor: Binghamton Valley Composition
Text: 10/14 Palatino
Display: Bauer Bodoni